Bangkok Is Ringing

BANGKOK IS RINGING

Sound, Protest, and Constraint

Benjamin Tausig

Oxford University Press is a department of the University of Oxford. It furthers
the University's objective of excellence in research, scholarship, and education
by publishing worldwide. Oxford is a registered trade mark of Oxford University
Press in the UK and certain other countries.

Published in the United States of America by Oxford University Press
198 Madison Avenue, New York, NY 10016, United States of America.

Library of Congress Cataloging-in-Publication Data
Names: Tausig, Benjamin, author.
Title: Bangkok is ringing : sound, protest, and constraint / Benjamin Tausig.
Description: New York, NY : Oxford University Press, 2019. |
Includes bibliographical references and index.
Identifiers: LCCN 2018011263 (print) | LCCN 2018013389 (ebook) |
ISBN 9780190847548 (Updf) | ISBN 9780190847555 (Epub) | ISBN 9780190847524 (cloth) |
ISBN 9780190847531 (pbk.) | ISBN 9780190847562 (companion website)
Subjects: LCSH: Protest movements—Thailand—Bangkok—History. |
Demonstrations—Thailand—Bangkok—History. | Sounds—Social aspects—Thailand—Bangkok. |
Music--Social aspects—Thailand—Bangkok. | Thailand—Politics and government—1988-
Classification: LCC HN700.55.B38 (ebook) | LCC HN700.55.B38 T38 2018 (print) |
DDC 303.609593—dc23
LC record available at https://lccn.loc.gov/2018011263

To Neil Smith, and a future that is radically open.

CONTENTS

ACKNOWLEDGMENTS

I pledge to one day write a book structured as one long acknowledgments section; such are the depths of my debt to many people and institutions. *Thank you.*

I wish to first thank Serena Roth, my wife. We went to Thailand on something like an ambitious, extended quasi-honeymoon, which included dark experiences as well as unrepeatably beautiful ones. This period became an on-ramp to our lives together. She is a brilliant interlocutor and partner, the center of all good things for me.

Among those I met for the first time during fieldwork, I first acknowledge *ajarn* (professor) Jup, who has been an ally, friend, and teacher for many years. She has been far more than a language instructor; she is a brilliant reader, thinker, observer, and critic. The curiosity and intellect she brings to her work led me to many of my most important readings, and her generosity has been boundless. This book would be a far more limited document without her aid.

My doctaural committee has been extraordinary, not only for their guidance but for allowing me to experiment, by using puns among other things. This committee includes my advisor, Jason Stanyek, who opened the door to me at NYU and thus to academia, and who taught several seminars that guided my thinking throughout this project. Jason introduced me to the field of sound studies, and consented to advise an ethnographic project in an unfamiliar country and political context. It includes Deborah Wong, who (and I can only now recognize the extent of this) sacrificed time and energy to help me solidify my project in its early days, who was the first to orient me in the anthropology of Thailand, and whose own scholarship paved the way for much of what I eventually wrote and thought. To this day she is my favorite ethnomusicologist to read, assign, and think with. It includes Martin Daughtry, a dedicated, brilliant friend who has served in equal parts as scholarly and familial model. It includes Rosalind Morris, whose intellectual depth I could only ever hope to emulate, and whose course in optic theory at Columbia was one of the most productive classes I have ever taken. Every reading and rereading of her scholarship provides new provocations. Each of these figures remains a staunch advocate.

I am fortunate to have been surrounded by many other great minds at NYU. I feel deeply lucky to have taken a seminar with Suzanne Cusick, and to have received her invariably wise comments about professional matters. Karen Shimekawa stepped in, with generosity and skill, as an outside reader at the last minute. Elizabeth Hoffman, Michael Beckerman, Maureen Mahon, Ana María Ochoa Gautier, and Helen Nissenbaum were important presences in the classroom and in many intellectual matters. Neil Smith, who sadly passed away in 2012, did not get to read the final draft of the manuscript. His seminar on "ideology and space" at the Graduate Center at CUNY did a great deal for the book, however, and I have completed it with him in mind as an exemplary reader of the left.

My cohort at NYU was a special group. Among those in my year or above who influenced the book, and who were supportive otherwise, include Bill Boyer, Andrew Burgard, Amy Cimini, Michael Gallope, Ivan Goff, Nicol Hammond, Jenny Johnson, Clara Latham, Rachel Mundy, Michael Birenbaum Quintero, Allen Roda, Jessica Schwartz, Tes Slominski, Steve Smith, Hila Tamir, Senti Toy Threadgill, and Emily Wilbourne. I apologize if I have neglected to include anyone; it was an incredible and an incredibly robust collective.

Many of the people whose lives are represented in the book were also allies, friends, and collaborators. *Ajarn* Mii, Orn, and Sombat aided this project throughout 2010 and 2011, and have continued to do so since then. Each has given me more than I can hope to repay; I will remain obliged to them. I recognize how fortunate I am to have an instrument teacher as skilled and devoted to his craft as Mii; his time and wisdom are a gift. My thanks to his entire family as well. Likewise Orn, comrade and friend, who helped me even when her own life was turbulent. She opened spaces to me that expanded my fieldwork, in ways that were especially generous. Thanks also to everyone at Red Sunday: Sombat, Bic, Gunn, Dear, Nop, Meow, Jin, Ben, and many others. I thank journalist Pravit Rojanaphruk for his ongoing updates and sharp insights, as well as his own bravery. I thank journalist Nick Nostitz for the very same reasons under a different set of circumstances.

I met a number of lifelong friends during fieldwork. This includes Peter Doolan, whose extraordinary archive of Thai recordings at Monrakplengthai.blogspot.com has been my most important source of musical information in a variety of genres, more so than any single academic reference. Terry Miller, Ros Phoasavadi and the Faculty of Fine Arts at Chulalongkorn University, James Mitchell, Peter Garrity, and Jenphop Jopgrabuanwan were also each gracious in helping me learn about genres and musicians over the course of several years. Alexandra Dalferro, who was in my Fulbright cohort, was an important source of friendship and insight throughout fieldwork. She is today positioned to be one of the most exciting and important ethnographers of Thailand, and I am humbled to know her and to watch her sensitive and incisive work come to fruition. Will Shattuck, Bonnie Chang, and Anthony Irwin—the Madison crew—have been dear friends since SEASSI, and throughout all of our fieldwork. Alexander Nanni connected me to opportunities at Mahidol University, to several great interviews, and to plenty of music and drinking spots throughout Bangkok.

I am lucky to have done research in Thailand at a time when the academic community was both outspoken and brilliant. No single person has been as influential as both scholar and activist than Tyrell Haberkorn, whose work remains a model, and none has been as supportive as she in helping me make connections in this scholarly community. Tyrell has done the tireless work of a committee member on my behalf, despite not being one formally; her contributions to the anthropology of Thailand are breathtaking. Above all, her example has led me to pause and reflect duly on injustice, with slowness and dignifying attention.

Malavika Reddy, Claudio Sopranzetti, Felicity Aulino, Eli Elinoff, Prakirati Satasut ("Biek"), and Aim Sinpeng have been wonderful readers of early chapter drafts, and/or conversation partners. I am humbled to be part of their cohort. Special mention must also be made of Chiranuch Premchaiporn, whose bravery during dark days has helped mobilize a community of dissidents, to Eef Vermeij, and to Fai Suluck and others at *Prachatai* for producing quality journalism in a place where print media has been unable to do so. Thanks to those who visited during fieldwork, notably including my parents and Serena's parents, and my brother-in-law and sister-in-law David Roth and Kate Garroway. Among my most important language teachers were *ajarn* Sidhorn and Robert Bickner at SEASSI, who guided me in the early years of language instruction. I extend sincere thanks to Fulbright for financial support for ten months of fieldwork, and to P'tip and Siriporn specifically.

Moving into the writing phase, I am grateful to Oxford University Press for their faith in this project, and their energy in developing it, including editor Suzanne Ryan and two anonymous readers whose comments made the final product far better and clearer. Mack Hagood, Kariann Goldschmitt, Stefan Helmreich, Anthony Irwin, and Michael Heller have also helped me workshop material.

At Stony Brook University, where I have taught since 2014, a new cohort has helped me polish the book. Summer feedback sessions with Erika Honisch and Maggie Adams helped in crafting the book proposal, and a fellowship at the Stony Brook Humanities Center provided time and support. For this opportunity, I thank Kathleen Wilson and Adrienne Unger. Judy Lochhead, Brook Belisle, Matt Brounley, and Sohl Lee have each provided invaluable feedback as well. Rebecca Lentjes graciously created the book's index. Ryan Minor and Shirley Lim have been *extraordinary* faculty mentors.

Finally—and this is not quite a thank-you, but it is the most important acknowledgement I have to offer—the victims of conflict matter immensely. At least ninety-one people were killed in the streets in 2010 during protests, as the Thai government confronted multitudes of the discontented. Thousands more were injured, and an untold number were traumatized. Scholarship concerned with Thailand owes the dead, wounded, and emotionally scarred a certain ethical debt. In light of conversation with victims' relatives, friends, colleagues, and supporters, I am convinced that an important if not urgent way to move forward is through open, critical analysis of the political changes afoot in Thailand, from governance to citizenship, from nationalism to economic participation, which they sought in their way to improve. In an environment of active censorship, serious treatments of political topics can have tremendous value, regardless of methodology or discipline. I offer no higher justification for my research. I acknowledge and in fact submit this book above all to the people whose lives it presumes to write.

NOTE ON TRANSLITERATION

All transliterations from Thai rendered in English in this book use a modified version of the Haas system, as specified in Mary Haas's *Thai-English Student's Dictionary* (1964). The modifications are intended to make the transliterations easier to sound out for those who are unfamiliar with the system. Thus, for example, ŋ is transliterated as "ng," the glottal stop marker "ʔ" is omitted, and "j" is used instead of "c" to represent the first consonant in words such as จะ. Although this compromise is imperfect, I hope it represents a middle path between serving readers of Thai, who may wish to identify the precise word, including its tonality, and those who do not read Thai but may want to follow terms more easily.

In instances where a person, title, or genre is commonly represented in English in a way that differs from the Haas system, I have used the common representation. This includes terms like *luk thung* and *mor lam*, as well as many individual names.

Introduction

On Sound, Protest Space, and Constraint

The protests at the center of this book resonated across vast, crowded expanses. From far off, the din seemed singular. But from within, it was a mosaic of strident chants, buoyant songs, alarmed shouts, and sober discussions. These sounds and many others adhered to spaces, and the spaces adhered to meanings. Clusters of sound, space, and meaning behaved like *niches*—local, audible adaptations within a broad ecology of political expression.[1] But, as in any ecology, these spaces were not permanent containers. Their contours changed with time and circumstance. They were sustained while their sounds rang, and then they dissolved or transformed. Walking between and among them, the spaces revealed rough linear borders. Marking time, if one had patience, these borders lasted between a few seconds and a few months. Relative to each other, the vibrant core of the spaces gave way to ecotonal zones, where sounds faded, clashed, abutted, or overlapped with other sounds. Inside the spaces, protesters gathered intimately around media objects—radios, megaphones, car stereos, VCD players, cellphone screens, sound trucks, stages, walkie-talkies, human voices, police whistles, bass drums, or plastic clappers, for instance. Each space pulsed with meaning, and each abutted other meaningful spaces. Sometimes these spaces were politically discordant with one another. The remainder of this book will offer context specific to the spaces of my case study. So far, though, I have generalized. Perhaps you have filled in this general description with specific memories of a sonic expanse that you yourself have experienced, of niches of dissent and transformation that have moved you. I encourage the reader to continue taking that liberty.

1. Jean-François Augoyard and Henry Torgue, *Sonic Experience: A Guide to Everyday Sounds* (McGill-Queen's University Press, 2005), 78. A sonic *niche* is "an occurrence of a sound emission at the moment that it is most favourable and that offers a particularly well-adapted place for its expression."

The sonic spaces of protest described in *Bangkok Is Ringing* were thickly imbricated. On February 13, 2011, I left a tent where a woman was collecting charitable donations, and within a few meters saw a crowd gathered near a television watching aggregated footage of military violence against protesters, with a live narrator nearby—a middle-aged man standing and speaking through a microphone, commenting on the footage as it played. I watched the crowd watch and listen. I asked one man why he was there, and he answered as though it were self-evident: he wanted to know more about the truth. Fading out, I spotted a regular protester, a communist bookseller. He recognized me. We smiled at each other and reintroduced ourselves. He showed me the newest issue of the leftist journal *Fah Diaw Kan*, which had a stoplight showing a row of three red lights on its cover. I leafed through it; we made small talk. Moments later, a vendor pressed play on a CD connected to some tabletop speakers, overwhelming our discussion. Mingling restively with his music, five meters off, a young girl begged for money. Her father was dead. She repeated the horror again and again. A little further, past a small crowd, the main stage became visible, with its speaker stacks suspended in gently arcing vertical towers. Black police trucks topped with cream-colored loudspeakers massed in front of the stage, ready to reply to its imperious noise. This was all in a one-minute walk. The gatherings were dense, unresolved networks of sound and political energy.

During my fieldwork in Bangkok in 2010 and 2011, protests of this size were ordinary—visited routinely by partisans and journalists, dodged like a heavy rain by nearly everyone else. Their sounds rang out daily, on roads and in parks, near monuments and in malls, whether or not one wished to hear. A national political faction called the Red Shirts, who denounced coups, censorship, and other antidemocratic abuses in Thailand, organized most of the events, which became part of the fabric of daily life. Most of the time, the gatherings felt like outdoor marketplaces or temple fairs, the sort one encounters throughout the country, with vendors in every available space selling food and other goods, and with people whiling away countless hours saying and doing nothing much.

But the protests were also extraordinary. On a few terrible days, open combat arose between protest, counterprotest, military, and paramilitary groups, especially in the period from March through May 2010. Those days were among the gravest in the history of the nation, and have left scars on its political consciousness. Alongside the violence, there was a palpable sense that the protests were catalyzing a fundamental change in Thailand. This change was imagined as the emergence of an authentic democracy, which would include the heightened self-identification of rural and working-class people as active participants in the public affairs of the nation. The protests seemed to promise a new era of political citizenship. Whether such changes were welcome or terrifying or something else depended on who was observing them. Some Red Shirts regarded their showdown with the government as the possible coming of end-times, but most were driven by optimism about the reforms that might come. Most had hope. Many outside of the movement, however, felt deeply unsettled.

Still, on most days the marches and occupations sounded less like a big bang than a prolonged and anxious hum, albeit one with rich overtones. Much has been written about the spectacular violence that drew international attention to Thailand on May 19, 2010 and other major dates (a brief timeline of the Red Shirt movement is included later in this introduction), but comparatively little research exists about the everyday oscillations of the movement and its events, about its internal structure and heterogeneity, about its niches and their thick interrelations, which transformed Thailand in still-unclear ways. What did it sound like to be at these protests? What was said, unsaid, expressed, implied, echoed, and heard?

Bangkok Is Ringing is an ethnographic study of the mediated sonic spaces of the Red Shirt protests. While I foreground sound, other analyses are possible. Protest movements can be understood as visual spectacles or through the lenses of the haptic, the olfactory, the culinary, the sanitary, the medical, the demographic, the economic, or the legal, for example.[2] The Red Shirt protests were multisensory experiences, often to an exhausting degree, and were socially and politically complex. This book will engage many sensory modalities. However, it is addressed above all to the anthropology of music and sound, to Thai studies, and to scholarship on protest and media. I argue that the constrained mobility of the Red Shirt movement was closely linked to the constrained mobility of its sound, and that in general the constraints visited upon sound and upon the mobility of transformative political action may be read in tandem.

The Red Shirt movement serves this discussion well, because it was constrained so thoroughly. In some sense, the movement faltered in its goals, particularly upon reflection several years later. The Red Shirts did not diminish the power of unelected elites or strengthen Thailand's commitment to democratic representation, as many in the movement hoped it would. The movement's effects have been slow and uneven (not to say non-existent), and its aims have frequently been out of alignment with its results. The "webs of significance" in Thai political life are tangled indeed; transformations, though possible, meet many obstacles of meaning and power.[3] The Red Shirts faced long slogs and backsliding along a path that could not guarantee their vision of democracy. Indeed, as of 2018, the movement has not only been rebuffed but pushed backward. A military coup in 2014 resulted in a lengthy constitutional vacuum (and eventually a new, military-drafted constitution), secret trials, and repeatedly deferred elections. The lesson of all this is familiar: *movements do*

2. There is some precedent for the sensory analysis of Thai protest. Alan Klima, *The Funeral Casino: Meditation, Massacre, and Exchange with the Dead in Thailand* (Princeton: Princeton University Press, 2002) focuses on modes of seeing within the 1992 anti-government protests in Bangkok. Klima's ethnography is a historically and religiously grounded analysis of the ethics of witnessing death and violence.

3. Clifford Geertz, *The Interpretation of Cultures: Selected Essays* (New York: Basic Books, 1973).

not always *move* things as intended.[4] As James Scott noted several decades ago, the gains wrought by revolutions are "uncertain, while the carnage, the repression, and the demoralization of defeat are all too certain and real."[5] All political movements must wade into this field of uncertainty. I will argue that the constrained mobility of movements—the uncertainties borne when attempting to move—is not only analogous to the constrained mobility of sound, but closely connected to it. For heterogeneous political movements like that of the Red Shirts, sound is both an emblem and a cause of constrained mobility.

CONSTRAINED SOUND, CONSTRAINED MOVEMENT

Sound, like political movements, often irrupts with the hope of an explicit transformation, before diffusing and distorting as it touches and is touched by the world. Indeed, there is perhaps no safer generalization about sound than to say that it is constantly running into things. But what is meant by "things"? One cannot readily separate sound-as-materiality from sound-as-meaning. Sound's materiality is always enmeshed with its own conceptual ground.[6] Sound is therefore not reducible to an acoustical analysis; acoustics is but one explanatory possibility, and not necessarily a foundation for understanding sonority. Sound does not begin life as a waveform, adding meaning later. Sound is *from its inception as an object* multiply defined, and multiply definable. Stefan Helmreich stresses that reverberation is not inherently a physical phenomenon, but always in some wise a rhetorical one, a product of "echoes and reinforcements of auditory analogies, echoes and reinforcements of explicit similes and implicit metaphors."[7] The "things" that sound runs into thus depends on how sound is understood, described, practiced, and heard in context. Sound, like political movements, is caught in webs of significance that prevent it from moving freely. Sound is transduced, refracted, and circulated *simultaneously* within architectures of concrete and semantics. These architectures erect barriers to what sound can do and where it can go. A chanted slogan at a protest event may be inhibited by a row of tall buildings, just as it may be inhibited by a moral sense of which sounds belong where, by people tuning it out, or by the differing auditory

4. Sara Ahmed, *Living a Feminist Life* (Durham, NC: Duke University Press, 2017). Ahmed plays usefully with this terminology.
5. James Scott, *Weapons of the Weak: Everyday Forms of Peasant Resistance* (New Haven: Yale University Press, 1985), 29.
6. Ana María Ochoa Gautier, "Acoustic Multinaturalism, the Value of Nature, and the Nature of Music in Ecomusicology," *boundary* 2 43, no. 1 (2016): 107–141. Tara Rodgers, "Toward a Feminist Epistemology of Sound: Refiguring Waves in Audio-Technical Discourse," in *Engaging the World: Thinking After Irigaray*, Mary Rawlinson, ed. (SUNY Press, 2016).
7. Stefan Helmreich, "Gravity's Reverb: Listening to Space-Time, or Articulating the Sounds of Gravitational-Wave Detection," Cultural Anthropology 31, no. 4 (2016): 464–492.

abilities of listeners. It may be inhibited by being classified, epistemologically, as noise. Most sounds never resound, if they sound at all.

For this reason, I dispute the claim to an "unbounded nature of sound" that is advanced in some sound studies writing, especially near philosophy and sound art.[8] Sound is not always marked by its "power to penetrate boundaries."[9] It is dubious whether "all the sounds that have ever occurred still reverberate" in any meaningful sense.[10] In most contexts, sound fails to act as a "sinister resonance," and does not help us escape from a prison of logic.[11] Each of these quotations from sources in the field of sound studies claims that sound is especially powerful or subversive, that it can disregard and interrupt the constraints of modernity.[12] Sound has even been treated in some literature as if it were transcendent, as Kane notes.[13] The notion that sound is impervious to spatial and temporal boundaries could be appended to Jonathan Sterne's "audiovisual litany," a catalog of common presumptions in sound studies.[14] Sound does of course move and act, but the world is crowded. At Red Shirt protests, any given sound contended with many others in a network of sonic niches, which were constrained by their interrelations with other present sounds. Much can be gleaned from considering how sound's mobility is limited in settings like this. It has been suggested that sound became a major topic of academic, artistic, and scientific interest because it is "paradigmatic" in an age of mobility, flows, and malleable subjectivity.[15] Instead, in this book I argue that sound may be an equally useful figure for explaining *limited political mobility*. Sound might in fact

8. Brandon LaBelle, *Acoustic Territories: Sound Culture and Everyday Life* (New York: Continuum, 2010), xxiii.

9. Steven Connor, "The Helping of Your Good Hands: Reports on Clapping," in Les Back and Michael Bull, eds., *The Auditory Culture Reader* (New York: Berg, 2004), 71.

10. Bruce R. Smith, "Into the Wild Blue Yonder: The Challenges of Acoustic Ecology," in Veit Erlmann, ed., *Hearing Cultures: Essays on Sound, Listening, and Modernity* (London: Berg, 2004), 21.

11. David Toop, *Sinister Resonance: The Mediumship of the Listener* (New York: Continuum, 2011).

12. The impulse to imagine sound as a shortcut through spatial constraints is at least five or six decades old. In 1966, Marvel Comics introduced a villain named Klaw who could transform himself into "pure sound" to become deviously mobile. See https://comicvine.gamespot.com/klaw/4005-3171/. Just three years later, R. Murray Schafer coined the term "schizophonia" to refer to sound delinked from its originary source. See R. Murray Schafer, *The New Soundscape: A Handbook for the Modern Music Teacher* (Toronto: Berandol Music Limited, 1969). Desire and anxiety alike may be projected onto the fantasy of sound as an immaterial materiality.

13. Brian Kane, *Sound Unseen: Acousmatic Sound in Theory and Practice* (New York: Oxford University Press, 2014), 9

14. Jonathan Sterne, *The Audible Past: Cultural Origins of Sound Reproduction.* (Durham, NC: Duke University Press, 2003). 15. Sterne, elsewhere, has located a strain of cultural evolutionism in such assumptions. He quotes Marshall McLuhan: "[U]ntil WRITING was invented, we lived in acoustic space, where the Eskimo now lives: boundless, directionless, horizonless, dark of the mind, the world of emotion, primordial intuition, terror." Jonathan Sterne, "The Theology of Sound: A Critique of Orality," *Canadian Journal of Communication*, 36, no. 2 (2011): 207–225.

15. LaBelle, *Acoustic Territories*, xxv.

be enlisted to help us understand how agency caroms and fractures, how political actors often find themselves bouncing off walls rather than passing frictionlessly through them. An ethnographic study of the sonic niches of the Red Shirt protests shows the contours of constraint in the sound of one political movement.

Mediation and media technologies frame this book's structure. Each of the sixteen chapters is oriented around one media object, or one related cluster of media objects. Media is a crucial consideration: there are no perfectly free fields, acoustically, and certainly not once technology and audition are considered. Recent literature has stressed the perils of overlooking mediation. Frances Dyson identifies sound and vibration as figures enlisted by sound studies and new media studies in a quixotic effort to "resolve[] the problem of representation and mediation."[16] The desire to transcend mediation is, Dyson argues, ideological, and has long characterized scientific modernity. The roots of this ideology are capitalist. They dovetail with marketers' promises of a pure presence through audio devices—high-end headphones, say—an equivalence of being and hearing so tightly fused that "one finds the technological apparatus in retrograde."[17] (Many have noted the old ad slogan "Is it real or is it Memorex?" as an expression of this idealogy.) Dyson's critique applies readily to sound studies scholarship that romanticizes vibratory transcendence. Mindful of such a critique, this book will foreground how media objects in every instance shape sonic niches.

And the constrained, mediated niches felt like this: I was in a crowd at a Red Shirt rally in late 2010. The temperature was above 95 degrees Fahrenheit, with the humidity unforgiving even after sunset. Bodies sweated shoulder-to-shoulder on the slim sidewalk curving around the famous Democracy Monument, just in front of the bright lights of a McDonald's restaurant. Each of the bodies was trying to go somewhere, to meet a friend, grab a bite, stand closer to the stage, or find a spot to sit down. But with thousands of people proceeding through a single, narrow bottleneck, the effort to move was futile. I stood in the throng, as necks craned all around. To my right and left, vendors squatted on the pavement, with literature and T-shirts spread for sale on blankets. People browsed or bought things while inching forward. We all had plenty of time. Meanwhile, other elbows and legs already occupied the sliver of space where I might have shifted my weight. My knees ached after standing for eight hours. My feet, exposed in flip-flops, recoiled against a warm liquid that I could not look down to identify, so compact were the bodies. Truck-mounted loudspeakers blared crackling music in the near field, while the sound from the stage echoed jumpily across Ratchadamnoen Avenue's corridor of low-slung buildings. The gamy odor of chicken hearts wafted from an open grill. I felt heat on my forearm from the coals. Propane hit my nose, followed by the plasticky *patapatapat* sound of a handheld clapper shaken vigorously. Two enormous video

16. Frances Dyson, *Sounding New Media: Immersion and Embodiment in the Arts and Culture* (Berkeley, CA: University of California Press, 2009), 11.
17. Dyson, *Sounding New Media*, 14.

screens flanking the main stage simultaneously flickered a bright digital blue as the monitor searched for its input. I felt nauseous and dazed.

Of all the intense sensory forms that engaged and impelled protesters, an analysis of sound will not offer the only possible vantage into the motivations or structure of the protests. What it offers, what it helps to explain, is limited or constrained mobility, which is so routinely felt at political rallies and by entire political movements. Limited mobility is the short- and long-term condition of political movements, and it is also the general condition of sound. This book will examine how the two phenomena meet limits of mobility together.

STUDYING CONSTRAINT AS AN OPTIMISTIC PROJECT

Emphasizing constraints is not, as it may seem so far, necessarily pessimistic. The aim of this book is in part to analyze a set of strategic challenges in one place, so that similar challenges may be met with clarity and imagination elsewhere. It may thus be read, if one chooses, as a case study for comparison when reflecting upon, joining, or organizing political movements. The stakes and circumstances of two movements will never be identical, but they may yet bear comparison. The first strategic step for a political movement is to reckon with its constraints by understanding what forces are arrayed around it, deliberately or incidentally, in deep contextual detail. In moving things, the obstacles are immense, and there are no shortcuts, as the title of one recent book on union organizing aptly puts it.[18] *Bangkok Is Ringing* is about the profound challenge of navigating constraints, but not at all about impossibility.[19]

Other scholars have examined the limits of musical and sonic mobility with optimistic ears. Gavin Steingo has conducted fieldwork in Soweto, South Africa, a "musical context where obduracy is far more common than mobility," casting doubt on the notion that musical flows and musical actors within modernity are

18. Jane F. McAlevey, *No Shortcuts Organizing for Power* (New York: Oxford University Press, 2016).

19. An extended note is due here to the following recent monograph: Claudio Sopranzetti, *Owners of the Map: Motorcycle Taxi Drivers, Mobility, and Politics in Bangkok* (University of California Press, 2017). Sopranzetti's research overlapped substantially with mine, both temporally and geographically, and not by coincidence given the subject matter, our analyses both focus on questions of mobility, albeit through different methods and framings. Sopranzetti argues that motorcycle taxi drivers in Bangkok did in fact enjoy a special kind of mobility, and that in some sense these drivers succeeded in finding shortcuts. "Their mobility through traffic was based on using information and skills to find a route across static traffic," he notes, near the end of an analysis that links these drivers' street-level mobility to the pursuit of political and economic mobility (249). However, the shortcuts that these drivers discovered were neither permanent nor always directed towards satisfactory destinations. In other words, their unique mobility was not without complicating roadblocks.

unimpeded.[20] Of course, limited mobility, of both sound and human beings, is not always the same as a lack of physical movement through space.[21] Rather, limited mobility signals a lack of determination over motion, and an often violent subjectification to the turbulence of the journey. Migrant labor, for example, is a type of mobility marked by displacement, uncertainty, and exploitation, in every respect unlike leisure travel. A mobile and an immobile body can move at the same velocity, along the same routes, perhaps even aboard the same vessel. These might be distinguished as *whole mobiles* and *ruptured mobiles*, with wholeness and rupture describing vastly different conditions of political subjectivity.[22] Limited mobility, however, need not evacuate agency. Steingo notes that obduracy in Soweto can in fact be generative, both musically and socially, and Sopranzetti writes against a "praxis of political immobility" that would cede too much power to forces of political domination.[23] These points are vital, and will be echoed sympathetically throughout this book. In Chapter 2, for example, I argue that histories of constraint and repression were, for many Red Shirts, breeding grounds for the possibility of a radical politics. Constraints may offer opportunities as well as limits.

But before recognizing such opportunities, it is necessary to acknowledge power differentials. Navigating between opportunities and limits requires a delicate analytical balance. The most relevant and eloquent poetics of power differentials from my fieldwork were found in Thai popular music. One genre to be discussed at length in this book, *luk thung*, is especially insightful about constrained mobility.[24] The most popular commercial genre currently produced in Thailand, *luk thung* has thematized the hardships of rural laborers in northeast Thailand (called Isan) since the mid-twentieth century, often through stories about migrant work:

> The theme of longing and separation [in *luk thung*] taps into . . . fifty years of seasonal migration to Bangkok, and almost two hundred years of separation from Lao people on the northern bank of the Mekong. Reaching further into the past, *luk thung* echoes the ancient Siamese travel literature genre *nirat* (literally "separation," or departing from something that is dearly desired) . . . Up until the nineteenth century, travel was not a desirable activity. For the Thai working class that is still the case: for them the purpose

20. Gavin Steingo, "Sound and Circulation: Immobility and Obduracy in South African Electronic Music," *Ethnomusicology Forum* 24, no. 1 (2015): 102–123.

21. Noel Salazar, "Towards an Anthropology of Cultural Mobilities," *Crossings: Journal of Migration and Culture*, 53, no.1 (2010): 53–68.

22. These terms are only fleetingly related to Latour's "immutable mobiles," which are textual inscriptions of objects that can traverse contexts. Bruno Latour, *Science in Action: How to Follow Scientists and Engineers Through Society* (Open University Press, 1987).

23. Sopranzetti, *Owners of the Map*, 280.

24. Matt Sakakeeny, writing in a different context about the constraints experienced by New Orleans brass bands (in a chapter called "Constraints"), also considers mobility and constraint in tandem. Matt Sakakeeny, *Roll With It: Brass Bands in the Streets of New Orleans* (Durham: Duke University Press, 2013).

of travel is to find employment, and so *luk thung* songs are full of accounts of loss and forced separation.[25]

Many Red Shirts have experienced such forced separation, both as members of a laboring class that must travel away from home and family for employment, and as members of a political movement whose epicenter, Bangkok, is a difficult and alien place. Power differentials are explained in *luk thung* through stories of ruptured mobile subjectivity. Unsurprisingly, this music was enormously popular at Red Shirt protests. Its lyrics and musical gestures serve as a rebuke to the Thai state, which has long sought to deny the very existence of political inequality. *luk thung* trenchantly highlights ruptures and power imbalances, ranging from the Siamese colonization of Isan in the eighteenth and nineteenth century to the class-inflected burden of migrant labor in the present. Before optimistically exploring how constraint can bring about transformative politics, the kinds of inequities that *luk thung* foregrounds must be acknowledged. This music, as I will discuss, describes an uneven political geography.

UNEVEN GEOGRAPHIES OF SOUND

Just a few days after the most violent clashes that took place between Red Shirt protesters and the military, in late May 2010, I encountered two sonically rich scenes over the course of an hour that plainly demonstrated the gap in Thailand between mobility and obduracy, between whole and ruptured mobiles. The first scene was the filming of a music video for a pop song, called *khɔ̀ɔ kwaamsùk* ("Bring Back the Happiness"), that had been hastily recorded on May 20, the day after the Thai military attacked the central occupied Red Shirt protest area in downtown Bangkok with weapons of war, resulting in dozens of deaths and thousands of injuries. Everyone then was gripped by fear. "Bring Back the Happiness" was recorded to help restore tranquility. To aid this reactionary political benefit project, 301 celebrities agreed to appear in the video and sing on the recording. The video would soon play ceaselessly on television and on the elevated mass transit lines of the Skytrain. The song's ubiquity lent it an air of propaganda, which was matched by its saccharine lyrics:

> *We used to smile, smile at each other, do you remember?*
> *Wherever Thai people would meet, they would smile at each other.*
> *Our house was like a city in a dream.*
> *But in the middle of all that happiness in the Thai house,*

25. James Mitchell, *Luk Thung: The Culture and Politics of Thailand's Most Popular Music* (Seattle: Washington University Press, 2016).

not long ago, the wind of conflict blew in.

It blew into our hearts, that dry air.

The happiness, the purity, and the everlasting smiles from the hearts of Thai
*   people were no more.*

May the happiness return to us, may the happiness and the abundant, everlasting
*   smiles come back.*

Generous, giving people, supportive people, come back and make Thailand
*   peaceful again.*[26]

The video for "Bring Back the Happiness" was directed by nationalist filmmaker Prachya Pinkaew. The celebrities wore matching white shirts that read, in Thai, "shirt without color," signifying that they did not identify with any color-coded political faction, only with a pure love of Thailand. But as with whiteness elsewhere, what these shirts in fact expressed was not a desire for unity but a presumption that entrenched political power should remain invisible. In the music video, the singers wear concerned expressions while standing (sometimes in front of a video backdrop) next to tire barricades and inside the burnt interiors of downtown commercial spaces destroyed during the crackdown.[27] These shots alternate with footage of smoldering rubble, firefighters, medics, people crying, and soldiers gazing into the distance through binoculars. Conspicuously absent from the video are the Red Shirt protesters, their discontent reduced in the lyrics to a transient "wind." Political alterity was thus figured as menacing and chaotic, but in the end manageable, like a heavy rain.

Just after the crackdown, wandering downtown disconsolately in the immediate aftermath of a violence unlike any I had witnessed, I came upon an outdoor shoot for part of the "Bring Back the Happiness" video. The setting for the shoot was a pile of debris at the base of the Siam Theatre, an old movie house that had been burned beyond repair during the recent conflict, and about which many forlorn articles had appeared in the press.[28] As I approached the theater, I saw soap opera actor "Por" Nattawut Skidjai surrounded by a film and makeup crew. One member of the crew carried a small plastic boombox so Por could lip-sync as he faced the camera. The boombox was low-tech compared to the giant video camera. Coming out of the boombox speakers, the song sounded tinny and small under two exposed stories of melted steel and blackened walls. Por sang under his breath as he lip-synced and danced. The megastar's performance was strangely unglamorous,

26. Translated from the original Thai.

27. Kitchana Lersakvanitchakul, "Bringing Back the Smiles," *The Nation*, May 26, 2010. Prachya is best-known for directing the popular jingoistic martial arts film *Ong-Bak: Muay Thai Warrior*, in which a sequence of fighters who negatively stereotype various Southeast Asian ethnicities are defeated by the Thai protagonist.

28. Parinyaporn Pajee, "A Farewell to Siam Theatre," *The Nation*, May 21, 2010; Wise Kwai, "Saying Goodbye to the Siam Theater," May 26, 2010, http://travel.cnn.com/bangkok/life/saying-goodbye-siam-theatre-595259.

Figure I.1 Soap opera star "Por" Nattawut Skidjai before shooting his portion of the video for "Bring Back the Happiness." Por and his assistant wear the same shirt, which on the back reads "shirt that has no color." Photograph by the author.

though post-production would add all the requisite polish. Between takes, an assistant wiped sweat from Por's smooth brow, a constant task with both temperature and humidity in the mid-90s (see figure I.1).

I stood watching among a crowd of starstruck fans behind a barricade. Por's TV costar, an actress named Ae Porntip, chatted with the fans while her partner performed. She spoke with a practiced confidence, and her comments echoed the themes of the lyrics to "Bring Back the Happiness." "We've always been taught to love our country, religion, and king, and not to forget these words," Ae told me and a few others, her face chalk-white with makeup and her expression stoic. "We've had these words instilled in us since we were children; we should never forget them . . . Right now is the moment for us to recover our sense of mutual obligation, to encourage each other, and to have unity. We must insist to everyone that they not forget this word—'unity.'"[29] Later Por, between takes, added, "What we did was make a mistake. Now we have to forgive each other, and go back to the way Thailand was before." Por was not alone in his wish to return to the supposed innocence of an earlier time. The aftermath of May 19 was marked by attempts to clean up the affected parts of downtown. Many Thais, racked with disbelief, wanted

29. Ae Porntip and Nattawut Skidjai, interview with the author, May 23, 2010. Translated from the original Thai.

Figure I.2 The exterior of a truck, damaged in the May 19 military attack. It is covered with handwritten memorials to the dead driver, and political invective. Photograph by the author.

familiar environments to be neat and orderly once more. This led to gestures like "Bring Back the Happiness," recorded and filmed at the same time that groups of volunteers scrubbed graffiti from buildings and tossed the remnants of the Red Shirt camps into garbage trucks. The restoration of space dramatized the desire for a restoration of the national political order. Because this desire was shared by the state as well as by agents of global capital, the song circulated widely, with relatively few constraints.

Immediately after this chance encounter, I walked to Lumphini Park, a manicured green area in the middle of Bangkok that was originally commissioned by King Rama VI in the 1920s. East of the park, just past the iconic red gate along the side of the road, a small pickup truck caught my eye. Still parked neatly flush with the curb several days after the crackdown, the truck appeared to have been hit with a concussion grenade (see figure I.2). Shards of metal were ripped from the chassis, but the engine was intact and nearly undamaged. The windshield was shattered; specks of glass sparkled on the pavement. Upon the gray paint of the vehicle's body, anonymous authors had scribbled messages in permanent marker, including "damn the vile [prime minister] Abhisit!" and "we will be back."[30] Some of the messages referred to the driver in the past tense, and I began to suspect that

30. Translated from the original Thai.

the notes were memorials. At last, I read a message that confirmed my suspicion. It translated as: "The man who died here did not die in vain." I looked down to the sidewalk, which was streaked with blood seared almost black under the May sun. I surmised that the driver must have died on that sidewalk, or later from injuries sustained there. Inside the cab and the truck bed lay the things that had belonged to the man, almost certainly a rural laborer and likely a migrant—pairs of shoes, empty bottles of energy drinks, and a camouflage fisherman's hat (see figure I.3). I was less than half a mile from the site of Por's "Bring Back the Happiness" video shoot, and I reflected on the distances and differences between the two scenes.

What did it sound like during this man's ride into the city to join the protests? Did he and his fellow travelers—ruptured mobiles—listen to music in a reverie of optimism? Or did they sit quietly, perhaps nervously, as the wind slapped coldly at their faces in the open truck bed during a nightlong drive? Did they shout into the air? Did they talk politics? And then what did it sound like as the attack came? Did the army bullets grow audibly closer? I try to imagine silence. Did the marker gripped by an enraged Red Shirt squeak beneath her sobs and curses as she wrote the driver's eulogy? These sounds will never resound like "Bring Back the Happiness" did, just a short walk up the road, if they ever sounded at all. They do not, among other things, present themselves positively to the ethnographic ear. In an uneven geography of sound, their mobility is constrained. (Though perhaps we are ethically called to refuse to stop listening).

Figure I.3 Interior of the truck; the driver's things. Photograph by the author.

The mobility of sound is constrained along politically uneven terrain. What structures propel a reactionary pop song while constraining the sound-world of rural laborers who join protests? Suzanne Cusick has cautioned against the impulse, in work using a "vibration-centered model" of sonic analysis, to ignore such power imbalances.[31] To borrow her example, when guards in Guantanamo Bay detention camp played music to weaken the will of prisoners, sound was not simply causing bodies to resonate sympathetically. Sound violated the subjectivity of one body at the behest of another. A vibration-centered model may fail to account for the operations of resonance amidst profound power imbalance, such as in torture.[32] Sound moves through channels of power and privilege that precede it, that have already politicized its vibrations. Red Shirt music and sound was constrained in this same way. *Bangkok Is Ringing* will explore how sound and power were spatialized within the Red Shirt gatherings. There, sonorous material did not break down borders, nor create a resonant equivalence between politically neutral bodies. Sound's movement, rather, was governed by channels and relations that sound itself could not easily escape, no less reshape. This book listens carefully to the resulting spaces, to their constraining histories, and to their transformative interactions.

In Thailand, certain sounds are absolutely constrained, especially critical public speech about the royal family. Early in my fieldwork, on a rainy night, some friends and I rode home from a rally in Ayuthaya in the back of a covered pickup truck. During our long drive, one woman shared the story of how she and her family had first gotten involved with the Red Shirts. The beating of the rain on the canvas above was so loud that it gave the two of us a private conversational corner, even though the truck was packed with people. The woman confided in me that she and her husband had nearly divorced in 2009, after she admitted to him that she no longer loved the king. The monarchy is unassailable in Thailand, protected by severe *lèse-majesté* laws, by online "Cyber Scouts" who monitor social media, and by daily norms that compel demonstrations of love for its deified human avatars. Public dissent against the monarchy is illegal and harshly punished.[33]

31. Suzanne Cusick, "An Acoustemology of Detention in the "Global War on Terror,"" in *Music, Sound and the Reconfiguration of Public and Private Space,* ed. Georgina Born (Cambridge: Cambridge University Press, 2013), 275–291.

32. Although some sound studies work has combined vibration-centered analysis with a consideration of political power differentials, notably including Steve Goodman, *Sonic Warfare: Sound, Affect, and the Ecology of Fear* (Cambridge, MA: MIT Press, 2009) and J. Martin Daughtry, *Listening to War: Sound, Music, Trauma, and Survival in Wartime Iraq* (New York: Oxford University Press, 2015)

33. The king died in October 2016, at the age of 88. Even in death, his image and name remain sacred symbols. The government announced a mandatory one-year mourning period after his death, during which time citizens were expected to wear black and to refrain from amusement. Music was banned throughout the country for 90 days, except that which was explicitly memorializing. This included the king's favorite genre, swing-era jazz, an idiom in which he himself had composed.

The rain pounded above, and the woman shouted into its insulating frequencies. Loud as she yelled, only the two of us could hear. She told me she had privately doubted the king for years after reading some dissident literature about the monarchy's great wealth in a nation beset by poverty and inequality. But she kept her feelings hidden from her staunchly nationalist and royalist family. She finally decided to break the news to her husband on a Friday night in late 2009. The husband flew into a rage. As their two young daughters cowered upstairs, the couple argued loudly through the night. Her husband, fed up, demanded a divorce in the early morning. No reconciliation was possible, he said, with a partner who had turned away from the foundation of their country. Hurt but not ready to give up, she agreed to grant him a divorce on the condition that they wait until Monday—government offices would be closed until then, anyway. He agreed, and even consented to hear out her position after tiring of the screaming matches. She pressed her case as coolly as she could and, remarkably, he began to relent, conceding many of her points. In the coming days, her husband marveled at his own transformation—for forty-two years, his love for the monarchy had been ironclad. Soon after the fight, he became an active Red Shirt organizer. The couple and their daughters participated in political activities multiple times a week during my fieldwork, and I got to know all four of them. The couple now agrees that the husband's dedication to the Red Shirts (he is now the most politically radical member of his family) is a result of the intensity of his political awakening.

This couple's story is not unusual. I met many Red Shirts who furtively dissented against sacred state symbols. There were several risky, powerful slogans, such as *taa sàwàang* ("eyes bright," or "eyes wide open"), a coded reference to those who had been awakened to critiques of the monarchy and political inequity, that circulated at rallies. And yet, our conversation was limited to one corner of the little pickup truck bed. Neither of us would have dreamed of having such a frank discussion if other Red Shirts could eavesdrop, let alone of having it in a more public place. It felt risky simply to *hear* protesters speaking this way, to feel the words brushing one's ears. But such dissent was almost always whispered, or cautiously encrypted. Thailand's uneven geography of power conditions the places where, and the extent to which, this critique can be voiced. Moreover, notably, it was not only language that was legally and normatively constrained. Any kind of sound, be it a chant, a song, or even a rhythm could be judged seditious (by the police, usually) if it was thought to be critical of a sensitive state or royal symbol.

The urgent need for unity (*khwaamsǎamákkhii*) was an excuse to suppress critiques like the one described above. Unity is invoked almost obsessively in Thai political discourse, much as it was by Por and Ae after the crackdown. Elites and conservatives do not suffer pluralism gladly. For them, Thailand either enjoys total political consensus, or it is hopelessly divided.[34] Absolutist ideas overwhelmed the

34. Pavin Chachavalpongpun, "'Unity' as a Discourse in Thailand's Polarized Politics," *Southeast Asian Affairs* no.1 (2010): 332–342.

airwaves as well as daily conversation in 2010 and 2011, crowding out other po- litical positions. The state has long advanced *khwaampenthai* (Thainess) as a local form of ethnic essentialism. Its precepts are taught to Thai students from a very young age, especially in school and the media. The reminders continue in adult life through twice-daily open-air broadcasts of the national anthem, state censorship of dissident voices in the media, the highly demonstrative use of *lèse-majesté* laws, and compulsory airing of nationalist content on television and radio. Thailand's Queen Sirikit summed up the ethos of Thainess in a poem she wrote for her 79th birthday in 2011, which read in part: "The Thai national anthem reminds Thais, day and night, to always remember that for Thailand to continue to exist, Thais must adhere to unity."[35] Not everyone agrees, assuredly, but those who do are resolute.[36] After the crackdown, anxiety over division was rampant. Drawings in art exhibitions depicted Thailand as a single body with two heads attacking each other. Musicians wrote songs about families pulled apart by divided political loyalties.[37] The anxiety in these representations explains why the need for unity was such a powerful con- straint for the Red Shirts' sonic practices, and ultimately for their political goals.

TIMELINE OF PROTESTS

Why did the Red Shirts organize and mobilize? The answer evolved in tandem with the protests themselves. The most visible and significant phase of the Red Shirt movement (which had been developing in some form since at least 2006) began in mid-March 2010, when tens of thousands of its members gathered in Bangkok. Former prime minister Thaksin Shinawatra, in exile from the country to avoid cor- ruption charges, had had over $1 billion of his assets frozen by the Thai Supreme Court two weeks earlier. Many Red Shirts were diehard supporters of Thaksin, whom they had helped elect democratically as prime minister in 2001 and again in 2005. Both of these elections were viewed by most outside observers as procedur- ally legitimate. When Thaksin was ousted in a 2006 military coup, and then even- tually replaced by an unelected member of the opposition party (democrat Abhisit Vejjajiva) through questionable parliamentary maneuvers, the Red Shirts concluded that Thai democracy was a farce, and that working-class, rural people were being

35. Pavin Chachavalpongpun, "Royal Motherhood Statement," August 4, 2011, http:// asiapacific.anu.edu.au/newmandala/2011/08/04/royal-motherhood-statement/.

36. The silence surrounding expressions of disunity is such that few written trails are left. However, the critiques that do circulate tend to be dramatic. For example, a Thai blogger using the handle timeupthailand posted a widely-read and highly personal account of disillusionment titled "Why I Don't Love the King" on her website, and freelance journalist Andrew MacGregor Marshall distributed a multi-part critique of the Thai monarchy in 2010.

37. For example, Rung Suriya's 2009 self-released single "The Land Weeps" describes a fic- tional household in which a mother and father who disagree about politics grapple with the division under their roof.

selectively shut out of governmental power. Daily protests began all around the city, including large rallies at a military base called RAB 11. There was a ritual cursing ceremony at which hundreds of gallons of human blood were spilled on the ground at the threshold of Abhisit's home. At these rallies, the top spokespeople from the central Red Shirt organizing faction, called the United Front for Democracy Against Dictatorship (UDD), gave speeches from impromptu stages to large crowds in the sweltering air of the hot season. The Red Shirt protesters braved the heat to make demands including *abhisit 'ɔɔkpay* ("Abhisit get out") and *yúp sàphaa* ("dissolve parliament").

Two weeks after these protests began, on March 31, I landed in Bangkok to begin my fieldwork. Lumphini Park, near my apartment, was one of several downtown bases for the growing ranks of the Red Shirts. Within a week, the army had closed the park entirely. Protesters also gathered near Ratchaprasong intersection, site of the nearest Skytrain station. The walk to the station took me south on Lang Suan Road, where in the shadow of insurance and apartment towers, street vendors made up a cheering section for passing Red Shirts. Exuberant protesters drove up and down all day in motorcycles or trucks, blasting music and waving truly enormous red flags. Lang Suan connects at one end with Phloen Chit, a major east-west route through the city where protesters had begun camping out beneath the broad cement slabs of the Skytrain. Near the camps, the UDD trucked in stacks of speakers for music and oratory, so large that they were rumored to be on loan or rented from politically sympathetic concert organizers. Just one block west from that point is Ratchaprasong intersection, where several of the swankest shopping centers in Asia are clustered near luxury car showrooms and international hotels. The architecture around the intersection is vertical, open-air, glassy, and imposing in its displays of wealth. It was, historically speaking, an unusual place to hold a political protest. This is where the occupation began to take shape, and where it eventually coalesced.

In fact, the Red Shirts were canny in occupying Ratchaprasong. In decades past, a park in the old city called Sanam Luang, near where most government and royal administrative buildings are located, was the principal site for political rallies. Sanam Luang was preferred because of its proximity to a group of buildings that were the seat of power in Bangkok, and thus the entire country. Certain landmarks nearby, especially Democracy Monument, were also vital gathering points because they were near Sanam Luang and its unrivaled royal gravitas. Near there, protesters had historically confronted the apex of the nation's political and moral hierarchy. Almost all of Bangkok's major protest events in the twentieth century happened within a mile of Sanam Luang. In 2010, however, the Red Shirts congregated instead mostly in business districts, including Ratchaprasong and a banking and insurance hub called Sala Daeng. The Red Shirts recognized that at this stage in history, disrupting shopping could provide more leverage than disrupting parliament. Evers and Korff note this shift in Thailand's symbolic geography: "While the centrality of the palaces, the temples and the ceremonial grounds was based on an intrinsic sacredness of the locality, and their constellation was based on cosmological principles, the centrality of the modern buildings, the temples in which the economy is now celebrated, is based on the sacrality of the modern economy."[38] The malls were now as important as the temples. They had become the center of attention, and therefore also the fulcrum of political negotiation.

In April and May 2010, there were many violent exchanges between protesters and the military, both in Ratchaprasong and elsewhere. Much of the fighting occurred in darkness. Confusion ensued about who was fighting whom, for what reasons, on whose behalf, and with what weapons. On April 10, as soldiers attempted to occupy a bridge, twenty-five people were killed in a long night of fighting. Among these were ten protesters, nine bystanders, five soldiers, and a Japanese cameraman working for Reuters (see Chapter 7). Both the government and the UDD blamed an invisible "third hand," a secretive force that was supposedly inciting violence. Further muddying the water was the fact that many soldiers and police were sympathetic to the Red Shirts. Some reportedly defied their superiors' orders. In the press, these were called "watermelon soldiers" (green on the outside, but red in their hearts) and "tomato policemen" (openly red). The military scrambled to bring their troops in line. These months were full of disquiet and doubt on all sides.

By mid-April, the Red Shirts occupied Ratchaprasong intersection fully and securely, and the protesters began to see themselves as permanent residents of the tent cities they had constructed. As would happen with Occupy Wall Street in the United States and the Arab Spring in multiple countries the following year, spaces of dissent became utopian models of daily living. The Red Shirt protests, in retrospect, prefigured those later international movements in many ways. People slept on foam mats just inches from the painted yellow lines on the road, attempting to build a new kind of political community among the symbols and materials of the existing order. At either end of a large, gated encampment, trucks blocked the way in, and volunteer Red Shirt guards checked everyone entering at a single point. Soon, tire and bamboo barricades were erected in place of the trucks. An opaque blue sheet covered the road like a canopy to block the view of helicopters and other overhead surveillance by the government. Within the protest space, which was closed to motor traffic and the military, but accessible to Red Shirts as well as some outside observers, thousands of people settled into a new and strange normalcy. Food stalls, political paraphernalia, laundry, and toilets were set up by networks of volunteers, as well as by independent Red Shirt vendors (see Chapter 10). These suggested the possibility of a parallel economy or society. Music played throughout the day, and pirate radio stations broadcast speeches and solicited call-in donations. In the evening, the main stage at Ratchaprasong—a huge structure set up in the middle of the road—was used by upstart Red Shirt musicians like the gritty-voiced *mor lam* singer Esompo Palui (see Chapter 4). Esompo and others were thrust into

38. Hans-Dieter Evers and Rüdiger Korff, *Southeast Asian Urbanism: The Meaning and Power of Social Space* (Hampshire, UK: Palgrave Macmillan, 2001), 228.

the spotlight by the daily demand for politicized entertainment. Crowds danced into the night, grateful to be engaged after long, repetitive days of occupation. Then, on May 19, the Thai military began a violent crackdown to disperse the movement, bringing tanks, assault rifles, and grenades to downtown Bangkok. During the assault, dozens were killed and thousands were injured. When the fighting and destruction ended, large sections of the city's downtown lay in charred ruin.

The Red Shirt rallies, remarkably, paused for only a few weeks after this violence. Many protesters were at first quite reluctant to return. But a few notable figures, including activist Sombat Boonngamanong (see Chapter 2), explored new and more theatrical modes of resistance. Sombat began organizing weekly coffee shop discussions called "Red Sunday," which evolved into happenings meant to surrogate the movement's martyrs. The first time this happened, Sombat was arrested, but since he had broken no laws, he was released by the police within hours. Sombat's theatrics exemplified a new set of nonviolent activist tactics that many Red Shirts adopted after May 19. These tactics were artful in every sense, emphasizing decentralization and indirect critique of the government. Protesters also adopted new sonic principles. One Red Shirt organizer, posting on a prominent UDD blog under the name banphai4, said that one of the core principals of the post-crackdown Red Shirt movement was its newly minimal approach to broadcasting. "The Red Shirts can protest without amplification, without stages, and without speeches. These will be protests of conversation. Of singing songs."[39] Fearing confrontation and arrest, some Red Shirts began developing techniques that would be potent but still legally compliant, allowing them to move lithely through the abiding field of constraints. By mid-2010, the giant speaker systems used earlier in the year were rapidly falling out of fashion.

In the coming months, the new wave of protests increased in frequency, size, and sophistication. On some weekends, events were small and scattered, with concerts in the provinces and small picnics in parks among friends. But sometimes, especially on dates of great significance such as the monthly anniversaries of the crackdown, thousands or even tens of thousands of people gathered. By October 2010, the events had become highly regular and were announced weeks in advance on Facebook, through SMS updates, and especially by flyers at smaller events. There were concerts, speeches, dances, lectures, meals, and flash mobs, often all in the same area. If the UDD had once been the primary voice of the Red Shirts, splinter groups increasingly commanded their own constituencies, and wielded their own organizing forces.[40] The iteration of the Red Shirt movement that followed

39. "New Dimensions of Protest," accessed January 22, 2013, http://www.norporchoreu.com/board/index.php?topic=635.0;wap2. Translated from the original Thai.
40. This book does not interrogate the structure of the UDD. Although UDD orators were quite important, and protesters spent a great deal of time listening to them, I am less concerned with crowds at the scale of mass audition than with the fine-grained divisions of sonic and auditory life within the gatherings.

the crackdown, for this reason, was more diffuse. The rallies were less focused on one large main stage, and increasingly marked by small sonic niches that had distinct aesthetics and ideologies. Every performance was surrounded by many other performances, each of which differed in purpose and style. This phase of the protests lasted for at least a year, until a Red Shirt-friendly prime minister, Yingluck Shinawatra (Thaksin's sister), was elected in July 2011. The research for this book took place between March 2010 and July 2011, but the period after the crackdown and before Yingluck's election—June 2010 through July 2011—is its primary focus.[41] This phase of relative stability offered an opportunity to examine the spaces of protest gatherings in ethnographic depth over a long period.

MEDIA MANAGEMENT

As the military and Red Shirts each strategized to control their tense showdown in spring 2010, media management became a priority. The Red Shirts relied on a nimble, loose national network of thousands of tiny local radio stations that kept protesters abreast of new developments, organized donation drives, played music, and criticized the government (see Chapter 4). Such criticism was unheard of on free-to-air television and radio stations, most of which are owned and overseen by the military. Red Shirt organizers also ran a satellite television station called People Channel that aired partisan news and talk shows, and that also supplied the rallies with broadcasting equipment. The military and government used the media for countercriticism, for example by promulgating a viral photograph of a Red Shirt protester hoisting his young son onto a stack of tires as the Thai army massed on the horizon.[42] This image was used to imply that the Red Shirts were fundamentally malicious, stupid, and immoral. A pro-government friend of mine mentioned a clip she saw on television in which a journalist asked a dark-skinned Red Shirt a question to which he gave no reply, instead staring silently ahead. The journalist wondered aloud, on the basis of this silent treatment, whether the Red Shirts were not actually Thai people, but instead Cambodian or Burmese mercenaries being paid to protest by Thaksin. My friend considered the report credible.

Struggles over media were central to the political crisis. The army raided the headquarters of People Channel in April 2010. Soldiers began shutting down radio

---

41. The brief description above covers only a fraction of the potentially important details about the political scene into which the Red Shirts stepped. For more information in English, see for instance Charles Keyes, *Finding Their Voice: Northeastern Villagers and the Thai State* (Seattle: University of Washington Press, 2014); Tyrell Haberkorn, "Hannah Arendt, Nidhi Eoseewong, and the Spectre of Totalitarianism in Thailand," *The Asia-Pacific Journal: Japan Focus*, 12, no. 14 (No.4, 2014): 1–6; Pavin Chachavalpongpun, *Good Coup Gone Bad: Thailand's Political Development Since Thaksin's Downfall* (Singapore: Institute of Southeast Asian Studies, 2014); and Sopranzetti, *Owners of the Map*.

42. "Thai Protesters Using Children as Shields, Army Claims," *The Guardian*, May 17, 2010.

stations as well, claiming that station DJs were inciting listeners to "disturb the peace."[43] Tens of thousands of anti-government websites were also shut down under the Computer Crimes Act of 2007, which was designed to control pornography, criticism of the monarchy, and other unlawful material. Though criticism of secular political officials was not at that time illegal, the Emergency Decree issued by prime minister Abhisit early in the year nevertheless gave security forces broad powers to regulate speech according to their personal judgment. The Computer Crimes Act thus became a potent and highly unpredictable instrument. The army, meanwhile, maintained a special media-focused subunit of its special forces division tasked with psychological operations (see Chapter 14). The military's own publicly available post-mortem report declared its media operations a success, concluding that: "The CRES (Center for the Resolution of the Emergency Situation) was able to capitalize on control of TV coverage" and that "the complete censorship of all kinds of communication was a major strategic operation."[44]

A systematic analysis of the media environment of the Red Shirt protests was difficult before the May 19 crackdown, because of the legal and physical risks of being inside the occupied area. Foreign journalists and researchers were scrutinized and surveilled by the government, and extended conversation with Red Shirt partisans invited suspicion. There was also significant danger of violence, especially as the crackdown approached. The protest space, once teeming, had been abandoned by many fearful protesters after the government publicly warned that it planned to "take back" the occupied spaces. Many Red Shirt leaders fled the country altogether. The remaining protesters understood that they might be taking a last stand before death. As military tanks plowed through the bamboo barricades and live rifle shots pierced the air, a handful of people fought back, mostly with small arms. Downtown was a battle zone during an operation called *sàlǎay kaanchumnum* (protest dispersal). The dispersal and the time leading up to it were not conducive to research, except perhaps into the phenomenology of fear and confusion. Subsequent obfuscations by the government make this period almost as difficult to research archivally. The Thai government often deflects crucial questions, such as when Colonel Sansern Kaewkamnerd infamously claimed that "it is hard for the army to give explanations about every single dead body."[45] Most evidence is fragmentary, or has been destroyed. This is as true for a musical or sonic accounting as it is for any other kind of inquiry. Among the wrecked remains after May 19 were felled stacks of speakers, wires, stage rigging, and vending tables. The fragile ecology of

43. "เช็กบิลวิทยุชุมชน เครื่องมือปลุกระดมคนเสื้อแดง" ("It's 'Check, Please' for Community Radio, a Tool of Incitement for the Red Shirts"). Translated from the original Thai. http://www.manager.co.th/Local/ViewNews.aspx?NewsID=9530000074366, May 30, 2010.

44. "Lessons from Operation Encirclement at Ratchaprasong," *Prachatai*, June 7, 2011. https://prachatai.com/english/node/2642.

45. Human Rights Watch, "Descent into Chaos: Thailand's 2010 Red Shirt Protests and the Government Crackdown," May 3, 2011, 4. https://www.hrw.org/report/2011/05/03/descent-chaos/thailands-2010-red-shirt-protests-and-government-crackdown.

the protest space, with all of its media and sonic niches, was wiped out in short order, and proved enormously challenging to piece back together.

BRIEF NOTES ON POLITICAL INFLUENCE AND GENRE

A discussion of music, sound, and media at the Red Shirt protests requires a few words about Thaksin, a deeply contradictory figure, and a few more about musical genre. Thaksin, the deposed former prime minister beloved by many Red Shirts, did not set foot in Thailand during 2010 and 2011, but his presence was powerfully felt. He communicated with protest leaders, and may have directed and funded parts of the protests. At many larger protest rallies, he appeared by Skype in the early evening, as the highlight of the night's scheduled entertainment, speaking remotely on a humongous screen to his throngs of fans. Thaksin was also present in less overt ways. He earned his billions in media and communications, and was in a sense responsible for creating the market for the very technologies that many of the Red Shirt protesters now used. The media world of the Red Shirt protests owed a sort of debt to Thaksin's entrepreneurialism.

The former prime minister has often been described as neoliberal because, as prime minister, he privatized major industries and granted concessions for public infrastructure and agriculture projects to large corporations. But the economic program known as "Thaksinomics" also ran contrary in many ways to the explicitly neoliberal restructuring of the Thai economy by the International Monetary Fund in 1997.[46] Thaksin was a nationalist, even a statist, rather than a globalist. Moreover, Thaksin's major accomplishments were in forms of social welfare, including policies of poverty alleviation that gave the poor debt forgiveness, low-interest loans, and improved access to health care. Thus, while Thailand's economy as it ran under Thaksin may exemplify neoliberalism in some ways, it diverged sharply from it in others. Of course, Thaksin knew that as a businessman he could sell more goods when his consumer base had money to spend, and when the poor were more dependent upon the national economy. His version of government welfare was arguably a boon to no one more than himself and his businesses, as Kasian Tejapira has noted.[47] On the other hand again, Thaksin helped bring rural Thais into the fold of democratic participation. And yet he was also responsible for major human rights violations that affected marginal people enormously, particularly in the Muslim south.[48] He is a figure of many contradictions, with which all the music

46. Claudio Sopranzetti, *Owners of the Map*, 123. Sopranzetti argues forcefully for a subtler understanding of neoliberalism, especially with regard to Thaksin, that can account for how the approach functions contextually. He details how Thaksin's political rise was in fact predicated, at least rhetorically, on a rejection of neoliberalism.

47. Kasian Tejapira, "Toppling Thaksin," *New Left Review*, May 22, 2006.

48. Thaksin committed vast human rights violations as prime minister. He oversaw a violent war on drugs, and bore at least some direct responsibility for the Tak Bai massacre in Southern

written as an ode to him (and there was a lot of it among the Red Shirts) is likewise saddled. Neoliberalism is only at best partially explanatory for Red Shirt music and its economies (Chapter 11, Chapter 13).[49] This music must be understood, rather, as relating to neoliberalism in an irreducibly local fashion. In Chapters 11 and 13, money and economy are presented as constraints that limited the mobility of the Red Shirt movement and its sounds. Thaksin is an important point of reference throughout these discussions.

Contradictions around money pervaded everyday exchanges among Red Shirt protesters. For example, Red Shirt musicians spoke of their fundamentally moral duty (*nâathîi*) to the movement, even as some of them made a great deal of money by participating in it. These exchanges and conceptions of duty remediated the genre of *mor lam*, a largely temple-based genre grounded in moral and religious ritual and pedagogy. The traditional values of *mor lam* were, at Red Shirt protests, ported to a setting of protest, which required those values to adapt significantly. I describe these values ethnographically in several chapters, including one about a master *phin* player named Mii with whom I studied for a year (see Chapter 13). Mii and I met while he was playing at a political rally. But the implications of his performance turned out to be complex, typifying the knots of music, morality, dissent, and money that entangled Red Shirt performers and listeners.

The Red Shirt membership drew heavily from the provinces outside Bangkok, especially the northeast, reflecting a transformation in the ethnic makeup of the capital. Since the 1960s and perhaps earlier, the profitability of rice farming has been hampered by consolidation of land ownership and low crop values.[50] Thais born into farming families now increasingly migrate to Bangkok—the political, financial, and touristic capital of the country—for work. Many people have started families in the city, while others labor seasonally, maintaining connections to their villages and returning home for the rice planting season, the harvest, or annual festivals. Many older residents of provincial areas have children in Bangkok who are students, retail workers, maids, taxi drivers, recyclers, or sex workers. Often, these children send part of their earnings home. But in any case, few can rely entirely on farming any longer for their livelihoods. A major consequence of this change has been a steady increase in Bangkok's ethnic diversity over the course of five or

Thailand in 2004, when 85 political demonstrators were killed after being loaded into an army truck, then beaten or suffocated to death.

49. Neoliberalism (*sěeriinîyom mài*) was of greatest concern in everyday politics in the late 1990s and early 2000s, when the IMF sought to impose broad economic reforms on the Thai economy after the Asian financial crisis of 1997. Thaksin was elected partly on the strength of promises he made to resist these alien reforms. However, Thaksin's policies ultimately included dimensions of a neoliberal agenda, and neoliberal subjectivities were arguably present among the Red Shirts. While neoliberalism remained a topic of some interest to both the left and right during the period of my fieldwork, it was not a word used often by Red Shirts.

50. Chris Baker and Pasuk Pongpaichat, *A History of Thailand* (New York: Cambridge University Press, 2009).

six decades. The number of northerners, northeasterners, Cambodians, Burmese, Malaysians, and Laotians in the capital has swelled. Because of internal migration, many outlying regions of the country now know firsthand the vast gulf between the austerity of the villages and the decadence of the city. Bangkok's many spoken accents reflect the region's migratory patterns. During my fieldwork, daily conversation with blue-collar workers often revolved around the noise, bustle, and conspicuous consumption of the city, which served as everyday foils to peaceful and ostensibly more moral small towns. This notion of an urban/rural binary animated the protests in key ways.

In song lyrics, particularly in the cross-pollinating genres of *luk thung* and *mor lam*, the imagined difference between the urban and the rural is central. *Luk thung* has been a popular genre since the mid-twentieth century, while *mor lam* describes a range of Lao and northeastern Thai ritual styles. The two genres share some instrumentation, and many artists have fused them. Other musicians have pioneered subgenres, especially devolving from *mor lam*, that exhibit almost totally new features. But nearly all varieties of the two genres, no matter their musical structure, share an ethos of rural purity. "The smell of country boys and girls blends with the buffaloes. It may not be as good as the smell of city boys' and girls' skins, which blend well with perfume. This makes them different from farmers," goes a line from the mid-twentieth century *luk thung* classic "The Odor of Buffalo."[51] Similar sentiments persist today. Ekkaphon Montrakan's 2010 ballad "Sweat for my Mother" describes the protagonist's thankless, low-paying physical labor in Bangkok as a repayment of debt to his hardworking mother. The song's video contrasts verdant provincial fields with the city's gray smog. The environmental comparison meanwhile suggests a moral gap; the farm may be a place of hardship, but the city is one of exploitation. Ethnomusicologist Yukti Mukdawijit suggests that *luk thung* and *mor lam* imply as a kind of trope that rural people "cannot communicate directly with the city people, who take advantage of them and are individualistic, selfish, aloof, and alienated."[52]

The music of the northeast, near the Laotian border, may be heard by the middle- and upper-classes as coarse and nonnative, perhaps even dangerous. Sedition might grow in those rice fields. Miller cites a royal decree from 1865 that rings familiar in discussions of provincial music, even today:

> Alien singing and dancing should not have priority over ours . . . Thai have abandoned their own entertainments . . . both men and women now play laokaen [mawlum] throughout the kingdom . . . His Majesty the King finds this kind of situation unfavorable. We cannot give the priority to Lao entertainments. Laokaen must serve the Thai; the Thai have never been the Lao's servants . . . You are

---

51. Translated from the original Thai.

52. Yukti Mukdawijitra, "The Sound of Politics in the Sound of Music," *Siam Rath*, March 18, 2009. Translated from the original Thai.

requested to stop performing laokaen . . . Anyone who disobeys this proclamation will be taxed. [53]

These same tensions were present in the music of the Red Shirts. Mitchell suggests that *luk thung* has stronger political themes than is often acknowledged, for instance in its use by the Communist Party in the 1970s.[54] The class and social difference sung about in much *luk thung* and *mor lam* was certainly apparent to the Red Shirts. The link between these genres and well-worn feelings of exclusion by provincial people is so strong that a minor-key accordion melody or *phin* riff can immediately raise the specter of class-based difference. Sound and music, suffused with symbols of identity, were thus already politicized—especially around issues of class—when they came to the capital city.

However, *mor lam* and *luk thung* have not remained stagnant, and have themselves been transformed by migration. *Luk thung* has urbanized, owing both to the influx of migrant laborers to Bangkok and to urban sprawl.[55] In truth *luk thung* has always been a polyglot genre, keeping pace with the modern global pop music industry since the 1930s. *Mor lam*, in branching out into a bevy of subgenres, has embraced ever-brighter stage shows and bawdier outfits, even while retaining a close relationship with regional Buddhist temples. Stylistic markers of the improvised central Thai ritual courtship genre *phleeng iiseew*, acoustic folk, Cambodian *kantrum*, ska, and Korean boy band music are routinely woven into *luk thung* and *mor lam*. These genres, provincial as they may be, have kept an ear open to global popular music.

As a final note on genre, this monograph pointedly avoids the term "protest music." Much American and European writing on "protest music" has focused on the U.S. labor movement and mid-twentieth century political movements.[56] Some scholarship uses "protest music" to categorize or explain later genres including hip-hop, heavy metal, and punk rock, though still usually through an Anglophone lens.[57] Recent work has considered sound, song, and dissent from the Global South,

53. Terry E. Miller, *Traditional Music of the Lao: Kaen Playing and Mawlum Singing in Northeast Thailand* (Westport, CT: Praeger, 1985), 38–39. The decree was given by King Mongkut.

54. James Mitchell, "Red and Yellow Songs: A Historical Analysis of the Use of Music by the United Front for Democracy against Dictatorship (UDD) and the People's Alliance for Democracy (PAD) in Thailand," *South East Asia Research* 19, no. 3 (2011): 457–494.

55. Terry Miller, "From Country Hick to Rural Hip: A New Identity Through Music for Northeast Thailand," *Asian Music* 36, 2 (Summer-Autumn 2005): 96–106.

56. For example, see Ron Eyerman and Andrew Jamison, *Music and Social Movements: Mobilizing Traditions in the Twentieth Century* (New York: Cambridge, 1998); Thomas Turino, *Music as Social Life* (Chicago: University of Chicago Press, 2008); and Ian Peddie, ed., *The Resisting Muse: Popular Music and Social Protest* (Burlington, VT: Ashgate, 2006). While Reebee Garofalo ed., *Rockin' the Boat: Mass Music and Mass Movements* (Cambridge, MA: South End Press, 1992) includes more international case studies, the majority of these are framed in terms gleaned from U.S.-based political movements.

57. Courtney Brown, *Politics in Music: Political Transformation from Beethoven to Hip-Hop* (Atlanta, GA: Farsight Press, 2007); Ellen C. Leichtman, "The Different Sounds of American Protest: From Freedom Songs to Punk Rock," in Mathieu Deflem, ed., *Popular Culture,*

or at least outside of the U.S.[58] But the term "protest music" (which was not, in fact, coined until the mid-twentieth century) is often imprecise. The use of "protest music" to describe all modes of sounded dissent may reinforce a set of presumptions about what dissent is *supposed* to sound like, thereby excluding modes of expression that perform resistance or refusal but that do not narrowly match the aesthetics of, say, Bob Dylan or Woody Guthrie.[59] Commitment to understanding different modes of sounded dissent thus requires avoiding historically narrow terms like "protest music," which is better understood as a genre.

MEDIA SPACES

To return to and elaborate upon the opening moments of this introduction, *Bangkok Is Ringing* is structured around media technologies and their sonic spaces. The larger and longer Red Shirt rallies could be heard as subdivided, usually by media, into sonic niches. Myriad small factions within the Red Shirt movement distinguished themselves spatially and ideologically through music and sound. Sonic niches were not ordered by media alone, however. Media mingled with longstanding habits of public gathering to produce events that were both familiar and novel. Miller's *Traditional Music of the Lao*, researched in the mid-1970s, briefly describes an outdoor entertainment scene that might be described as a terrain of sonic niches. The author's description could be applied nearly verbatim to the Red Shirt protests four decades later: "The Red Cross Fair in Mahasarakam held January,

Crime and Social Control (Bingley, United Kingdom: Emerald Group Publishing Limited, 2010): 173–91.

58. For example, see Farzaneh Hemmasi, "Intimating Dissent: Popular Song, Poetry, and Politics in Pre-Revolutionary Iran," *Ethnomusicology* 57, no. 1 (Winter 2013): 57–87; Jonathan Sterne, "Quebec's #casseroles: On Participation, Percussion, and Protest," *Sounding Out!*, June 4, 2012, http:// soundstudiesblog.com/2012/06/04/casseroles; Noriko Manabe, "The No Nukes 2012 Concert and the Role of Musicians in the Anti-Nuclear Movement," *Japan Focus* http://www.japanfocus.org/-Noriko-MANABE/3799; Michael Bodden, "Rap in Indonesian Youth Music of the 1990s: "Globalization," "Outlaw Genres," and Social Protest" *sian Music* 36, no. 2 (Summer/Fall 2005): 1–26; Oded Heilbronner, "Resistance Through Rituals"— Urban Subcultures of Israeli Youth from the Late 1950s to the 1980s," *Israel Studies* 16, no. 3 (Fall 2011): 28–50; Sharon Hayashi and Anne McKnight, "Good-bye Kitty, Hello War: The Tactics of Spectacle and New Youth Movements in Urban Japan," *positions: east asia cultures critique* 13, no. 1 (Spring 2005): 87–113; Tse-Hsiung Lin, "Mountain Songs, Hakka Songs, Protest Songs: A Case Study of Two Hakka Singers from Taiwan" *Asian Music* 42, no. 1 (Winter/ Spring 2011): 85–122; Heather MacLachlan, *Burma's Pop Music Industry: Creators, Distributors, Censors* (Rochester, NY: University of Rochester, 2011); Jeffrey E. Taffet, "My Guitar is Not For the Rich: The New Chilean Song Movement and the Politics of Culture," *Journal of American Culture* 20 (1997); James Mitchell, "Kon Baan Diaokan or 'We're from the Same Village' - Star/ Fan Interaction in Thai Lukthung," *Perfect Beat* 12, no. 2 2011); and Peter Manuel, "World Music and Activism Since the End of History," *Music & Politics* XI, no. 1 (2017).

59. Benjamin Tausig, "Sound and Movement: Vernaculars of Sonic Dissent," *Social Text* 36, no. 3 (2018).

1974, included outdoor movies, games, restaurants, rumwong dancing, boxing, rides, popular music groups, mawlum moo, mawlum plün, and mawlum glawn. In such festivals each troupe, ride, restaurant, or entertainment attempts to overpower the competition with badly worn recordings of popular music played through powerful amplifiers and giant speakers."[60] Charles Keyes, similarly, notes that he was "struck in looking at video of the Red Shirt demonstrators . . . by how similar the gatherings were to Isan temple fairs."[61] Media forms thus did not by themselves determine the shape and relationship of sonic niches, but reworked these spaces in tandem with rituals and hierarchies of public life. I hope to demonstrate sonic media's role in a context where, as Neil Smith has put it, "socially divided societies reproduce their forms of social differentiation in geographical space."[62] A constructivist reading of boundaries is central to both sound studies and critical geography, and thus provides a disciplinary nexus for an examination of sonic space.[63] A close study of media and space is one means of carrying out such a reading.

Red Shirt protests were iterative—massive events took place every couple of weeks (sometimes more frequently), and tended to resemble previous events. Between June 2010 and July 2011, the protests settled into well-worn patterns. Relationships between smaller factions of the Red Shirts, as well as with local authorities, ran the gamut from cooperative to deeply suspicious. The niches within the rallies changed subtly over time, but the same broadcasters and listeners showed up routinely, and I got to know many of them well.[64] My methods involved walking, driving, running, trudging, ambling, bicycling, pacing, chatting, interviewing, networking, and hearing through the sonic niches at the events I attended.[65] I balanced individual and small group interviews with recordings of media broadcasts and live stage performances, and also recorded while moving through the spaces of the rallies. I once recorded from the top of a moving truck, once on the main UDD

60. Terry E. Miller, *Traditional Music of the Lao*, 36–37. The different forms of mawlum (or *mor lam*, as it is transliterated in this book) in the quote refer to different poetic idioms.

61. Charles Keyes, *Finding Their Voice*.

62. Neil Smith, "Neo-Critical Geography, Or, The Flat Pluralist World of Business Class," *Antipode* 37, no. 5 (2005): 887–899.

63. In this regard, "Bangkok Is Ringing" is also indebted to Thongchai Winichakul's *Siam Mapped: A History of the Geo-Body of a Nation* (Honolulu, HI: University of Hawaii Press, 1997). See also Georgina Born, ed., *Music, Sound, and Space*.

64. I use the term "broadcasting" to refer to the action of spreading an announcement, performance, or program to an audience, however widely. Although the term is typically used in reference to mass media, I also use it to describe small-scale transmissions such as concerts or even unamplified singalongs. Interestingly, both the English term "broadcast" and the Thai equivalent, *kràjaay*, are metaphors drawn from agriculture, in which the word refers to the scattering of seeds.

65. I recorded with a Sony PCM D50 portable digital audio recorder, just a little larger than pocket-sized and inconspicuous aside from a windscreen invariably described as looking like a head of hair. The recorder was set to a bitrate of 24 and a sampling rate of 48 kHz/s except in certain situations. For still-photos and video, I used a Canon D90 DSLR camera. All attributed interviews were recorded with verbal consent, although I occasionally used a binaural microphone for ambient sound in public settings.

stage while facing a crowd of 50,000 people, and many times among the grieving and dead.

Over the course of sixteen months, I attended as many dissident gatherings as possible, most in Bangkok but many outside the capital as well. I became acquainted or close with people of varying ages, occupations, and backgrounds. The faces and voices of many others became at least passingly familiar. By mid-2011, I knew a handful of regulars quite well, including the man who taught me to play the *phin* (Chapter 13), the organizers of Red Sunday (Chapter 2), many performing musicians and CD vendors (Chapters 10 and 11), and rank-and-file protesters (Chapters 3, 6, 7, et al.) I sought out my contacts at each event, asking for updates, lending assistance and, in many cases, arranging to hang out informally. Some people were quite familiar with the arcana of the American academy (a few even had degrees conferred by it), while others had little sense of why a foreigner would research Thai protests at all. This of course affected the dynamics of field-work. Meanwhile, many of my contacts were engaged in documentation or media projects themselves, in which case I was typically expected to reciprocate their help. If I followed one group, for example, I might be asked to serve as an ambassador for their political program abroad. (Not to say that I always did so). I edited text for the English-language version of a blog, recorded English-language voice-over audio for a film project, translated printed material from Thai to English, and appeared in promotional photographs, to name a few small acts. Those who asked for these things had little time for principles of objectivity—they wanted help with their ac-tivism. There is no fieldwork without favors, and in this case there was no fieldwork without alliance.

At some events I sat for hours, assisting a lone CD vendor, watching people listen in a single spot, or spending idle time with musicians. At others I kept moving. My emphasis depended on the gathering, and on the pertinent questions that it raised. I was surveilled as well, both by the military and protesters, with varying degrees of seriousness. *Farang*, a catchall category for light-skinned foreigners from many countries, often came to observe protests, but only a few came regularly, and even fewer were not journalists linked to well-known media outlets. As an ethnogra-pher practicing long-term participant-observation without press credentials, I was a curiosity, an object of interest, for better or worse a chattering part of the scene (see Chapter 16). After several months of regular attendance, I began to sketch a typology of the sonic niches of the Red Shirt protests, so that I might begin to explain how each expressed ideological significance. I noted the broadcasting technologies in each spatial type, which ranged from professional sound systems to tiny, barely functional amplifiers—and the extents and contours of their range. As the book stands, incomplete even in its published form, these comprise spaces of traffic (Chapter 1); republican middle-class activism (Chapter 2); atrocity video viewing (Chapter 3); regional radio station trucks (Chapter 4); megaphone singing (Chapter 5); megaphone lecturing (Chapter 6); quiet and silence (Chapter 7); whistle-blowing (Chapter 8); vehicular audio (Chapter 9); CD vending tables

(Chapter 10); stage music (Chapter 11); chanting (Chapter 12); entrepreneurial busking (Chapter 13); surveillance and propaganda (Chapter 14); fatigue and respite (Chapter 15); and the imaginary points from which some of us tried, neckdeep and witless, to parse everything (Chapter 16).

I asked questions and was in response invited to dinners and protests in new places, to study instruments and to train choirs. The typology is of course incomplete. With more time and resources, the scope of the study could have been much wider without losing focus. The longer my fieldwork continued, the longer the list of niches grew. Eventually it became clear that the breadth of the typology, its messiness, was a revelation in itself. The structure of this book, with its abnormally high number of chapters, is an attempt to represent the heterogeneity of media and sonic space at Red Shirt protests, to portray the mess without enervating it. The chapters are laid out in ways that reflect the relations between spaces. Each, in effect, represents a sonic niche. The chapters are a heaped, heterogeneous bundle that sometimes resonate with each other, and sometimes conflict. Some of the chapters describe a linear space produced by resonant sound, while others are full of the temporal deferrals and oddly shaped diffusions produced by media technology.

Media stratification is also an important analytic, as it was an important constraint for the mobility of communication. The Red Shirts were often described as the opponents of a group called the Yellow Shirts. In pro-government media, the Reds were stereotyped as upcountry rabble, and the Yellows as nationalists, while international channels like the BBC and CNN tended to frame the schism as a matter of candidate or party preference. Both characterizations carry a grain of truth, but the issues were never really so streamlined. Conservative media in Thailand was particularly harsh in its coverage of the Red Shirts. ASTV, a satellite television station owned by Yellow Shirt media tycoon Sondhi Limthongkul, established some of the most enduring invective early in the history of the Red Shirt movement. After a 2007 rally (at that point, the movement was still small, and the color red was not yet in wide symbolic use), a daily television program called *yaamfâw phèndin* ("Protecting the Land") featured a conversation between the hosts about a proto-Red rally the previous day. They claimed that these protesters had been hired by Thaksin, that they were "seeking chaos," and that the movement was inorganic and funded through murky channels.[66] Furthermore, said one host, the protesters were people "of low quality" who "lacked human hearts."[67] The dehumanization of Red Shirts on ASTV was normalized very early, and spread quickly beyond the channel

66. "มอบไข่แม้ว"เริ่มพ่ายแพ้ทางการเมือง หลังสลัดภาพท่อน้ำเลี้ยงอำนาจเก่า และความถ่อย-เถื่อนไม่พ้น" ("An Analysis of the 'Cat' Mob Leaving the Picture; Whether They are Bogus, For-Hire Protesters is Not Clear"), June 14, 2007, http://www.manager.co.th/Home/ViewNews.aspx?NewsID=9500000068844. (Transcript from an episode of the television show "Protecting the Land").
67. Ibid.

on which it began. ASTV and others who appealed to a far-right, nationalist audience would not moderate their message.

Meanwhile the Red Shirts, along with political centrists, communists, leftist intellectuals, global pop culture enthusiasts, and devout Buddhists, could also each access broadcast outlets and websites that delivered politically targeted content. Mediated sonic niches in the in-person spaces of Red Shirt protests were constrained by the same ideological partitioning that characterized the media more generally in Thailand. Journalist Nick Nostitz, reporting on a 2011 Red Shirt rally in the northeastern city of Udon Thani, described the frustration of experiencing this stratification, which resulted from constrained mobility:

> Behind the brightly lit new building of the radio station, Udon Lovers staff sold 'Red Radios' for 340 baht and Red mobile phones for 990 baht . . . I noticed no journalists other than Red Shirt media. There was no TV coverage; no coverage of this event in any newspapers I know of. I wonder how it can be possible that such a large event can go completely unnoticed by the local media? I understand that every small Red Shirt stage cannot be covered by the media . . . but isn't the largest Red Shirt gathering since last year's rallies a news event important to cover?[68]

Nostitz's two questions ("how can it be possible that such a large event can go completely unnoticed?" and "isn't [this large gathering] important to cover?") drive to the heart of how both the Red Shirt movement and its media circulations were constrained. Large events *could* go unnoticed, and *could* be dismissed as unimportant, when certain constraints were present. All too often, they were. The task of *Bangkok Is Ringing* is to feel out the contours of these constraints ethnographically, through sound in particular, and to understand how such limitations both reiterated existing power structures and at times offered opportunities for political transformation. The constrained mobility of sound and the constrained mobility of movements might thus speak to one another.

68. Nick Nostitz, "A Mass Rally and a Funeral," *New Mandala*, April 8, 2011. http://asiapacific. anu.edu.au/newmandala/2011/04/08/a-mass-rally-and-a-funeral/.

CHAPTER 1
Completely Packed In

The bus came to rest at another intersection, where it parked quietly and for a long time because of a stalled car in the middle of the street. The rain fell. Through the window, I could see a man pushing his car. But he couldn't push it anywhere because, all around, the cars were completely packed in. If he pushed it, I guess it would just hit the other cars.

He looked pitiful out there, his body all soaked by the rain. The people sitting on the bus with me looked out with dispassionate expressions, perhaps thinking that you get what you deserve. Isn't that how it always goes?

This is the torture I had to sit through. I'd been on that hellish bus for almost two hours already. It was hot. The heat baking the bus didn't relent at all. Both sides of my face were itching from the lines of sweat running down, which I tried desperately to blow onto my chest.

No one on the bus said a word. People were packed in right in front of me, some standing and some sitting. Some people hung their heads, others stared forward with no sense of purpose. Still others watched the street flood with water. I knew very well that everyone was being restrained and patient. I thought to myself that the patience of human beings is tremendous indeed. Even in wrenching conditions like this, no one complained. No one even spoke. No one looked like they were about to get off the bus.

Wanich Charungkichanan, *"The Royal City"*[1]

The Red Shirts praised patience, the patience they'd displayed already and that which they would soon need. The struggle might not advance for years. Worse still, nothing might happen today. Patience was a mantra that could ward off tedium, so the word *òt thon* was repeated when tedium struck.

Most Red Shirt protests were mobile, beginning at Ratchaprasong and traveling to Democracy Monument or Bangkok Remand Prison. But in Bangkok, the royal city, mobility often means going nowhere. It means patience. Protesters idled for hours, like commuters, just like they did when they weren't protesting. Red Shirt

1. Wanich Charungkichanan, "เมืองหลวง" ("The Royal City"), in *Wanich 60.5: มองผ่านชีวิตหกสิบปีครึ่ง* (*Wanich 60.5: Looking Back at My Life of 60.5 Years*) (Bangkok: Open Books, 2010). Translated from the original Thai.

cars and trucks crept along roads and highways, baking with the buses. (To part the seas of traffic, as royal convoys do daily, is a sacred act). As these caravans entered the traffic swell, they were subsumed. Their music was masked by the great slow roar of engines after the light turned green. At Makkasan Bridge, the traffic met a thousand cars which became a lumbering mass groaning left toward the highway, all color and sound greyed out.

I walked along the caravan, inching through the thin steam lingering over the road, chatting with people in truck beds. No one could broadcast further than the sphere around their own vehicle. The stuck protesters each jubilated in a space like a hot closet. Launching a movement might mean embracing this inertia. No one complained. No one, literally or figuratively, looked like they were about to get off the bus.

CHAPTER 2

Red Sunday

Power and Connections

W e urged Mae to sing.[1] Though drunk, and years out of practice, she shook the rust from her vocal cords and agreed, straightening in her seat. The chatter in the garden fell away as she began, and into the clearing of quiet came the song's first line, soft and melismatic:

tɔɔn thamnaa khâa chûu daawrɯang
("When I was a rice farmer, my name was Shimmering Star. . . .")[2]

Ten of us—volunteers, friends, members of a movement—sat on Mae's patio in Bangkok on a sticky night in late April 2011. On the picnic table lay half-devoured plates of grilled eggplant, gray-brown Singha beer bottles smudged with oily fingerprints, and the bright white bones of salted *plaa kràphong*. The range still fired, sending a whiff of propane and food into the air, though we were long past full. Orn, Mae's daughter, my closest confidante among Red Shirt activists, played sober, hovering hostess, while her mother sang and spoke about her cabaret years, democracy, and the bittersweet history of her house, as long as her guests would stay. She bounced boozily between nostalgic anecdotes from her career as a singer and politically charged invective about the oppression of working people in the early twenty-first century. The past met the present; in fact, they were difficult to tell apart. *daawrɯang daawrooy* ("Shimmering Star, Fading Star"), the song she sang,

1. For another treatment of the case study at the end of this chapter, see Benjamin Tausig, "Sound and Movement: Vernaculars of Sonic Dissent," which was originally published in *Social Text* 36, no. 3. Copyright 2018, Duke University Press. All rights reserved. Republished by permission of the copyright holder, Duke University Press. www.dukeupress.edu.
2. Mae's singing, and all the conversation during the evening described, took place in Thai.

is a vintage *luk thung* hit, made famous over twenty years earlier by the tragic diva Pumpuang Duangjan. The song narrates a young girl's journey from the provinces of Thailand to Bangkok in search of fame or, at least, success. The song echoes Mae's own experience; as a young woman, she too traveled from the provinces to perform in Bangkok's night clubs. She continued:

> *phɔɔ khâw nay mɯang chɯ̂ɯ khâa fɯ̂ang lɯ̂anglɯɯ*
> ("When I came to the city, I grew famous. . . .")

Mae took care to articulate each *ɯ̂an*, or melismatic run, precisely as her favorite singer Pumpuang does in the studio version, recorded in 1989. There is substantial disjunct motion in the melody, and many of the notes are extensively decorated, making the tune an acrobatic feat to sing. The last syllable of the line, *lɯɯ*, jumps from the dominant note to the seventh, where it oscillates up to the octave and back down, landing tensely on the leading tone at the end of the measure. But Pumpuang's renown was not for her vocality alone. She melded blue-collar story-telling with a diva's stagecraft so well that many fans now insist that the entire genre of *luk thung* died with her. As Mae channeled Pumpuang, she could not suppress the rasp of age in her voice, but she could summon the defiant sweetness for which Pumpuang remains posthumously adored, and that Mae in imitation had long ago committed to full-throated memory. She seemed to plead with her lungs and vocal folds until they divulged their latent luster. Mae went on, to the part of the song where the protagonist audaciously forgets her roots:

> *khâa plìan chɯ̂ɯ pen wɛɛwdaaw*
> ("I changed my name to 'Starlight'. . . .")

The occasion was late—at night and in my fieldwork. Orn and I had been friends for nearly a year. She brought me into the inner circle of a small activist collective called Red Sunday, which consumed nearly all her free time, and which played an outsize role in the Red Shirt movement. Orn introduced me to a group of dedicated colleagues and composers, alerted me to protest performances, and brought me to dinners and strategy sessions and to work with her choir. But the invitation to meet Orn's mother was special, opening a view to a world at once intimate, historical, and political, as all familial worlds are. Mae's vocal perfor-mance encapsulated central themes of my fieldwork with Red Sunday, for whom bitter recollections of past failures animated new forms of optimism. Tragedy acted as a precondition for refiguring a hopeful futurity. Mae brought the song to its bitter coda:

> *ʔànítjang khâa mây thandang dây, sǎaw klaaypen khàaw klàp naa, daawrooy*
> ("Alas, I couldn't manage my fame, this girl went back to the fields, a fading star. . . .")

We clapped, awed and drunk, while Mae assumed a *luk thung* singer's humble posture before her fans.[3] Though the performance was informal, and though she has not sung professionally in decades, Mae still identifies as a musician. On this occasion, she performed the hierarchical rules that govern contact between musicians and audiences in Thailand—the audience pays a debt of gratitude by listening, which the singer acknowledges through steadfast humility and individual attention to loyal fans. Mae bowed her head slightly, aiming her eyes forward, and mouthed the ending particle *khâ* deferentially several times, pursing her lips seriously after each recitation, offering the word in recognition of our attention. I sensed while listening that she connected with Pumpuang not only as an artist, but as a working-class Thai woman emotionally chiseled by hardship. Political energy surged in the affective connection Mae felt with Pumpuang, who like the protagonist of her own song came from the fields to the city to find fame, and who died young there. After Mae's performance, this energy rose to the surface dramatically.

"I'm not afraid of you fuckers," Mae spat, grabbing my sound recorder like a microphone, as if on a stage, training her dangerous words not on the listeners in her midst but on Thailand's political elites, the constrainers of the Red Shirt movement, to everyone's righteous delight and amusement. Body rigid, eyes wide, and playing it deadpan, she repeated her brazen challenge. The grim joke was that, through the medium of the recorder, powerful people would hear her. "Are you gonna have problems if I say that, Ben?" she asked with a sudden softness that contrasted with her blunt outburst from a moment ago. "I won't," I answered, a little nervous. My entrainment in the rhythm of the conversation was, as ever, a half-beat behind. The table erupted in laughter. Mae's quasi-comic performance teetered at the edge of control. It was unpredictable, but subtle, funny, sincere, *intense*. My nervous answer provided a release. Mae was not afraid. "Democracy has no divisions. It has liberty, equality," she said, her tone briefly sober. She had no fear of being heard.

This chapter follows Red Sunday's performative protest work over the course of a year, from mid-2010, when it first emerged, toward 2011, when it adapted strategically to a new political climate. At issue is Red Sunday's use of historical protest symbols, especially sonic ones, and the ways that these were both useful and constraining. Red Sunday experienced the kind of constrained mobility described in the introduction. I follow Eric Drott, Judith Butler, and others in suggesting that dissident performance is steeped in conditions, often constraining ones (like Mae tangled in her own life-history) that would-be reformers or revolutionaries cannot outrun. These conditions precede the decision-making of social actors, including protesters. And yet these conditions are not only hindrances, but at times resources. Their symbols may become the basis of performative repertoires.[4]

---

3. Mitchell, "Kon Baan Diokan."

4. Diana Taylor, *The Archive and the Repertoire: Performing Cultural Memory in the Americas* (Durham, NC: Duke University Press, 2003). Taylor theorizes the *repertoire* as a storehouse of embodied knowledge analytically opposed to the lettered *archive*. The repertoire is a process of

Drott, for example, in his study of the music of the May 1968 protests in Paris, describes the "symbolic repertoire" of music and other practices that people drew upon in reimagining themselves as dissidents.[5] This repertoire referred to idealized figures from the French historical imagination, harking back at least to the French Revolution, which could be usefully mobilized, not least of all in addressing an audience that knew and related to those figures. But pulling from a historical repertoire also posed risks, as when student protesters abandoned singing "La Marseillaise" for its perceived nationalistic chauvinism, turning instead to "The Internationale," which seemed to better signify a unified left. In adopting the latter song, however, the students were branded as inauthentic by the working classes, because as students they had a weak claim to the political symbolism borne by "The Internationale." They were not thought to be *true* revolutionaries, and so a *true* revolutionary song seemed absurd coming from their mouths. The students fell prey to assignations of musical meaning that they could not control, to which they were a priori susceptible. Such are the perils of interpretation. Red Sunday acted through historical symbols, much like the Parisian students of May 1968, especially in sonic performance. This entailed both opportunity and risk.

For Butler, protesters (or queer figures of many kinds) must discover ways to act in spite of such risk, within the "very domain of susceptibility, this condition of being affected," that historical norms and symbols produce.[6] Like Mae, living and singing in the shadow of Pumpuang and her resonant musical *roman à clef*, so full of pain and failure, but straining toward a different political future, Red Sunday was susceptible to history even as it pursued reform. History provided the only legible symbolic language, and yet this language threatened at every turn to choke the movement by rendering it conventional, impotent, feckless, or embarrassing. The challenge for Red Sunday, as for all political movements, was to engage in the creative work of figuration, refiguration, and configuration of norms, to use historical symbols to build new worlds.

Such world-building, however, is not just rhetorical, but always also performative. World-building requires the articulation of claims, a task that in protest is often delegated to politicized sound in depoliticized public spaces—shopping areas, religious buildings, settings of state ritual, and the like. Those who make sound presume (or seize) the right to hold the floor, prior to speech-qua-language, by performing. This act presumes political equality, often forcefully. As Butler writes, "to be a participant in politics, to become part of concerted and collective action, one needs not only to make the claim for equality, but to act and petition within the terms of

performative repetition that allows knowledge to be transmitted without textualization, or at times language of any kind.

5. Eric Drott, *Music and the Elusive Revolution: Cultural Politics and Political Culture in France, 1968–1981* (Berkeley: University of California Press, 2011), 27.

6. Judith Butler, *Notes Toward a Performative Theory of Assembly* (Cambridge, MA: Harvard University Press, 2015), 64.

equality, as an actor on equal standing with others."[7] Blocking a major intersection with bodies shouting, for example, is a performance in which the meaning of the act precedes the semantic content of whatever one shouts. This assumption of the right to speak is always part of a field of political communication. In their transformative work, Red Sunday activists were not only claimants but sonic performers. Sonic performance—*the tenuous act of saying something aloud*—adds a layer of risk on top of that already assumed by making specific claims or petitions.

Red Sunday's membership was small (roughly a few hundred people), but it was politically significant because it invented some of the most potent visual and performative symbols used by the larger Red Shirt movement, which had millions of adherents. Many of the iconic slogans, happenings, and graphics of the Red Shirts were created by tiny Red Sunday before being adopted by the larger faction. The hierarchical UDD, the national group that organized most of the large Red Shirt events, had an uncertain relationship with Red Sunday, recognizing its cleverness but remaining skeptical of its middle-class sensibilities. Periodically, when the group was in the news, a Red Sunday speaker would be invited onstage at a major Red Shirt rally. But a similar invitation might not come the next week. Red Sunday thus never quite became a household name in Thailand. But the media diffusion of its performances, precisely because they seemed meek and spontaneous, had significant ripples. Like Mae singing and speaking frankly among friends, the intimate *feel* of Red Sunday's live events was critical to their impact.

However, mass mediation always loomed, and could not be disentangled from performance. This calls to mind Philip Auslander's reading of "liveness" as a flexible concept whose definition can shift.[8] Red Sunday was skilled at framing its happenings as spontaneous and authentic, at creating a live feel even amidst performances that were steeped in mediation and temporal deferral. Auslander argues that liveness is contingent: "how live and mediatized forms are used is determined not by their ostensibly intrinsic characteristics, but by their positions within cultural economy."[9] This complicates Butler's argument, which steers away from the question of how media redefine the boundaries of bodily presence. As will be described below, Red Sunday was not only concerned with what Stanyek and Piekut call "fleshy presence," but with deftly handling media in order to create a live and intimate *feel*.[10] In this way, the group could be seen as claimants through sonic performance, while mitigating some of the risks that such performance entailed.

Red Sunday's pursuit of a live feel might be understood through Václav Havel's notion of the "power of the powerless."[11] In Havel's samizdat essay on dissent in

7. Ibid., 52.
8. Philip Auslander, *Liveness: Performance in a Mediatized Culture* (London: Routledge, 1999).
9. Ibid., 51.
10. Jason Stanyek and Benjamin Piekut, "Deadness: Technologies of the Intermundane," *The Drama Review* 54, no. 1 (Spring 2010): 14–38.
11. Václav Havel, *The Power of the Powerless: Citizens Against the State in Central-Eastern Europe* (Armonk, NY: M.E. Sharpe, 1985).

Soviet-controlled Czechoslovakia, the titular concept describes how subjects, once their consciousness has been raised, can exclaim their liberation through speech acts. Havel, who was a playwright by trade and a dissident by circumstance, argues in a manner consonant with Butler that normative silence invests the speech of the oppressed with disruptive agency.[12] It is useful to think about powerlessness as both a political and technological condition. To be powerless can mean to lack access to decision-making and self-determination, but it can also mean simply to be disconnected from an electrical outlet. The two meanings converge in the performative sonic work of protest, as both political and sonic liminality can bestow the power to speak frankly. Mae, for instance, enjoying no legitimate claim to discursive public space, used the weak, oblique medium of the recorder to shout into that space, saying almost whatever she pleased (because she was powerless), and experiencing no fear as a result.

Powerless sonority in the Red Shirt case has been governed by what I call, metonymically, the politics of *kuu maa'eeng*. The phrase *kuu maa'eeng* ("I came by my goddamn self") was chanted by Red Shirts during and especially after the crackdown in order to signal their independence from the hierarchical constraints of centralized leadership. I have had to take some license in translating "I came by my goddamn self" from *kuu maa'eeng mây tɔ̂ɔng jâang* (กูมาเองไม่ต้องจ้าง). The literal translation of the full slogan is "I came myself—I didn't need to be hired." But the pronominal form of "I" used here, *kuu*, is rude because it is coarse and rural (and thus profane in certain contexts). The word thus requires a comparably coarse form in translation. "I came by my fucking self" would be a bit too strong, and "I came by myself" misleadingly weak. "I came by my goddamn self" approximates the vulgarity as well as the fierce determination contained in the words. The slogan was chanted everywhere, by many different protesters. Such a rebuke to authority was part of a broader trend among Red Shirts, one with both strategic and ideological aims. On the one hand, this approach closed avenues of attack from political opponents (especially the charge that the movement was populated by paid mercenaries) while on the other it rehearsed political relationships said to be more egalitarian than those defended by the current bureaucracy. Red Sunday was quietly integral to this shift away from strong leadership and toward self-directed protest (which pre-echoed the approach of Occupy Wall Street), fomenting it through music, speech, and drama. Tracing this shift must take careful account of how norms and historical symbols operated, and how claims were articulated through media technologies, in the context of susceptibility and powerlessness, to figure new political worlds.

12. Havel's position should be differentiated from James Scott's in *Weapons of the Weak* for its alignment with a revolutionary politics. Undoubtedly, Red Sunday members would describe their strategies as much closer to Havel's fruit seller than Scott's tenant farmers.

Red Sunday has a leader but, aptly, one who plays that role reluctantly. Sombat Boonngamanong is an NGO activist who studied theater in college, turning to politics only later. Sombat is affable and earnest, with a shy streak. He rejects the headstrong masculinity expected of Thai male authority figures. Sombat's first NGO was the Chiang Rai-based Mirror Foundation, begun in 1991 and committed to various humanitarian initiatives in rural Thailand, including flood relief and combating human trafficking. After the 2006 coup that deposed then-prime minister Thaksin, Sombat turned his attention to pro-democracy issues, including the burgeoning Red Shirt movement, recruiting volunteers like Orn who soon became the core of the Red Sunday group. Sombat had minor involvement with the UDD during the initial phase of the 2010 protests, but emerged as a more recognizable and influential figure only after the military assault on the Red Shirt occupation in May 2010, when he struck out on his own by launching Red Sunday.

On Sunday, June 13, 2010, just a few weeks after the crackdown, Sombat arrived at Ratchaprasong intersection, epicenter of the recent violence, with a crowd of a few hundred supporters who held handfuls of red ribbons. This happening was the beginning of the long, tentative process of discerning what kinds of political gestures would be legal and legitimate in the aftermath of conflict. The police had been told about the plan in advance, and a battalion of riot officers lined up along the curb to keep order. Sombat spoke briefly and cordially to one officer as he prepared for the lone planned action—tying a red ribbon around the tall blue sign that displays the name of the intersection. As Sombat tied the ribbon, his supporters chanted in unison: *thîi nîi mii khon taay* ("people died here," or "there are dead people here"). After a few minutes, just long enough for the happening to be witnessed and documented, the crowd left. The ribbons were quickly removed by the police, but the sound of chanting seemed to linger, even as the hum of traffic reinstalled itself.

The malleability of the phrase *thîi nîi mii khon taay* is apparent in its direct translation: "right here, there are people dead." Thai verb structure leaves a grammatical loophole, so that the presence of the dead may be construed in several different ways. First, the corpses were indeed still fresh, with still more bodies fallen victim to unreported disappearance. Material remainders of the protests could still be found scattered about the area—broken windows, scraps of pamphlets, even bloodstains. The literal flesh of the dead remained, right here. Second, ghosts were felt to haunt the intersection through the mediation of the living, as when the refrain of *thîi nîi mii khon taay* slapped back from the concrete underbelly of the Skytrain while soldiers and other agents of the state gave dispassionate audience. The dead remained as specters, right here. Third, the chant could be heard as a historical report, a sonic declaration of past events not yet properly acknowledged or rectified. The dead remained an ongoing political problem, right here. English translations on placards took further inventive license, ranging from the blunt "people died here" to the winking "I see dead people," borrowed from the 1999 American horror film,

"The Sixth Sense." In all cases, the presence of the dead was symbolically linked with the injustice of their death. Chanting sustained this link. Aloud, the slogan was broken into two phrases separated by a pause, *"thîi nîi"* and *"mii khon taay."* The tone of each of the first two words— *thîi* and *nîi* —are falling, and their vowels are long, giving them an insistent quality that the protesters stressed in their delivery: *thîiiii nîiiiii*, "riiight heeere." The emphasis of the second part was squarely on *taay*, which the crowd shouted in a manner that extended its normal pronunciation, giving it a falling tone (*tâay*) rather than a neutral one. This brief, dramatic episode of chanting in Ratchaprasong, shared on YouTube and elsewhere online in the ensuing weeks, insisted that the memory of those killed during the crackdown be preserved in the name of justice.

The happening also helped Sombat gain a following. For the next few Sundays, he convened discussion groups in coffee shops around Bangkok, refiguring the Red Shirt movement as one more informed about political theory, and more focused on reform and media strategy than confrontation. The meetings became known as the Red Sunday group (*klùm wan'aathít sĭidɛɛng*), and grew rapidly in attendance and complexity. By August, five hundred to a thousand people routinely showed up for weekly singalongs, reenactments of the Ratchaprasong killings, and picnics. By now Sombat was regularly profiled in the media, including a front-page article in the national weekly newspaper *Matichon*.[13] The group rented an office on Bangkok's Vipavadi Road, stocked with equipment, where a core group of volunteers began planning future events.

On August 15, 2010, Red Sunday held its largest gathering to that point, in a section of the sprawling and manicured Chatuchak Park, near where the right-wing People's Alliance for Democracy (PAD) had held many of its own rallies before the May 2010 crackdown. Roughly two thousand people attended, by my estimate, many of them older than fifty and carrying bottles of red wine and plastic Tupperware filled with picnic food. They wore shirts with slogans such as "Liberty Egality Fraternity Thailand," [*sic*] which spelled LEFT by its initials, in English rather than French or Thai. On the snaking pathway around the central lawn, representatives of small non-profit groups with names like the People's Information Center sat on blankets, speaking to passersby through microphones plugged into portable karaoke machines. Songs played from laptops plugged into speakers. Volunteers distributed literature and collected donations for victims of the military crackdown and their families. Red Sunday had designed a series of graphics that were by now widely visible on T-shirts and buttons at Red Shirt events, including the group's stylized red sun logo and a hand giving the middle finger to the government (a comparatively mild gesture). Overall the gathering was so subdued and

---

13. "การแสดงเชิงสัญลักษณ์ของคนเสื้อแดงที่สวนลุมฯ: 'ชาติ' แบบอื่น และ นาฏกรรมนอกรัฐ" ("The Symbolic Performances of the Red Shirts at Lumphini Park: Another Kind of Nation and Dramatic Performance Outside the State"), *Matichon*, July 26, 2010.

bourgeois-seeming that it might have been difficult to recognize the risks that the protesters were taking.

Not far from the picnic area, as sunset approached, roughly one hundred people of various ages, many wearing red shirts, danced in an aerobics session on a small paved lot. Aerobics is a common form of public exercise throughout Southeast Asia, and the setup in this instance was typical. Two lithe, muscular instructors stood on an elevated hill in front of the lot, each atop a large wooden box. Speaking through a wireless microphone pinned to her spandex shirt, one of the instructors counted out the *nùng-sɔ̌ɔng-sǎam-sìi* (four-on-the-floor) rhythm, and she and her male assistant demonstrated the steps as the crowd followed. An audio technician wearing red shorts and sandals slouched on a bench next to a wheeled cart containing an audio mixing board, which ran out to a quartet of gray, swiveling loudspeakers arrayed in a semicircle around the lot. The dance mix played from a CD that included uptempo tracks like the Danish Safri Duo's remix of Pat Boone's "Speedy Gonzalez" and a wackily sped-up version of MC Hammer's "U Can't Touch This." The playful public event was almost exactly like what one would see and hear after work in parks from Phnom Penh to Kuala Lumpur, including the musical selections, the dance moves, and the choice of location.

Despite its apparent banality, however, the gathering was subversive, an act undertaken in deliberate defiance of the government. Butler refers to "assemblies," in which the mere act of togetherness makes a claim to equality even in the absence of speech. "Concerted bodily action—gathering, gesturing, standing still, all of the component parts of 'assembly' that are not quickly assimilated to verbal speech—can signify principles of freedom and equality."[14] The aerobics event's political content first became clear when I snapped a few pictures, and the instructor hopped down from her box to warn me that documentation was forbidden, a rare admonition in photo-friendly Thailand. I watched as other casual photographers were given the same warning. The aerobics session was an excuse to gather and perform in tacit solidarity at a moment when direct political expression was dangerous. Even in such a seemingly benign setting, the dancers worked to preserve their anonymity—if a government official happened to photograph and identify them, they could easily be harassed or added to a government blacklist. The military was so unpredictable, so unencumbered by any pretense to legal transparency, that this level of caution was merited. Legs pumped and arms swung in time to the pulse of a drum machine, rows of eyes fixed forward together. The performance was a blaring secret.

"Under the Emergency Decree we cannot gather," said Orn, Mae's daughter, standing on a patch of grass nearby, when I asked her about the aerobics. "We cannot create political activities. But doing exercise is something that people can join, you know? Because we just aerobic dance. Nobody can catch us, nobody can

14. Butler, *Notes Toward a Performative Theory of Assembly*, 48.

take us to the prison. . . . It's music, it's peaceful manner, you know? We should have this right to express, we should have this legitimacy."[15]

The "legitimacy" to which Orn refers is the right to assembly and shared expressive performance. Red Sunday's aerobics session did not derive its subversive power through liveness as an inherent result of fleshy presence. Rather, this power emerged from a combination of political circumstance and collective agency that gave specific actions legitimacy, or positioned them as challenges to existing forms of legitimacy. Stanyek and Piekut argue that there is an "unhelpful and overvalued schism between presence and absence that undergirds much literature on performance," and they argue further that all performance entails "distended temporalities and spatialities."[16] What one perceives in a performative moment cannot fully account for the ways that that moment bears meaning, as Drott makes clear in his discussion of symbolic repertoires. In performance, presence is not the binary opposite of absence, nor a metaphysical condition. Understanding the subversive value of Red Sunday's aerobics session as an assembly compels us to ask how "presence" was made legible in this context.

The Emergency Decree mentioned above by Orn was a temporary state of emergency in place during most of 2010, which at the time governed the legal value of presence in Thailand. An appointed body under military supervision called the Center for the Resolution of the Emergency Situation (CRES) had been granted sweeping powers to investigate, arrest, and at times wage armed battle with civilians. The center's mandate used vague language, allowing it for instance to forbid "communications that might inspire fear. . . or affect the good morals of the people."[17] Because the legal language was so general, no one was sure what constituted a violation. Among other incidents, at a rally I attended in Ayuthaya, the military at the behest of CRES arrested an older woman for selling sandals adorned with the prime minister's face (a highly insulting gesture) and the words "people died at Ratchaprasong." The potential for legal trouble under the Emergency Decree explains the cautious and indirect character of the aerobics protest. Red Sunday was feeling out how *the movement itself* could be made present in public space, because the meaning of presence was opaque. When would a gathering count as a Red Shirt event? When was the movement understood to be present by the authorities? These were unsettled questions.

The next weekend, Red Sunday planned a rally in Chiang Mai—the first major event organized by Sombat outside Bangkok—to try to reach beyond the capital. Chiang Mai was among the first provinces where the Emergency Decree was lifted,

15. Orn, interview with the author, August 15, 2010. This conversation was in English.
16. Stanyek and Piekut, "Deadness."
17. "คำสั่งนายกรัฐมนตรี ที่ พิเศษ ๑/๒๕๕๓ เรื่องการจัดตั้งศูนย์อำนวยการแก้ไขสถานการณ์ฉุกเฉิน" ("Special Order of the Prime Minister, 1/2010, on the Establishment of a Center for the Resolution of the Emergency Situation"). http://www.ratchakitcha.soc.go.th/DATA/PDF/2553/E/045/3.PDF.

four months before Bangkok, so the trip was also an opportunity to speak and sing somewhat more openly. But Red Sunday was still finding its feet strategically, still exploring how it might use media and especially sound to mobilize historical symbols. Around fifty Red Sunday volunteers traveled fourteen hours north from Bangkok on Saturday night, riding an attention-demanding chartered bus with seven rows of parallel lamps across the front, a glowing green neon light below, and elaborate psychedelic drawings on the sides. Speakers were built in to the walls from front to back, and the driver had access to a four-channel mixer, amplifier, microphone, and several large analog volume meters on the dashboard. The Red Sunday members who joined the trip spent much of it listening to music through this system. I tried in vain to sleep and ended up joining a whiskey-soaked card game instead. On arrival in Chiang Mai in the morning, with all of us unshowered and groggy, the bus crawled through the city, surrounded by cheering Red Shirts on every block, blaring a song called "Love the Red Shirts." (This song will be described in greater detail in Chapter 11). In a mode that Red Sunday would soon disavow, the passage through town felt and sounded like a political campaign rally.

"At Phan Fa bridge, 'Love the Red Shirts' is the song (we sang) when the soldiers began to shoot," said Red Sunday volunteer Meow, recalling the violence of April 10 as we passed time on the bus.[18] "We sang it together, and then the soldiers began to shoot at the people," she added. Meow was one of Orn's closest friends. She held stronger republican leanings than most members of Red Sunday, which caused tension that later led her to leave for a more radical subgroup. Like many Red Shirts, her positions hardened after events like the Phan Fa shootings on April 10. The coincidence of soldiers firing as this song played imbued it with enormous weight for Meow and others.

The fact that musical meaning is made present not merely through composition, but also through audition and performance, is a foundational concept in the anthropology of music.[19] Meow and the other members of Red Sunday were intuitively sensitive to this as activists. "Love the Red Shirts" was a part of the repertoire that evoked shared associations among listeners with vivid memories of the violence of one particular night. As with the political content of the Red Sunday aerobics session, much of the meaning accrued by the song, *much of the value of its presence,* was impossible to apprehend without reference to the effects of temporally and spatially distant events that clung stubbornly to it each time it played.

But these associations also made Red Sunday susceptible when they deployed the song for its historical symbolism. "Love the Red Shirts" had for months been a

18. This conversation was in Thai.
19. Yukti Mukdawijitra, "The Sound of Politics in the Sound of Music"; Gregory Barz, "Meaning in Benga Music of Western Kenya," *British Journal of Ethnomusicology* 10 (2001): 109–17; Louise Meintjes, "Paul Simon's Graceland, South Africa, and the Mediation of Musical Meaning," *Ethnomusicology* 34, no. 1 (Winter 1990): 37–73; John Blacking, *How Musical Is Man?* (Seattle: University of Washington Press, 1973),

standby selection for the UDD, a hierarchical organization from which Red Sunday preferred to keep its distance. The bright, bouncy hook in the chorus was perfect for warming up crowds, and the UDD had laid informal claim to it as an anthem. This linked the song with the UDD in the minds of many listeners, especially during mass events like those that took place in Ratchaprasong and near Democracy Monument in the second half of 2010 and first half of 2011. Such massive, forceful demonstrations were at odds with Red Sunday's "power of the powerless" ethos. Sombat was therefore caught in a bind over whether to rely on the Red Shirts' collective favorite song, which would always draw more listeners and more attention, or avoid it and distance himself from a type of protest activity that many moderate Bangkokians loathed. Ultimately, Red Sunday disavowed "Love the Red Shirts," and by extension the strategies that accompanied its broadcast. Like "La Marseillaise," whose fate in French political life has been "tied to that of Republicanism as an ideology and political movement," the value of "Love the Red Shirts" changed rapidly with the political currents.[20]

As we drove home after the Chiang Mai rally, Orn suggested that the Red Shirts "lost support from the masses because of the media," referring to Bangkokians who failed to sympathize with the Red Shirts before the May crackdown.[21] "We took a key area, the business area, of the middle class. That's why Red Shirts lack support from the middle class in Bangkok. . . . The middle class doesn't understand how the Red Shirt people are suffering. They just see Reds as pro-Thaksin, yeah. What they can imagine is that we are hired by somebody, we are nominees of somebody. It's not the truth, but it is what the media makes us to be. . . . The CRES blocks our websites, community radio, everywhere. Many Reds might hate the elite people, but Sombat thinks we shouldn't go that way, we should try to draw support from the middle class. It is time to change the way Red people fight. We need to draw support from the middle class."

The strategic trajectory of Red Sunday was clear from Orn's comments: the group hoped to court the middle class. But they were nevertheless caught between this decision and their role as a satellite of the broader Red Shirt movement. The Chiang Mai rally illustrated this double-bind. Even as Orn and Sombat looked toward new strategies, they found themselves tied to old symbols. For example, the sound system Red Sunday used was on loan from the UDD, who also provided a volunteer sound engineer—the UDD's size and structure made this an easy favor. And most of the songs played through the speakers were crowd-pleasers that many listeners remembered from the long, dull days in the tent cities of Ratchaprasong in April and May, when the UDD was the main organizing body. The emotions and strategies that these songs called to mind sat uneasily beside Sombat's media-directed, middle-class-friendly approach. Even the schedule of the Chiang Mai rally

20. Drott, *Music and the Elusive Revolution*, 29.
21. Orn, interview with the author, August 22, 2010. This conversation was in English.

borrowed almost note-for-note from UDD events—a DJ cycled through the same eight or ten songs while people danced (with great endurance) near the stage, an emcee warmed up the crowd in a central area with jokes and greetings, vendors sold CDs, clothing, and food from rows of tables and tents along the sidewalk near the main stage, and a succession of increasingly high-profile orators took the stage. The arc of the show was meant to engage the audience with a steadily climaxing display of volume and force, a formula that the UDD had honed, and that Red Sunday was now rehashing to some extent. The event was like a day in the tent cities of Ratchaprasong in miniature. But this was the last time that a Red Sunday event would take such an approach.

A week after the Chiang Mai rally, Sombat and I met in the Red Sunday office for an interview, sitting on perpendicular red couches near a picture window facing the street. It was a bright Saturday morning after a brief but torrential early rain, and no one else had come into the office yet. Birds in wooden cages sang on the *soi* outside. On one wall, a large whiteboard listed office supplies to be purchased (table, chairs, clock, a new computer) along with a schedule of recent and upcoming events. On the desk were a computer and two laptops, all three plastered in haphazard zeal with Red Sunday stickers. The office resembled a political campaign headquarters but would (like "Love the Red Shirts") be left behind by Red Sunday before the end of the year. For Sombat, a new strategic approach to protest performance was beginning to take form. "I am trying to give a new solution for the fight," he explained, choosing his words thoughtfully. "If it's like last time, there will be violence again. . . . This is a political game, not an army game. If the government starts an army game again, I will not play. I am trying to play a political game. . . . If they don't like to play my game, I will play alone."[22]

Sombat made clear that Red Sunday would not repeat the semi-permanent occupations of public space that the Red Shirts had pursued earlier in the year. This turn away from confrontation and toward symbolic action, a "political game," was an embrace of the symbolic historical repertoire. It was a pivot toward courting an educated middle-class, and toward non-hierarchical organization. Sombat stirred a cup of instant coffee and sat back against his couch in contemplation. "If (a lot of people) come, it creates problems for me. I need some scale, but nothing too big. If it's big, it's like a rally. That's difficult for me and for the management. I want people to join, but it's decentralized. We have many different activities—people go there, there, there, there, there. It's not too big."

The "political game" envisioned by Sombat would also entail greater attention to the production and effects of performance. If Red Sunday could successfully engage the vital topics that mattered to the Red Shirts (injustice, censorship, the role of the military in government) without being branded as agitators, then the

---

22. Sombat Boonngamanon, interview with the author, September 1, 2010. The interview took place primarily in Thai, occasionally switching to English.

movement could gain momentum. This meant that political content had to be present in every action, and yet at some level be plausibly deniable. Orn described the aerobics dancing in Chatuchak as merely a gathering, apolitical and thus not prosecutable. Here, Sombat strategized in the place where assembly shades into politics, auguring claims for legitimacy. Butler, writing about the Egyptian revolution of 2011, suggests that such acts of occupation can be "the most eloquent political statement[s]" in themselves.[23] Sombat's wager was that his happenings could function as political actions, but not be branded illegal because they were purely representational, so clearly choreographed that they could not be mistaken for spontaneous. The political content of assembly was fleeting, and thus outside the legal realm. And anything sufficiently choreographed could be excused as false, exterior to legality, even if Sombat knew well that the action was politically oriented. "I still use theater theory to think about the political," he added. "Drama is fake. We use fake to show real. We use fake to present the truth. It's art." His approach aimed at the long-term viability of the movement, which had to begin with the sustained safety and security of his volunteers. His challenge was to channel the energy of dissidents into political projects that could survive and persist without agitating the military. This required a studied application of artistic concepts, the performance of politics as an improvisatory symbolic game.

The historical symbolic repertoire was important here. Notably, Sombat's performance mirrored that of the historical Thai state, which since the dawn of the nation in 1932 has relied on drama to stage ideals of citizenship. Sombat suggested that his use of music and drama in political action arose, in part, from his personal experiences with state-propagated dramatic forms. In public grade school in the 1970s, he heard anticommunist songs that were played as part of the national curriculum.[24] "The politicians used art, drama, music, and film to control people's thinking," he explained. "When I was young, we had a crisis about the communists. For about ten years, the government created a lot of songs to increase nationalism. Every day the students had to sing these songs. For example, *nàkphèndin* ['Heavy on the Earth,' an anti-communist anthem with violent themes]. It's very strong. It separated the people, and set up the children to think that people who are against the government are evil, and should die. That no one would care if they died. . . . When I was young, I believed this. That changed after I studied and had discussions about culture with theater people. I joined political theater." The song to which Sombat refers, *nàkphèndin*, is a famous case. Historian Somsak Jeamteerasakul describes it as the single most popular example of its era in the genre of *phleeng*

23. Butler, *Notes Toward a Performative Theory of Assembly*, 90.
24. Benedict Anderson, "Withdrawal Symptoms: Social and Cultural Aspects of the October 6 Coup," *Bulletin of Concerned Asian Scholars* 3 (1977); Michael Kelly Connors, *Democracy and National Identity in Thailand* (London: RoutledgeCurzon, 2003); Katherine Bowie, *Rituals of National Loyalty* (New York: Columbia University Press, 1997).

plùkjay, a nationalistic right-wing style.[25] *Nàkphèndin* was recorded and sold by the Thai army orchestra in the mid-1970s. As the military worked in tandem with paramilitary groups to hunt, arrest, and in many cases murder students and others suspected of being communists, the song was a rallying cry.[26] Although Sombat eventually recognized the propagandistic character of the music and art he experienced as a student, and rejected it politically, he nevertheless acknowledged its role in the development of his own performative methods in protest.[27]

Sombat's "playing a political game," and especially the ways that this game engaged music, drama, art, and performance as modes of persuasion, was remarkably close to how the state itself used these modes historically. The state's methods offered performative models for the mobilization of historical symbols through media that Red Sunday now sought to use *against* the state. Michael Herzfeld notes a similar tendency in a separate context in Thailand, that of a fight over land rights between Bangkok government agencies and a small community, the latter who routinely "represent[]. . . their struggle as a small-scale replay of the national struggle for sovereignty."[28] For both the community described by Herzfeld and Red Sunday, historical symbols offered by state models of power and contestation were valuable but carried the risk of using the master's tools to tear down his house, to borrow Audre Lorde's phrase. Might Sombat's "political game" have ultimately reinforced the existing apparatus of power? The historical symbolic repertoire of the state, in this regard, was yet another constraint to consider.

25. Somsak Jeamteerasakul, " 'We Fight': Political Royal Songs and the Politics of 1975–1976." somsakwork.blogspot.com (blog), November 16, 2007. (สมศักดิ์ เจียมธีรสกุล. "เราสู้: เพลง พระราชนิพนธ์การเมืองกับการเมืองปี 2518–2519.")

26. Somsak also mentions that the Gammachon Band, a left-wing student group led by Jin Gammachon (discussed later in this chapter) played *nàkphèndin* as well, but in the context of their performance it was intended as an anticolonial anthem.

27. Beginning in the 1930s, the Culture Minister enjoyed tremendous influence, and followed an ambitious agenda in propagating nationalist concepts that were sustained into the 1970s and, arguably, the present. For instance, Luang Wichit Wathakan's 1933 song *rák châat* ("Love the Nation") included the lyrics: "Whatever kind of love, no matter how great, does not last long. Love of lovers, no matter how deep, may later turn bitter. But love of our motherland can be so deep to the utmost; this love provides us spirit; for it, lives can be sacrificed, flesh can be given, blood can run dry. Our earthly body we regret not; for when we die what are left but ashes? Sacrifice everything we can, except our motherland; we will never allow anyone to destroy this treasure." Thak Chaloemtiarana, Charnwit Kasetsiri, and Thinaphan Nakata, *Thai Politics: Extracts and Documents, 1932–1957* (Bangkok: Social Sciences Association of Thailand, 1978), 321. As one character in a propagandistic 1942 radio drama put it, "language, both plain and in the form of poetry which will seep into our hearts will have to go through music. It alone cannot go into the hearts of people unless through music" (316). For detailed information on the cultural policy of Luang Wichit Wathakan, see Scot Barmé, *Luang Wichit Wathakan and the Creation of a Thai identity* (Singapore: Social Issues in Southeast Asia–Institute of Southeast Asian studies, 1993).

28. Michael Herzfeld, *Siege of the Spirits: Community and Polity in Bangkok* (Chicago: University of Chicago Press, 2016), 90.

As Red Sunday's approach was refined, its rhetoric of *kuu maa'eeng* ("I came by my goddamn self") and horizontality sharpened, along with its preference for unamplified performances.[29] This shift occurred in the last few months of 2010, at the moment when Red Sunday's protests began to break away from the strategies of the UDD and pivot toward Sombat's "political game." Until then, the performative dimension of the Red Shirt movement had been comparable to that of similar movements in Southeast Asia, such as mid-1990s Indonesia, where cultural policy had likewise been a major part of nation-building, and where popular resistance to national mythology was articulated through music and public performance. Describing the music of Indonesian youth uprisings, Michael Bodden suggests that it was no coincidence that "such angry 'noise' has grown into an explosive rage, almost a cacophony, in a time when democratic reform has stalled in the face of an intransigent military and political elite."[30] But Red Shirt music did not grow louder in such a correlative fashion. Contra the Indonesian case, Red Sunday's "political game" was a turn toward de-electrification, a powerful mode of powerlessness. The trajectory of Thai dissident music was not one of increasing volume or intensity.

This was evident on Sunday, October 2, 2010, as Red Sunday traveled by train to Ayuthaya to hold a small rally. The two-hour trip was far less showy than the bus ride to Chiang Mai a few months before. We rode the ordinary train, which cost 15 baht (roughly fifty cents) per person, with no broadcasting equipment more powerful than a handheld plastic megaphone. Red Sunday volunteer Nop, an unusually tall young man with a wide smile who served as Sombat's bodyguard, jacked his cell phone into the megaphone. Towering above everyone on the packed train car, Nop held the megaphone aloft, and played a selection of upbeat Red Shirt songs through it, including the catchy theme to the political TV talk show *Truth Today*. This song's sunny, eight-bar chorus is performed by a man and woman who sing over a busy drum part and a buried electric guitar. The lyrics of the chorus (which translate as "Truth today! Truth today! Truth today! Truth Thailand!") are quite an earworm.

On television, the ditty plays while the hosts walk onstage to be greeted with applause by the studio audience. The raucous crowd on the train likewise stood and shouted in celebration between songs, engaging in impromptu chants, clapping, and whistling. Nop's megaphone was so weak and tinny that the group had to pause their own cheering between songs to discern what the next selection was. After figuring it out, they would commence singing again, drowning out the recorded version almost entirely. Several times, the crowd had to slow down after inadvertently racing ahead of the recording. Within a chorus of fifty voices and a steady

29. The notion of "horizontality," meaning an equal distribution of political power, is drawn from Argentinian dissident movements of the early twenty-first century. See Marina Sitrin, *Horizontalism: Voices of Popular Power in Argentina* (Oakland, CA: AK Press, 2006).

30. Bodden, "Rap in Indonesian Youth Music," 19.

clapping that echoed sharply within the tight, exposed metal interior of the train car, the megaphone itself was barely audible.

The feverish singing of the trip was documented by multiple journalists riding in the car to gather material for televised reports about the post-crackdown resurgence of the Red Shirts, including Aidan Hartley, a reporter for Channel 4's "Unreported World" program in Britain, and Neil Trevithick, host of the BBC World Service program "The Strand." I spent part of the trip explaining to these two journalists what Red Sunday was doing, how it differed from the Red Shirt movement as such, and about the meanings of the songs. Sombat also spoke to them. From watching similar encounters, I knew Sombat was expert at framing rich scenes for foreign media. The way that the group sang during the train ride exemplified this framing. The symbolic components of the performance (small size, minimal amplification, cheap logistics) embodied how Sombat now wanted Red Sunday to be represented.

The rally in Ayuthaya was also structurally different from the August event in Chiang Mai, and suggested new performative modes. I searched at the beginning for a main stage, but there was none. Consistent with the principle of non-hierarchical control, the gathering was not organized around a central visual or sonic point. Rather, vendors arrayed their wares along a stretch of sidewalk, and many different orators set up wherever they could find space. When Sombat finally addressed a large crowd, he did so with the aid of the very same handheld megaphone that Nop had used on the train a few hours earlier. In front of about a thousand people (a small fraction of the total attendees), and with only his megaphone for amplification, Sombat delivered a strategically self-effacing manifesto for Red Sunday. He stood on an open, neatly mowed grass field that made him look and sound small, and explained that he should be called not a kɛɛnnam (central leader), as the UDD's top brass had been termed, but instead a kɛɛnnɔɔn (horizontal line), a flat entity that does not rise above anyone or anything else. The phonetic proximity of kɛɛnnɔɔn to kɛɛnnam was fortuitous and made for great puns. The clever wordplay brought excited laughter from the crowd, who sat taking in Sombat's every word, reacting with amusement and agreement, periodically extending a middle finger in the symbolic direction of the government. Journalists always want to talk to people from political parties, those at the apex of power, Sombat explained to the crowd. But in a movement structured horizontally, without hierarchy, he himself could not properly be called a leader. "And so what am I?" he asked, allowing the whole group to answer as a collective: kɛɛnnɔɔn!

The title "horizontal line" implied that Sombat was a negation of the virile, self-assured leader figures of the UDD. The term is loosely drawn from the Argentinian dissident concept of *horizontalidad*, employed during that country's 2001 economic crisis. The word has roots in several different anarchist movements. Among the principles of *horizontalidad* is the concept of replacing "power-over" with a distributed "power-with," especially in decision-making.[31] Horizontalism has since

---

31. "แกนนอน: วิถีระนาบ Horizontalidad" ("Horizontal Line: The Flat Strategies of Horizontalided"), accessed February 21, 2012, http://www.tonkla.org/tag/แกนนอน/.

then been broadly adopted by movements including Occupy Wall Street, parts of the Arab Spring, and anti-austerity protests in Europe. In the person of Sombat, the notion of leadership was diminished, smoothed over until he and the crowd were equal, despite his physical position at the front of it. But the *kɛɛnnɔɔn*, no more important than any other protester, was in fact a present absence where the figure of the central leader should have been—not a lack of hierarchy, but hierarchy in effigy.[32] In that sense, the line was not entirely horizontal. Rather, it dipped at the point where the leader stood. Sombat mocked himself as a sacrificial avatar of the notion of authority. It was only appropriate for Red Shirts who had "come by their goddamn selves" to favor leaders who claimed no authority. *Kɛɛnnɔɔn* leadership and *kuu maa'eeng* protesting were thus animated by similar logics. To arrive by one's own motivation was, in this instance, to reject authority tout court.

Sound and performance were an important part of the political game that emerged in this moment. Sombat's megaphone was the medial centerpiece of his *kɛɛnnɔɔn* speech. Listeners were compelled to lean in to hear him, creating an intimate space in which bodies huddled to listen. Moreover, the projection of Sombat's already nasal voice was appropriately weak, underscoring his failure to reach the leadership ideal that he so avidly disavowed. At one moment during the speech, a very short, unrelated announcement from an overhead public address speaker overwhelmed the tiny megaphone. Sombat made physical comedy out of looking up at the booming acousmata above him, staggering backwards in an exaggerated fashion, as if struck by the sound. It was a bravura performance. A few weeks later, Channel Four in England ran a twenty-five-minute episode of *Unreported World* about the state of Thai politics. One of the reporters I spoke with on the train used several minutes of footage from the rally, including the singing on the bus and parts of Sombat's *kɛɛnnɔɔn* speech.[33] *Kuu maa'eeng*, a live feel, horizontality, and a new instantiation of the Red Shirt movement were, through international television, made globally present.

---

32. "ความหมายของ 'แกนนอน'" ("The Meaning of 'kɛɛnnɔɔn'"), https://www.facebook.com/note.php?note_id=160741693951264, September 28, 2010. (Translated here from the original Thai, Sombat defines *kɛɛnnɔɔn* with nine qualities, namely "1) A *kɛɛnnɔɔn* is not a *kɛɛnnam*; 2) a *kɛɛnnɔɔn* gives the highest importance to the people; 3) a *kɛɛnnɔɔn* moves in a horizontal line; 4) a *kɛɛnnɔɔn* has the duty to connect the masses to opportunities to participate on their own, and to facilitate leadership; 5) a *kɛɛnnɔɔn* must organize groups themselves no larger than 5–15 people to create organizations; 6) a *kɛɛnnɔɔn* must be clear about their targets and strategies and be capable of finding new tactics; 7) a *kɛɛnnɔɔn* must try to connect with other *kɛɛnnɔɔn* when necessary, and be capable of making decisions collectively with other groups; 8) a *kɛɛnnɔɔn* must study and adapt the lessons they have learned to improve their work continually; 9) a *kɛɛnnɔɔn* must be able to communicate, listen, and in fact be an *expert listener*." [emphasis mine]. Translated from the original Thai.

33. "Thailand's Red Fever," *Unreported World,* Channel 4, December 10, 2010. http://www.channel4.com/programmes/unreported-world/episode-guide/series-2010/episode-20.

Red Sunday was rapidly breaking away from the UDD. Later in the month, the Red Shirt-allied Pheu Thai Party held a rally at an outdoor football stadium, also in Ayutthaya, at which the increasingly in-demand Sombat was invited to give a speech. As the crowd streamed in, I stood with Orn behind the main stage in a muddy field. She was reticent about the event, explaining that it did not reflect how Red Sunday wanted to present itself. Among the scheduled stage performers were the pop singer Pae Bangsanan (see Chapter 11) and UDD leader Jatuporn Promphan, both major figures within the movement. Sombat, unavoidably yoked to a microphone and stadium PA system because of the size of the crowd, gave a hurried and tepid address. Ten thousand Pheu Thai partisans, covering an entire football field and the bleachers around it, gave him a merely polite response.

The sun had not yet set, and the rally had barely begun, but the moment Sombat left the stage Orn announced that Red Sunday's contingent was leaving the rally. The fifteen or so volunteers gathered their belongings and hustled to the parking lot behind the end of the field where the rally would continue until late at night. We loaded into our cars and left in the direction of a quiet seafood restaurant twenty minutes away. Red Sunday no longer wanted to associate itself with the methods of events like this one; even to stay and be seen would have communicated the wrong symbolic message.

FIGURES OF THE HISTORICAL SYMBOLIC REPERTOIRE

While the techniques of *kɛɛnnɔɔn* leadership were advancing, Sombat mined the historical symbolic repertoire by becoming close with an older dissident band-leader named Jin Gammachon. Jin, then in his mid-50s and living near Bangkok, was among the most important musicians affiliated with the Thai student political movements of the 1970s. His group, the Gammachon Band, had been at the fore-front of the "songs for life" genre, which blossomed in that decade. In addition to original march compositions, the Gammachon Band wrote musical arrangements for poems written by the murdered Marxist leader Jit Phumisak.[34] Although Jin had not actively performed in almost thirty years, and although his original band had long since broken up, he remained supportive of pro-democracy movements. Devastated by the 2006 coup against Thaksin, he was moved to write a poem that eventually became a song called "Waning Sky," his first work of political dissent in decades.[35] His former collaborators had grown politically conservative in the intervening decades, he told me, but Jin was drawn to the Red Shirt movement, and decided to join it as a songwriter. He even performed a few times on the UDD

---

34. Somsak, "We Fight."

35. Chiranuch Premchaiporn, "แรมฟ้า..บทเพลงจากห้วงรู้สึกในคืน 19 กันยาฯ ของจิน กรรมาชน" ("Waning Sky. Lyrics from Jin Gammachon's Hopes and Feelings on the night of September 19"), *Prachatai,* June 14, 2007. https://prachatai.com/journal/2007/06/13086.

stage, although his subdued demeanor was not well-suited to the UDD's crowds. Red Sunday's emphasis on dramatic symbolism matched Jin's aesthetics much more comfortably.

Jin wrote and recorded a song called *náksûu thúliidin* ("Warriors of the Dust") in 2009, which was heard periodically in the Ratchaprasong tent cities of March-May 2010. Much as "Love the Red Shirts" had grown in meaning for Meow and others after it played at a crucial moment on the night of April 10, "Warriors of the Dust" gained notoriety when it happened to be on the loudspeakers during the announcement of the death of controversial Red Shirt leader Seh Daeng, who was killed by a sniper on May 13 while being interviewed by a reporter from the *New York Times*.[36] Jin had performed "Warriors of the Dust" many times in late 2009 and early 2010, but after the death of Seh Daeng the recording became newly relevant. Furthermore, as the movement writ large began incorporating acts of mourning to commemorate the increasing number of dead protesters, somber ballads gained prominence in the repertoire. By the time of Red Sunday's rise in late 2010, "Warriors of the Dust" was without question the music of choice for candlelight vigils and other memorial events, which now happened at nearly every protest.

"Warriors of the Dust" is a brooding piece in E minor, over six minutes long, that rises in intensity over several verses toward a grandiose refrain that repeats until the song ends almost cold. A backing chorus, slow-rolling bass drum, and synthesized strings create a feeling of militaristic melodrama. The title refers to the longstanding hierarchical position of common people as "dust" beneath the feet of the Siamese (later Thai) royal elite. In Thailand, status is installed in everyday life, from the depth of a bowing *wây* to choices of pronominal address, from the height of one's head near social superiors to the central importance of the concepts of "face" and *baarámii* (a gauge of moral perfection).[37] For a speck of dust—that is, a social inferior—to be an agent rather than a passive subject of fate is to reject hierarchy as a given condition. Indeed, "Warriors of the Dust" extols the "nameless warrior" who "changes fate" while standing with "pride and dignity on the field of battle." The song was composed in Jin's signature march style, much closer to nationalistic, mid-century genres like *phleeng plùkjay* than to folk music, or déclassé rural styles like *luk thung* and *mor lam*. Within a Red Shirt canon that favored guitar-driven *luk thung*, hip-hop, and *mor lam sing*, Jin's marches were a stylistic anachronism. But they were also valuable tokens of past dissident movements.

Jin's lyrics had once been primarily about poverty and the inequities of capitalism. His famous song "Slum," for example, describes poverty as an invisible

36. Thomas Fuller and Seth Mydans, "Thai General Shot, Army Moves to Face Protesters," May 13, 2010, http://www.nytimes.com/2010/05/14/world/asia/14thai.html. By coincidence, I was a few hundred meters up the road when Seh Daeng was shot, and saw the crowd that formed, but did not know what happened until returning home and checking the news.

37. Deborah Wong, *Sounding the Center: History and Aesthetics in Thai Buddhist Performance* (Chicago: University of Chicago Press, 2001); Larry Scott Persons, "The Anatomy of Thai Face," *MANUSYA: Journal of Humanities* 11, no. 1 (2008).

tragedy. The "songs for life" and affiliated "art for life" movements, with which he was associated, drew attention to such injustices.[38] In his reemergence in the twenty-first century as a Red Shirt, Jin adapted to a movement not headed by students and farmers, but by a politically conscious working class that wanted their share of development's spoils. Rather than concern with a litany of leftist social issues, the Red Shirts strove for ownership. As Jin explained, "Many, many people who I know from back then, they would not associate with these people today. Nowadays when democracy spreads from the grassroots level, it adds meaning to what I did before. Before we talked about democracy only in college, only in elite groups. Right now the word 'democracy' is in the general population—common people understand how government affects their lives, how it can solve problems of hardship and suffering. It is deep and profound. You've asked if there's a difference between now and the old days, how is it different. . . . Nowadays people are capable of knowing. Because the people have taken ownership. Much greater ownership."[39]

"Warriors of the Dust" was thus an apt anthem for a *kuu maa'eeng* approach to protest. Even the song's recording reflects a proud amateurism, a sense of entrepreneurial self-starting. All instrumentation, including drums and keyboards, was created by digital presets. Compared even to the music of the UDD leaders, hardly professional musicians, the quality of Jin's production was low. However, when I discussed the song with Red Shirts, the issue of production was never a concern. Amateur production was in fact an asset; it was a good thing that it seemed like Jin had recorded the song with limited resources. For Jin's audience, professionalism and technical expertise did not signal authenticity. Only ownership did.

As "Warriors of the Dust" became common at rallies in late 2010, Sombat began featuring Jin as a performer at Red Sunday's events. The aesthetic qualities of Jin's music, combined with the popularity of "Warriors of the Dust," at last gave Red Sunday a musical symbol that could distinguish it from the UDD. In November 2010, Jin began spending time in Red Sunday's expansive new office space on the fifth floor of the Big C shopping mall in Lad Phrao, where it had moved from its previous and more campaign-like headquarters. Jin came on weekends to lead rehearsals and to help Sombat teach hour-long "democracy lessons" in front of small, mixed-age groups in the seminar room. On weeknights, he gave singing lessons to the children of Red Sunday's volunteers. Perhaps most importantly, Jin began working with Orn and a thirty-year-old composer named Dear to train Red Sunday's new choir, which Sombat hoped would perform at rallies and other events. The singers in the choir were drawn from Red Sunday's current crop of active volunteers, nearly all of whom were musical neophytes. They planned to rehearse a few pieces written by Jin, under his supervision. The seven-month anniversary of the May crackdown, December

38. "พัฒนาการเพลงเพื่อชีวิต" ("The Development of 'songs for life'"), accessed January 30, 2013. http://www.9dern.com/rsa/view.php?id=90.

39. Jin Gammachon, interview with the author, December 19, 2010. This interview took place in Thai.

19, happened to fall on a Sunday, and various Red Shirt groups were planning to hold the largest rally since the previous spring in Ratchaprasong. The Red Sunday choir would make its public debut, unamplified, in the middle of that event. The date was circled on the office calendar.

MEDIATED LAYERS OF THE SYMBOLIC REPERTOIRE

Orn, tears streaming down her cheek in the driver's seat, watched herself sing on a tiny iPhone screen. It was December 10, 2010, and she was driving me from Red Sunday's office across the city to Democracy Monument, where a massive Red Shirt rally commemorating the April 10 violence was taking place. Orn herself would not attend—after she dropped me off, she planned to go home. That morning she had decided, in a bitter revelation, that activism was interfering with her personal relationships, her professional obligations, and her ability to lead a healthy life. She was embroiled in an ongoing argument with another Red Sunday volunteer. For today, at least, she was going to catch up on other work. This decision was acutely painful because of the commitment she felt to the Red Shirt movement. To miss even one rally was hard, and it weighed on her throughout the ride. Our conversation turned to the past, and Orn strained not to cry.

"I do everything for my uncle, he is a true democracy fighter" she told me, explaining why she felt so dedicated to Red Sunday. The man she called her uncle was a friend of the family who had supported Orn and her mother after Orn's father died many years earlier. "This uncle supported my mother, and helped my family in hard times. . . and he was part of the October 6 fight, when many college students were killed by the army." That date, October 6, referred to the 1976 massacre of several hundred Thai student protesters at Thammasat University by military and paramilitary forces during the anti-communist period described earlier by Sombat. Orn understood her participation in the Red Shirt movement as a repayment of debt to her uncle, whose past struggles for democracy she had inherited.

Waiting at one of Bangkok's many interminably long red lights, Orn brought out her phone to play me a video clip of a song she had sung the previous week, at an event hosted by Sombat. The event was called *wɔɔn nɔɔn khúk* (officially styled in English as "Jail Me, Dude"), and used a talk-show format, with skits, stand-up comedy, and musical performances. It was held in front of a packed crowd in a small theater, and video of the show was later included on a DVD sold by Red Sunday. The gimmick of the event was to creep toward the line of various political taboos, each time with a dose of humor. For example, the event was originally scheduled for December 5, the King's birthday and one of the holiest days of the year—certainly no occasion for political satire. But the symbolism of the date proved too apparent. Sombat received death threats, and the event had to be pushed back by one day. Nevertheless, on December 6, he did sing "Happy Birthday"—this time, to the Red Shirt movement. Orn's contribution to the show was to sing a piece composed by

Dear called "19 Ratchaprasong." She sang in duet with a young man named Jom, who was facing *lèse-majesté* charges because of comments posted on his Facebook page deemed critical of the monarchy. "19 Ratchaprasong" was lyrically straightforward, praising the *wiiráchon* (heroes) who died during the military assault on Ratchaprasong on May 19. But Jom's participation gave the song a much sharper symbolic edge. Orn had been nervous about her own singing, but the crowd liked the song, and afterward Jin approached her to comment on how beautiful her voice sounded.

Orn turned up the volume on the side of her iPhone a few clicks, until it maxed out. The sound, already grainy on the recording, clipped through the phone's tiny speakers. The handheld cinematography caused the image to quaver gently. Each piano note landed with heavy distortion, and the lack of bass in the phone's speakers made the sound tinny. Nevertheless, Orn burst with pride on rehearing the performance. Given the decision she had made to skip that day's protest, the clip took on a heightened nostalgic quality, evidencing her continued commitment and depth of feeling. Her face brightened as she revisited the moment. We plodded through traffic for forty minutes before nearing the periphery of the protest. Small groups of Red Shirts sat on plastic stools eating bowls of *kǔaytǐaw* or walking out of 7-Eleven with plastic bags of bottled water and pork snacks. The part of downtown near the old city was very familiar to Orn, and she narrated her memories as we drove, watching their living indices through the window. The constrained, often painful past lay beneath the hopeful present like a foundation.[40] She gestured to the right, where the Pinklao bridge connects Bangkok to the nearby suburb of Thonburi. Orn's late father had once owned a shop just beyond there. "He had a printing business," she explained. "This bridge is a memory of him. I always sat in the car with my dad from my home to the company. We went home together, so I have memories of Ratchadamnoen Road since I was young. And my mother was a famous singer of that age. She sang in a night pub on Ratchadamnoen. My father and my mother met each other here. . . . She sang the music of other artists. Local Thai singers. *Luk thung.* You know *luk thung*, right?" I told her that of course I did. "Do you want to listen? I can sing Pumpuang, *na*. Because it's the kind of song I listened to when I was young. Do you want me to try? Ok, Pumpuang, *na*."

Orn straightened in her seat. The song she chose, that came easily, was by Pumpuang Duangjan, the same singer her mother would channel a few months later over dinner at her home. Orn sang a song called *fɛɛn Pumpuang*, the title of which has the subtle double-meaning of either "fan of Pumpuang" or "Pumpuang's lover." The recording, released in 1990, was probably calculated by the diva to assuage fans concerned with rumors that she had taken a lover who would distract

40. Rosalind Morris, *In the Place of Origins: Modernity and Its Mediums in Northern Thailand* (Durham, NC: Duke University Press, 2000). Morris explains representations of originary symbols that *already represent displacement* in Thailand as evidence of an "ambivalent self-consciousness" within modernity (14).

from her career, and thus also from her relationship with fans. The song is sung seductively, drawing out the affectionate particle *jǎa* again and again. Orn began:

> *fɛɛn jǎa mây tôɔng pen hùang thâa rák phûmphuang lɛ̀ɛw jà sambaay*
> ("My lover/fan, you don't have to worry, if you love Pumpuang, it'll be OK")

> *jà rɔ́ɔng phleeng hâyfɛɛn fang phleeng thay phleeng faràng*
> ("I'll sing songs for my lover/fans, Thai songs and foreign songs")

> *phûmphuang kɔ̂ɔ rɔ́ɔng dây fɛɛn jǎa khâw maa klâyklây*
> ("Pumpuang can sing, and my lover/fans can come close")

> *fɛɛn jǎa khâw maa klây klâyjà bɔ̀ɔk àray*
> ("My lover/fans, come close, what will you say?")

"Thank youuuuu!" said Orn with delight upon finishing. "But my mom, she is an expert, you know, I cannot compare. She sang Pumpuang songs very beautifully, Ben." Orn turned her attention back to the road in front of her; Ratchadamnoen and the protest were visibly ahead. "The night pub should be around here." As we reached the road that connected downtown to the bridge, Orn dropped me off. She turned right, toward home. I walked ahead, swallowed up by the protest's heat and noise.

DECEMBER 19

Orn called later that week to tell me that choir practices were on. Despite skipping the previous week's rally, she was determined to participate in the December 19 performance—whatever her future with Red Sunday might be, this was too important to miss. Because December 19 fell on a Sunday and was also the seven-month anniversary of the crackdown, it was a convenient as well as symbolically rich day to hold a Red Shirt event. An enormous turnout was expected.

The day before the rally, Jin and Sombat sat in Red Sunday's new office on the fifth floor of Big C for a daylong rehearsal, attended by nearly every volunteer who expected to sing the next day. The plan was to perform "Warriors of the Dust" and three other songs, all composed by Jin, in the early evening. The choir would sing unamplified in a part of the intersection that was typically crowded and close to the central stage. Given the size of the rally, the significance of the anniversary, and the fact that this would be the Red Sunday choir's debut, the performance was hotly anticipated.

Red Sunday's office in Big C was larger than its previous facility on Vipavadi Road. In addition to a computer room, the new space had a separate den with couches and televisions, a library, and two smaller multipurpose rooms used for everything from seminars to performance rehearsals. In fact, the entire fifth floor of the mall was leased to Red Shirt businesses. Near Red Sunday's headquarters, a pro-Thaksin television station housed its main broadcasting studio. Coffee and

CD vendors, their stalls covered in red streamers, set up on a veranda overlooking an ice skating rink thirty feet below. A souvenir shop sold teddy bears, shirts, and bags, all emblazoned with Red Shirt graphics and slogans. Several volunteer offices advertised assistance to victims of the crackdown, including anyone with medical or legal needs unmet by the government. Even the advertisements in this part of the mall were tailored to the movement—a large cardboard standee near the escalator pitching instant coffee featured an image of popular Red Shirt singer Muk Mekthini. Though Red Sunday's office was large, it was merely one among many Red Shirt organizations and businesses on the floor.

Choir rehearsal began in the late morning, in the smaller of two multipurpose rooms. Jin and Sombat sat on the floor, at the same level as the thirty or so volunteer singers, mostly middle-aged or older, who had squeezed inside. The only person standing up was a young conductor, brought in by Sombat to help coordinate the choir. The choral arrangements were simple, with a few alternations between the male and female singers. But there was no attempt to harmonize, even though the songs would have lent themselves to it. All four of the pieces were recent compositions by Jin, each in a military march style. Among these was *kam chay* ("Grasping Victory"), a rousing piece for drum, flute, and brass that Jin had sung onstage at one pre-crackdown Red Shirt event in March 2010. The conductor and Jin gave minimal instructions, explaining only that the volunteers should not be nervous about the size of the crowd around them, and that they should stay in close formation to keep the sidewalk clear. The singers' imperfect diction and other rudimentary issues were left uncorrected. If the purpose of the concert was to show what *kuu maa'eeng* protest meant in practice, then it made sense to recruit amateur singers to represent Red Sunday. In a portentous moment, the sound of a crowd cheering along to a televised video of Surachai Danwattananusorn, leader of another subgroup called Red Siam, seeped into the Red Sunday office from the hallway outside. The noise mingled with their singing, at times overpowering them. The choir's tender, self-motivated feel also left it at risk of being drowned out. Red Sunday dwelt on the tenuous line between a "power of the powerless" agency and vulnerability to louder, proximate sounds.

The December 19 rally turned out to be the largest Red Shirt event since the crackdown. Tens of thousands of people packed into the intersection from late morning until around midnight. Despite half-hearted efforts by the police to clear the road, vehicle traffic could no longer pass through by the early afternoon. And although the Emergency Decree still technically forbade amplification, many drivers parked cars in the intersection to play music from their stereos. Some protesters also brought long red strings, which they tied across the Skytrain railings and lamp posts, weaving them into a thick red patchwork overhead. Small origami birds were hung from the taut lines.

Red Sunday gathered in its usual spot, on and around the broad steps in front of McDonald's at the southeast corner of the intersection, not far from where Sombat had held the "people died here" happening in June. This was close to the center of the rally a few hundred meters away but set off just enough to allow the group some symbolic distance. Sombat spent the morning glad-handing Thai and foreign journalists, while Orn, Meow, and other volunteers prepared for the evening. "The government won't allow us to use amplifiers," Sombat told me, "so this is a method of communicating. It won't be loud, but it should be interesting. . . . We're concerned about the noise, but it will be full of feeling." Even as we spoke, recorded music was audible in the background, intruding impulsively into the conversation. Staging a performance that would show "feeling" rather than volume-based power was, for Red Sunday, not merely an effect of legality, but a strategic choice made by Sombat in the course of playing his political game.

Jin, meanwhile, was nervous. "The concert today is strange," he said a few hours before performing.[41] "It's something that hasn't really been done before, hasn't really been done in this way. We're singing without amplification, just singing with our mouths in a group. Just singing. It offers a new feeling." He paced in front of the steps, smiling only when a fan stopped to pose for a photograph with him. By the late afternoon, the rally had swelled to about one hundred thousand people. The sidewalk beneath the Skytrain was so packed that participants could only inch along, willing themselves to patience. The choir held a practice run earlier in the afternoon, close to the center of the rally, but it was subsumed by the surrounding noise, forcing them to end early. For Jin and most of the group, there was hope mixed with terror about what the evening concert might accomplish or fail to accomplish. I asked Jin how he felt hearing mass groups of protesters singing "Warriors of the Dust" in unison. The weight of historical symbolism and connection was clear in his answer. "It's like I'm connected to a thousand people," he replied. "As if we have the same mood. The same intentions. The same injuries and pain. The same resentment and sense that we want to fight injustice. The same. . . the same as our friends. It's like we've been friends and relatives forever, and we share the same pain. And so we want to fight." By coincidence, Mohamed Bouazizi, a Tunisian fruit vendor, had immolated himself in the town of Sidi Bouzid just thirty hours before this rally, catalyzing what would become the Arab Spring. The Red Shirts would soon become aware of that movement, and it would be figured as a kindred uprising. But no one knew about that connection yet.

The choir members began taking their places around 6:30 p.m., just after sunset, wearing identical black T-shirts displaying the number of known dead in the ongoing conflict in white chalk, as if on a prison cell wall. The choir director took his place in the center, almost invisible, a present-but-absent leader. Around him, on the broad steps of McDonald's, hundreds of Red Sunday members huddled together, a small island in the complex ecosystem of the protest. From above, on the

41. Jin Gammachon, interview with the author, December 19, 2010. The interview took place in Thai.

Skytrain platform, the rally could be seen to sprawl in every direction, into alleys and intersections and shops, everywhere cramped.

The choir director pulled out a clarinet, and the crowd hushed as he began playing the song's main motif, dark and cinematic. All around, arms shot up holding cell phone cameras and video recorders, many on tripods. Phones in neon rubber cases snapped quick shots, large black cameras swiveled and pointed ahead, their operators' faces hidden behind lenses, portable sound recorders aimed at an angle downward alongside microphones and camcorders and windscreens and cables. Some even documented as they sang; the concert is now on YouTube from many angles.

The clarinetist missed the highest note in the introduction. No one blinked. Into the ensuing four beat pause rushed distant undulating cheers and a woman's high laughter, which subsumed the choir director's snapping fingers. The male singers pulled in their breath and entered together on the first line, staggered by some accidental milliseconds. A woman cleared her voice in anticipation. Sitting on the sidewalk, audible underfoot, one Red Sunday regular wearing a shirt that said in bold letters "La Reforma," the name of a nineteenth century Mexican leftist movement, played a twinkly version of "La Marseillaise" from an iPod jacked into a toy megaphone. It was like being connected symbolically to a thousand people, whatever that might bring.

CHAPTER 3
Atrocity Broadcasts

Under a high sun, on a different corner and a different day, the monument appeared suddenly, as if sprouting from the asphalt. Across the sidewalk, a man sold CDs from a folding table. Facing him obliquely was another table, where donations were being collected for the family of a Red Shirt man killed by the Thai military. A young girl, too young for this, stood on a concrete block and shouted in a high register, hailing passersby to donate money. The CD vendor was garrulous, chatting without pause. His table was long and narrow, about fifteen feet from end to end. On the far end of it was a television showing unnerving footage of soldiers assaulting protesters. A pair of small speakers near the vendor played music, which clashed with the sound from the VCD. Onscreen, soldiers behind shields and plastic masks brought their batons down on an unarmed young man in a red T-shirt in the muddy darkness of the night of April 10. The footage was shot from behind an iron gate, which framed the action. Gut-turning screams and thuds vibrated the speakers. Hands behind his neck, the man lay on the ground in apparent submission. The soldiers began to walk away, only to return to issue more blows for a minute, until the man stopped moving—dead, unconscious, or beaten beyond resistance. One more black boot came down on his back, and his body shuddered.[1]

Near the screen, people came by and greeted the vendor. He smiled and shook their hands. Happy music came from the stage, making up one corner of a sonic triangle (along with the atrocity footage and the recorded music) that was impossible to cognize or process emotionally all at once. I set up a sound recorder to document the scene for ten minutes. In one channel of the stereo recording is guitar-based,

---

1. Mindful of the potentially exploitative character of this description, I have made every effort to present it as directly as possible based on what occurs in the video. The aim of selling the VCD was, of course, to represent the savagery of the military, so the footage was chosen precisely to represent the worst atrocities of the soldiers. The VCD is untitled and remains in my archive of fieldwork material. I do not know the ultimate extent of the man's injuries.

upbeat *luk thung*, and in the other the sound of popping bullets, screams, and tank engines. As a whole, the recording describes an excess.

Peace and war, represented on the same plane, create spectacular ironies. Alan Klima, who has analyzed the viewing of atrocity videos at Thai protest events, argues that violence and death are nested within a putatively peaceful Thai modernity.[2] Dissent is thus often predicated on exposing violence as a kind of hidden truth. "Death imagery has played a vital role in political transformations," Klima writes.[3] The neoliberal state has represented its version of modernity as a bloodless one, he suggests, despite that state's frequent recourse to violent repression. Neoliberalism is in fact rooted in death and war, and remains haunted by them.

But listening within the sonic triangle described above, the promise of a just future was fully co-present with, not distantly haunted by, the memory of a violent past. My sound recording explains this co-presence more readily than an image. It is, perhaps, a sonification of the existential noise of human experience, of the excess with which we live. This sound recording represented noisy co-presence both for the protesters and for the researcher listening among them. Both future and past were figured through sonic media. Atrocity videos perform a different kind of work when viewed than when heard in a field of contradictory and complementary sounds. (And I do not propose a Buddhalogical study of the Red Shirt ear). Hearing these videos calls upon auditors to mobilize figures of memory in the name of a future salvation. This might include further sacrifice. No one yet knows. The sounds are not synchronized. Perhaps there is an implication. It is left to the listener to make decisions about what strategies are both ethical and worthwhile. But the fact remains that the listener in that position (a very accessible and public position) listens to many things at once, often more than can be managed consciously. The listener listens in excess, to memory and to promises, which together make the present throb. The Red Shirt protests mixed memory and futurity, which enabled one another. Suffering and pleasure, heaven and hell, converged. The past becomes a malady that might cure the future.

2. Klima, *The Funeral Casino.*
3. Ibid., 5.

CHAPTER 4

Wireless Road and the Ground of Modernity

R adio was the ground of the Red Shirt protests. This claim has two meanings: first, radio was probably the most important Red Shirt media technology; second, the Red Shirt occupation was staged in the exact place (along a thoroughfare called Wireless Road) where radio had been inaugurated in Thailand nearly a century earlier (see Figures 4.1, 4.2 and 4.3). A ground, in electricity, is the origin point of a circuit, a physical connection to the earth that acts as a reservoir of electrical charge. Wireless Road, as the origin point of radio in Thailand, functioned in precisely this way for the Red Shirts, as a ground or reference point for modernity and its publics.

In the early twentieth century, radio arrived as a totem of modernity in Siam, which would soon become a constitutional monarchic nation called Thailand. Siam's first radio station (as well as the road along which it was built) was the project of a developer and real estate magnate named Nai Lert, who also introduced buses and commercial ice, among other new conveniences, to Thailand. Nai Lert's innovations made him a millionaire. Radio was among the technological wonders that connected the nation to global modernity, both symbolically and as a mass medium. The radio was highly centralized, both then and now. While broadcast regulations have shifted, the government has always maintained tight control over stations and their licensing, with the military playing an especially strong organizational role. Thailand's bureaucratic modernity, as Herzfeld notes, has long been marked by a centralization of power of which control over the radio is typical.[1]

The proliferation of unlicensed community radio in the early twenty-first century threatened the centralization of media that the Thai government had exerted over the past eighty years. This threat was realized when provincial radio broadcasts became openly political and even critical of the government beginning in the late

---

1. Herzfeld, *Siege of the Spirits*.

Figure 4.1 Wireless Road, site of Bangkok Radio Station, which was inaugurated in 1920. Courtesy of the National Archives of Thailand.

2000s. An article from the right-wing online newspaper *ASTV Manager* thus reported in satisfied tones about the mass closure of antigovernment community radio stations by the army on May 23, 2010.[2] The article claimed, using loaded language, that "in the mobilization of the Red Shirt group for the recent burning of the country (*phǎw bâan phǎw mɯang*), it cannot be denied that the community radio stations that sprouted like mushrooms were a tool of incitement (*khrɯ̂angmɯɯ plùkràdom*)."[3] The rhetoric of *Manager* highlighted the acute political threat of Red Shirt radio, which was decentralized and at least partly listener-supported, and which has been described as the foundation of the Red Shirt movement by critics, supporters, and non-partisan observers alike.[4]

The *Manager* article exemplified the critical response to Red Shirt radio, which dovetailed with the fears of the Thai government. In early 2010, as political protests

2. "เช็กบิลวิทยุชุมชน เครื่องมือปลุกระดมคนเสื้อแดง" ("It's 'Check, Please' for Community Radio, a Tool of Incitement for the Red Shirts"). Translated from the original Thai. http://www.manager.co.th/Local/ViewNews.aspx?NewsID=9530000074366, May 30, 2010. *ASTV Manager* was the online wing of Sondhi Limthongkul's media empire. A former business associate and friend of Thaksin Shinawatra, Sondhi began using the various outlets under his control to call for Thaksin's ouster after the two had a private falling out in the mid-1990s. Following the political orientation of its founder, *ASTV Manager* was thereafter consistently critical of the Red Shirts for their relationship with Thaksin.

3. Ibid.

4. Charoen Pengmoon (เจริญ เพ็งมูล), "วิทยุชุมชนกับการพัฒนาทางการเมืองท้องถิ่น เจริญ เพ็งมูล" ("Community Radio and Local Political Development"), *COLA Local Administration Journal* 8, no. 2 (2015): 60–72.

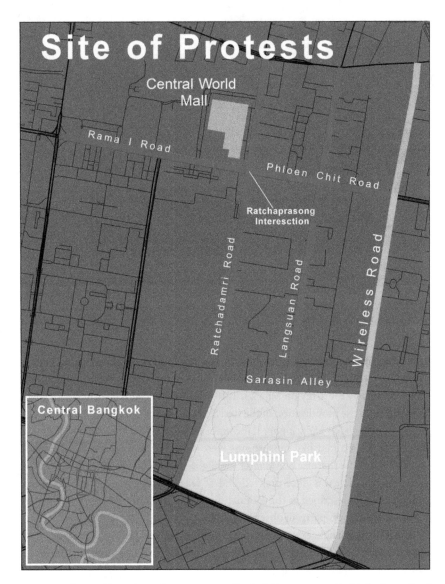

Figure 4.2 The map above shows the areas occupied by Red Shirt protesters (highlighted in red and orange) in Bangkok as of late April 2010. Wireless Road sits on the eastern edge of the occupation site. Each eastern terminus along Wireless included two "stockade defenses," or towers of sharpened bamboo poles around a vehicle checkpoint operated by guards. Map courtesy Margaret Randall.

grew, the army sought to rein in local radio by shutting down a handful of stations in several different provinces. After these stations were raided, however, some operators simply moved their transmitters to new facilities, or converted to online broadcasts, which were more difficult to trace. Others abandoned mass broadcasting entirely, instead trucking stacks of public address speakers directly to rallies in Bangkok and other cities, playing music from within converted cargo vans for

Figure 4.3 Red Shirt bamboo and razor wire stockade defense at the intersection of Wireless Road and Phloen Chit, May 15, 2010. Photograph by the author.

protest audiences who knew of the harassment that the stations had experienced. At these rallies, under banners that advertised the stations' original call letters and provinces, DJs engaged listeners face to face much as they had previously done on the air. If anything, the stations had decentralized further, despite sacrificing broadcast range.

Collective memory of the stations' role in mobilizing protesters in the provinces made radio sound trucks a powerful counterpublic medium. Through their speaker systems, even lyrically innocuous songs became charged with political meaning. Charles Hirschkind describes a counterpublic as "a domain of discourse and practice that stands in a disjunctive relationship to the public sphere of the nation and its media instruments."[5] As Michael Warner defines them, counterpublics operate very much like ordinary publics, but their discursive modes restrict the size of their audience. The return (and the transformation) of Red Shirt radio stations after the raids was an example of *kuu maa'eeng* protest action, in which leadership and centralization were shunned, independent motivation was prized, and marginality became virtuous.[6] *Kuu maa'eeng* was a discursive mode, embodied by the counterpublic

5. Charles Hirschkind, *The Ethical Soundscape: Cassette Sermons and Islamic Counterpublics* (New York: Columbia University Press, 2006), 117.
6. Duncan McCargo and Krisadawan Hangladarom, "Contesting Isan-ness: Discourses of Politics and Identity in Northeast Thailand," *Asian Ethnicity* 5, no. 2 (2004): 219–34.

broadcasts of radio sound trucks, that became "constitutive of membership and its affects."[7] As government censorship focused on mass broadcasting, the Red Shirts shifted to sections of the communicative bandwidth that remained accessible to them—small, intimate, often outmoded media such as sound trucks and pirate radio. Rather than being regarded as a retreat, however, these media were imagined as especially authentic.[8] "Small media" were valuable counterpublic instruments in part because they afforded dialogue (it is easier for a listener to respond directly to a small, local radio broadcast than a large, national one) and in part because of the censorship that led directly to their instantiation.[9]

At the peak of the raids, immediately following the Ratchaprasong crackdown in May 2010, forty-seven low-wattage stations across thirteen provinces were surveilled, searched, and permanently closed. The government did not offer a rationale for the targeting of these forty-seven stations in particular. According to Suthep Wilailert of the press-freedom advocacy group Campaign for Popular Media Reform, government-controlled media outlets reported that the closures were a response to *lèse-majesté* allegations. But in fact, the authorities usually cited technical violations.[10] The military also exploited ambiguous, moralistic language in the Thai Public Broadcasting Service Act, including the legal imperative that broadcasters "[protect children] and youth from the program that presents violence, illegal or immoral manner, allurement that leads to wrong-doing and coarse language [sic]" to justify their actions.[11] The number of outlets that were shut down was a small fraction of the estimated eight thousand community stations operating in Thailand at that time, but the raids served as warnings—if a few broadcasters were targeted, all were effectively threatened. This approach succeeded. In my experience as a listener in Bangkok, it became increasingly difficult to find community stations of any kind on the dial, but especially those sympathetic to the Red Shirts, as the May

7. Michael Warner, *Publics and Counterpublics* (New York: Zone Books, 2005), 122.

8. David Novak. *Japanoise: Music at the Edge of Circulation* (Durham, NC: Duke University Press, 2013). The chapter "The Future of Cassette Culture" analyzes the anachronistic fashion for tapes as an attempt "to impose technological, social, and aesthetic limits on the omnipresence of new media" (199). The resulting aesthetic is colored by a strong ethics and an emphasis on social intimacy. The Red Shirts' move to small, outmoded media after the radio station raids functioned similarly, although the limits were external rather than self-imposed.

9. See Annabelle Sreberny-Mohammadi and Ali Mohammadi, *Small Media, Big Revolution: Communication, Culture, and the Iranian Revolution* (Minneapolis: University of Minnesota Press, 1994) for a theorization of "small media."

10. "New Media and Political Mobilization," Heinrich Böll Stiftung Southeast Asia Foundation, 2012.

11. "Thai Public Broadcasting Service Act," B.E. 2551 (2008); see also Section 37 of the Radio and Television Broadcasting Services Act, B.E. 2551 (2008) which stipulates that "it is prohibited to broadcast programme that causes the destruction of the Democratic Regime with the King as Head of the State, or has an adverse effect on national security and the good moral of the public, or displays pornographic act, or has an adverse effect on the social psyche or detrimental to the health of the public. The authority or commissioner can ban the program or revoke the license of the station [sic]." English translations are the official versions provided by the Thai government.

19, 2010 crackdown approached, and even more so after it was carried out. Each day, there were fewer stations on the dial where one could hear Red Shirt news and broadcasts from Ratchaprasong. Eventually there were none at all. By mid-May, Chiang Mai had also been mostly purged of Red Shirt channels.

The raids were plainly political. Though the stations were not formally connected to each other, all were supportive of the Red Shirts and critical of state elites, and all were small, peripheral operations.[12] Many of these stations had launched in the mid-2000s as apolitical outlets, thanks to the increased availability of inexpensive, low-wattage transmitters and a strong demand for stations offering rural music and comedy. The turn toward political content came only after the 2006 coup, when provincial radio was still relatively free from government scrutiny. The musician Hongthong Dao Udon, for example, became a DJ for the northeastern Rak Udon community station in 2006. Though initially apolitical, she was convicted of incitement for statements she made on-air in 2010, and served twelve months in prison in 2015–16.[13] Community stations helped mobilize a diffuse group of dissidents into a self-aware counterpublic, which the government quickly came to recognize as a threat.

After the political turn, despite an uptick in talk-oriented programming, music remained an important emblem of political belief. Most of the musical repertoire on Red Shirt community radio was *luk thung*, a genre with mid-twentieth century roots in the agrarian provinces near Bangkok, but linked strongly with the north and northeast as well.[14] *Luk thung* singers' voices are judged by fans on the depth of emotional experience they convey, especially their capacity to express suffering through trilling and melisma. Tempos are slow, and vocals are elevated in the recorded mix. The personalities and poetic flourishes of singers drive the genre, which is replete with tragic and legendary stories such as that of Pumpuang Duangjan (see Chapter 2). Mitchell suggests that *luk thung* oriented something like a counterpublic as early as the 1940s, with its lyrics an open rebuke to the denial of class division by Bangkok's governing elite. *Luk thung* singers rhapsodized about the difference between city and country, and the hardships of traversing the two realms for poor people in

---

12. "เจ้าหน้าที่บุกค้น-ยึด วิทยุชุมชนเสื้อแดงหลายแห่ง" ("Officials Raid Many Red Shirt Community Radio Stations"), http://prachatai.com/journal/2011/04/34237, April 26, 2011.

13. James Mitchell, "Isaan Lives: Hongthong Dao Udon: From singing star to political prisoner," *Isaan Record* (http://isaanrecord.com/2016/09/12/isaan-lives-hongthong-dao-udon-from-singing-star-to-political-prisoner/) September 12, 2016.

14. It is not my aim to wade into the controversial (but largely moot) question of the "true" origins of *luk thung*. As the genre has shifted from associations of low morality to being a source of cultural pride for some, central Thailand has increasingly laid claim to its heritage, especially by way of famous singers like Suraphol Sombatcharoen and Pumpuang Duangjan, both of whom are from the province of Suphanburi in the central plains. On the other hand, some effort has been made to situate the origins or core identity of *luk thung* in the northeast, including the pseudonymous Weng Plangwarn's *Luk Thung Isan*, an exhaustively detailed, self-published Thai-language monograph that runs over six hundred pages.

particular.[15] Such themes have long been a source of anxiety for government officials, who have periodically censored *luk thung* recordings that suggest class division, among other unpalatable themes.[16] *Luk thung* songs in the twenty-first century may well be heard as mild, nostalgic oldies in certain contexts—say, on a film sound-track. But in other contexts, including that of politicized Red Shirt community radio, which paired the music with frank political discourse and fundraising, their political potential may reemerge forcefully. The government's radio station closures thus reasserted a hierarchical modernity that does not tolerate public suggestions of class and power difference (even as—or perhaps *because*—the government relies so powerfully on those differences in governing).

The very structure of community radio, especially its decentralization, was a threat to hierarchy and centrality. Stations typically had only one small transmitter and some basic equipment, which was controlled by two or three volunteer DJs and engineers. The stations had no leader and no accountability to a single, central organization. Government officials were concerned that structures like this would make it difficult to locate the exact origins of incitement. One legislative act about protest broadcasting, drafted in 2013, sought to empower authorities to crack down on leaderless events simply because they were leaderless: "the president of the Examining Committee shall have the authority to stop a gathering in a public place. . . if there is no organizer taking care of the gathering."[17] In other words, certain structures of political organization could be a priori illegal, regardless of their content. The proposed act thus sought to criminalize leaderlessness as such.

The radio stations raids included a great deal of forensic analysis. A photograph at the beginning of the *Manager* article shows police and National Broadcasting and Telecommunications Commission (NBTC) inspectors examining the equipment from one closed station, 92.5 FM in Chiang Mai, on a long wooden table. Such images are commonly seen in tabloid newspapers, and often depict seized caches of drugs or counterfeit goods. The image in this article shows a yellow, consumer-model satellite dish, a handful of coiled black cables, and an 8-channel mixing board,

15. John Clewley, "The Many Sounds of Siam: Thai music ranges from Classical to Bikers' Rock," in *The Rough Guide to World Music: Europe, Asia and Pacific*, Simon Broughton, Mark Ellingham, and Jon Lusk, eds. (London: Rough Guides, 2009). Monrakplengthai.com, "phumphuang duangchan: hang noi, thoi nit," July 19, 2009. Pumpuang's "Sao A.M." ("AM Girl") has been discussed independently by John Clewley and Peter Doolan as an example of a song that might have invited the wrath of the censors for its clear differentiation between naive country girls and exploitative city boys. Similarly, Dao Bandon's *khon khìi lăng khwaay* ("People Who Ride on the Backs of Buffaloes") signals class by contrasting the lifeworlds of the rich and poor.

16. Consider—ironically given his popularity in the north and northeast—Thaksin Shinawatra's own censorship of twenty *luk thung* songs in 2003.

17. "Act to 'Manage Gatherings in Public Places'" ("ร่างพระราชบัญญัติจัดระเบียบการชุมนุมในที่สาธารณะ พ.ศ. . . . ."), http://www.parliament.go.th/ewtadmin/ewt/parliament_parcy/ewt_news.php?nid=3175&filename=index08, accessed March 4, 2013. Translated from the original Thai.

all laid out in neat rows. A translucent plastic tub holds *luk thung* CDs, each of which is sealed in an individual plastic bag. DJs and other station employees are absent from the image, and the equipment splayed on the table is no more sophisticated than the setup in a bedroom recording studio. One can imagine the echoes of voices and footsteps in the room, a distinctly nonmusical atmosphere, while the roundup proceeded. The raid was like an autopsy of the tiny facility, carried out in an effort to reveal its connections to the elusive systems of a decentralized movement.[18]

Barred from mass media—Red Shirt opinions are unspeakable, for example, on free-to-air television—members of the movement turned to the counterpublics of small media instead. Dissent has no place in state media, and so as the protests in Bangkok escalated in March 2010, stations like 92.5 FM became key sources of reporting and opinion within limited geographic areas, often in a partisan register. Compared to television, radio stations were easy to set up and much more likely than websites to reach provincial listeners. According to a 2011 report by the Asian National Media Barometer (ANMB), a greater percentage of Thais (40%) at that time had access to community and local radio than to newspaper and print media (33%), cable TV (15%), or internet (20–22%).[19] Although mainstream radio and television are available almost everywhere (95% penetration rate), the majority of mainstream stations are either owned directly by the military or tightly managed by the government, and among critics of the government these are seen as better sources of soap operas than of news.[20] Mainstream radio resembles the corporatized formats of large stations in North America and many other places, with slick, repetitive jingles, a fixed rotation for playlists, and little if any participation from listeners beyond carefully tended call-in requests. The suppression of alternative voices, however, had the effect of fracturing the media.[21] The campaign

18. An etymological note may be useful here. The Thai word for propaganda is *kràbɔ̀ɔksǐang*, meaning also "mouthpiece of an organization," and translated literally as "sound cylinder." *Kràbɔ̀ɔksǐang* collapses a mediating device with the output shaped by its structure. This nexus of definitions seems to suggest that bias resides in the materiality of technologies of aural mediation. The police who raided Red Shirt radio stations likewise seemed to assume that by examining equipment, they could gain a better vantage on political "distortion" in community radio broadcasting. Tools of mediation were suspected of having the agency to distort truth within a state-controlled media network where communications are expected to reiterate a single, centralized political message.

19. "Asian Media Barometer: A Locally Based Analysis of the Media Landscape in Asia— Thailand 2010," Asian National Media Barometer, 6. The ANMB estimates the total number of community radio stations to be around 8,000, and estimates that there are 524 licensed mainstream stations. The report further suggests that radio is a vibrant medium, but highly politicized, and that the Thai government does not nurture its diversification.

20. Paul Wesley Chambers, "Thailand in Crisis: Resurgent Military, Diminished Democracy, Civil War?," briefing prepared for the United States National Intelligence Council and US Department of State, Washington DC, April 19–20, 2010. As for military control over the media, the armed forces as of 2010 controlled two television stations and 245 out of 524 licensed radio stations.

21. According to the ANMB report, the closures were based on the Emergency Decree of 2005. The report argues that because community radio is harassed by government, and given

to censor community radio, rather than restoring a centralized structure, produced the opposite outcome. Small media proliferated. The counterpublic of small media thus developed from strategic choices made in the face of censorship.

Thai historian Nidhi Eosriwong asked, as the protests continued in May 2011, "How much do these Red Shirt communities connect with provincial leaders? It is strange that there is no relationship among organizations. The provincial leaders usually have access to new media, especially community radio, self-publications, and the internet. The signals of the movement usually come from the radio stations, but the provincial leaders don't send anything down to the Red Shirt rank-and-file."[22] There was no hierarchical structure, as one might anticipate from a national movement that focused on acts of mass resistance. Nidhi stresses instead that the Red Shirt organization was "loose," with no clear command lines, and indeed that "the lower down, the looser the structure."[23]

One academic living in the northeastern city of Khon Khaen emailed me the following earwitness account of community radio in the provinces:

> On a given day, there is probably a good eight hours of red radio time that is local. Of that eight hours, a good portion—30 %? 40%—is given to reading off the names of those who donated: "From Nongluk village, Mae Sariang Phonthong, 20 Baht; Paw Jandee Panthawong, 50 Baht, Nai Khamthong Khamrong, 100 Baht."
>
> I asked a DJ of red radio here how much was donated in a day. He said it ranged from 30 or 40,000 [$1,000–1,333] Baht a day, to 150,000 [$5,000] on special event days, such as April 10. The average he estimated to be around 60 or 70,000 baht [$2,000–2,333]. This money goes toward the free [shows] at night, the operating costs for the rally, and maybe the buses for those going down to join the protest [in Bangkok].[24]

The stations that organized these fundraisers—that, to a significant financial extent, made it possible for the larger events to happen—converted to mobile setups after they were raided, or when they felt threatened. Typically, these stations loaded up a minivan or cargo van with CDs and audio equipment, including speaker cabinets that could be mounted on the roof of the vehicle, and then drove to Bangkok to join large rallies.

And so this chapter moves, as the stations did, from the studio to the ground of the street. When station DJs arrived at the rallies to perform live, protesters knew their histories. Those that I saw in person included 105.75 from Pattaya, 96.35 from Pathumthani, 96.75 from Bangkok, and 93.25 from Nongkhai, each of which

no assistance, stations are essentially forced to seek their own sources of support, preventing the growth of large independent networks.

22. Nidhi Eosriwong, http://www.matichon.co.th/news_detail.php?newsid=1316417310&grpid=&catid=02&subcatid=0207, May 2011. Translated from the original Thai.

23. Ibid.

24. Personal email from Dr. David Streckfuss, May 1, 2010.

Figure 4.4 Agents of a radio station in Pattaya play music from speakers on top of a pickup truck during a rally at Democracy Monument on March 12, 2011. The sign reads "Pattaya city radio loves democracy." Photograph by the author.

brought mobile rigs to events at Democracy Monument and Ratchaprasong intersection, drawing some of the largest crowds of any broadcaster aside from the main stage (see Figure 4.4).

The January 23, 2011 Red Shirt rally was held at the same time as a semi-permanent Yellow Shirt encampment continued to grow in front of Government House, less than a mile from Democracy Monument. The date held no specific importance as an anniversary or political deadline. Rather, the Yellow gathering made it vital that the Red Shirts offer a proportional response. A community station from Lam Luk Ka, a district in southern Pathumthani just a few miles from the outskirts of Bangkok, was among those that parked a vehicle in the middle of the Red Shirt crowds on January 23. The station, nicknamed LLK Radio, operated from inside a silver Chevrolet cargo van. Affixed to its left-rear windows with electrical tape was a red canvas banner listing the station's province, district, and subdistrict, as well as its website and phone number. Such details were commonly included as a matter of regional pride.[25] Pickup trucks and SUVs parked nearby, including some that also played music. But LLK Radio had by far the loudest equipment in the immediate area.

25. Claudio Sopranzetti, *Red Journeys: Inside the Thai Red-Shirt Movement* (Bangkok: Silkworm Books, 2012). The book describes how protesters identified themselves by province within the Red Shirt camps.

One station volunteer sat on top of the van, amidst a motley array of speakers, including twenty-four-inch cabinets pointing to either side, and smaller *lamphoong* (loudspeakers) trained in all four directions. The height of the equipment spread the sound quite far, and at least fifty dancers gyrated in the audience. One man swayed his hips while waving a Thai flag in the air. A middle-aged woman wearing sandals and a cowboy hat, with a plastic bag filled with food on her arm, danced joyfully, practicing swiveling *ram*-style arm gestures. The DJ, a middle-aged man nicknamed Doctor, mixed a set of songs by the upstart *mor lam* dissident musician Esompo Palui, an Udon Thani native who performed on the Ratchaprasong stage, near Wireless Road, in the days before the May 19, 2010 crackdown.[26] Although Esompo possesses the deep rasp that has been typical of female *mor lam* and *luk thung* singers during the past few decades, she has a limited range and tends to sing out of tune. Onstage, she frequently lip syncs to her own *phleeng lênkan* (prerecorded backing tracks), a practice unthinkable for most professional Thai singers, at least in live settings. Her lyrics are an editorialized reportage. She details current events, adding some commentary. Because she is a politically engaged amateur, her music denotes a *kuu maa'eeng* counterpublic. At one large rally in Ayuthaya, organizers played a full album of hers to warm up a crowd of over ten thousand people. The radio DJ Doctor used Esompo's songs for the same reason.

To the side of the LLK Radio van, the crowd spread out. They congregated in a single lane of Ratchadamnoen Avenue, the largest artery that runs directly into Democracy Monument. Ratchadamnoen has been developed since 1899 as a grand complement to the royal palaces and government buildings nearby. It is eight lanes wide, with ornate greenery in the median. Larger-than-life portraits of royal figures, past and present, run along either side. Much like Wireless Road, Ratchadamnoen's history is steeped in symbols of Thai modernity. By law, buildings in the area must remain below a certain height so that the avenue and its symbols will not be overshadowed. On the day that the LLK Radio van arrived, all but one of the lanes was filled with dissident vendors, broadcasting equipment, and audiences. The westernmost lane was used alternately as a traffic route and dance floor. Vehicles of all shapes and sizes worked their way through, including a man pushing an ice cream cart, several bicyclists, and a pickup truck covered in Thaksin banners that overflowed with passengers. The truck's girth forced the dancers to stand aside for a few seconds, and as it passed it played an anthemic hip-hop song called *yàak mee rûang* ("We Want the Truth"), a tribute to Red Shirt leader Jatuporn Promphan. The opening guitar notes crossed into Esompo's gritty soprano and the saxophone playing along with her, initiating a brief, woozy sonic moment. The dancers fluidly reconvened as the truck slowly

---

26. "Doctor" is also this DJ's on-air nickname. Nickname used by interviewee request.

pulled away, their sonic niche expanding and contracting along with the glacial flow of traffic.

The Esompo song playing at that moment included a long verse with minimal melodic variation, typical of *mor lam sing* compositions. It was dedicated breathlessly to Thaksin. The lyrics suggested that the former prime minister was *khwaamjay khonjon* (charitable to the poor) and suggested that he might return from his exile from Thailand after the new year, dating the song's recording to late 2010. The song called to mind how the former prime minister had framed himself as a man of the people, in spite of his extraordinary wealth. Instrumental breaks in Esompo's singing were punctuated by blistering saxophone and *phin* runs, and dancers in the crowd joined in with shouts of support. Many shook red, foot-shaped clappers representing their low social status, and blew noisemakers left over from recent New Year's celebrations. The generator used by LLK Radio to power their broadcast whirred busily at a low frequency. One woman in the audience wore a straw hat with a circular band reading *mâytôngjâang—kuu maa'eeng* ("I didn't need to be hired—I came by my goddamn self").

There was an incongruity in this scene. The counterpublic of the radio station trucks seemed, from a certain angle, to be allied with the billionaire Thaksin. How could adoration for a politician with so much money and influence be reconciled with the principles of *kuu maa'eeng* protest? Had censorship pushed community radio so far from the center (and the centralization) of modernity that it had cycled back to the ground, only now to be powered by a wholly different energy source—that of global capital? Was the fracturing of radio into more and more intimate and illicit splinters a *kuu maa'eeng* end-run around censorship, or was it an embrace of new modes of capitalism, different organizations of hierarchical power, perhaps even an ascendant modernity? These questions drove critique of the Red Shirts from both the left and right. The movement responded by straining to affirm its independence from Thaksin.

Inside the radio station van, DJ Doctor ran just one microphone and one CD player into his four-channel Yamaha mixer, which then led out to the cluster of speakers on the roof. His entire setup was perched on a large wooden box behind the black leather seats. Burned CDs of Red Shirt music were strewn about. The radio as a still-unsettled mediator of modern publics had brought us here. We sat inside for half an hour, with the rumble of the power generator and the sound of the music equally loud in our ears. Our conversation revolved, as I had expected, around injustice and self-motivation. Doctor, speaking with urgency, explained injustice as an economic problem. Harvesting rice and processing sugar had grown too expensive relative to their market value. This, along with media censorship, was his main political concern. The Red Shirt movement, in such moments, seemed as charged by economics as it was by politics. But when I asked whether he considered himself an employee of LLK Radio, he demurred: "We're just village people who come out to help. None of us are hired or paid, and any expenses we incur ourselves. There is no hiring. If there were hiring, we wouldn't come at all. It wouldn't be worth it. It would be more comfortable to stay home. We're here in solidarity."[27] "Thaksin can come or not," he added. "There's no association. We come to support ourselves."

---

27. "Doctor," interview with the author, January 23, 2011. Translated from the original Thai.

CHAPTER 5

Megaphone Singing

Once more near Red Sunday, a candlelight vigil began on the pavement where several protesters, dressed as corpses, had just now performed their own violent deaths. Fake gray matter glistened on the pavement, its verisimilitude foul. A monk poured holy water on the bodies, which had closed their eyes. The sun dropped wide and low; things were beginning. Orn was at the head of the circle, with some members of Red Sunday and others crowding around. She sang quietly, unamplified. I stood between the vigil and the stage of the large rally, and without warning large drops of rain began pelting my head. My camera and recorder were exposed, too, so I ducked back under the Red Sunday umbrella, now completely within their niche. Almost as quickly as the rain came, it subsided. The sun was mere minutes from fully setting, and those in the circle knelt with umbrellas above their heads as a sweet smell rose from the asphalt. No one left the circle during the flash rain, and the candles continued to burn. Orn knelt in front of the flames before the ebbing sunlight and the stage's spindly shadows. Then the sun set. She brought out the Red Sunday megaphone, the same one Sombat had used in Ayuthaya, and began singing Pumpuang, tender and resolute. The air from the megaphone appeared to stoke the fire.

I noticed that Orn was a bit out of tune, perhaps unable to hear herself. The rain returned, lighter now. Orn and one other young woman, wearing a long red dress, stayed out of the circle, exposed to the drizzle. They were soon soaked but remained unprotected. The rain relaxed and intensified through the evening. I took pictures from under the umbrella, packed in with protesters, emerging now and then when the downpour abated. There was cover by the metal railing in front of the press area, under a tarp I helped hold.

The large, central stage was sonically divided from Red Sunday's megaphone niche. The niches were not at all in sync. Thaksin was scheduled to give a remote address by Skype, broadcast on a gigantic monitor on the main stage, as he often did at prime time during major rallies. I asked a few protesters when his address might begin, and most guessed around 8:00 p.m. Orn curtly dismissed the question, though, replying that Thaksin was "not the reason why we are here." Red Sunday rejected Thaksin as a political force, and performed their disinterest whenever he was the center of attention. From within Red Sunday's little area, the sound of the stage was a faint echo, mostly ignored by the group members, despite its great volume. The stage's sound did not offer cues for Red Sunday's activities or timing. The group made a spectacle of death and sang songs of dissent on its own schedule, in its own niche. Observing these performances from the core of the niche, it was hard to hear the main stage at all. The division was hard, audible, and maintained on purpose.

CHAPTER 6
Megaphonic Somsak Comes by His Goddamn Self

This chapter introduces a discussion of *figuration* to explain the symbolic power of megaphone sound, and further proposes an analytic of *sonic figuration*. Figuration, as the term is used in rhetoric and anthropology, refers to a way of lending meaning and narrativity to lived experience by describing such experience through figures—mythical or qualitative beings. Figuration gives form to abstractions, creates unified stories from disjointed events, "makes real what is not thought of immediately or commonly."[1] In so doing, figurations conjure worlds. Figures can be of many types—consider figures of speech, legendary figures, and population figures. Each of these—respectively linguistic, moral, and numerical—weaves a tangle of concepts and conditions into a legible story, and becomes a resource for locating everyday experience in that story. For example, a vain person may be figured as narcissistic—that is, as an embodiment of the mythical figure of Narcissus, and may even be burdened with the presumption that their own fate will be similar. From loose details (a person's tendency to brag and preen, say), figurations suggest origins and resolutions. People become characters in willful stories. Figuration can be both empowering and constraining. This chapter considers *sonic* figures, which are often enlisted, optimistically, to tell the story of a political movement's narrative trajectory. How do these figures conjure new or transformed worlds?

Political movements rely not only on figuration, but on *re*figuration and *con*figuration, which tell new stories about already familiar things. Re- and configurations alter politics by situating the members of a movement within a transformative story. "A figure collects up the people," writes Donna Haraway, "a

---

1. Phillipe-Joseph Salazar, "Figuration—A Common Ground of Rhetoric and Anthropology," in Ivo Strecker and Stephen Tyler, eds., *Culture+Rhetoric* (Oxford, New York: Berghahn Books, 2009), 160.

figure embodies shared meanings in stories that inhabit their audiences."[2] An audience may understand itself to be linked to the narrative arc of a figure. The idea of *humanity*, in one of Haraway's examples, might be refigured as feminist. What it means to be human in this new figuration is reoriented away from a patriarchal genealogy and toward a radical sexual politics. The audience's conception of its own humanity is, in this example, the target of transformation. In a further example, Stefan Helmreich notes that coral has been refigured in many different ways throughout history—as architecture, as a living being, as a beacon of ecological damage, and so forth.[3] In each of these refigurings, coral tells a different story about the state of the planet.

Figures are not evidentiary, however. For instance, coral has sometimes recently been figured as sexually fluid, but this figuration is not meant to suggest that *all* species are sexually fluid, that everything lacks inherent sexual characteristics. Rather, figuring tells a story that mediates between one realm and another. And so, when reflecting on human sexuality, "corals are good to queer with."[4] That is, they allow us to think queerly, and are figured in order to conjure a world of sexual fluidity that people might inhabit (or, in Haraway's inversion, that might inhabit people).[5] Coral, as figures of queerness, allow us to imagine ourselves in different positions. Because figures are instruments that can shift thinking and drive social realignment, their utility for social movements is clear and powerful.

This chapter engages sonic figurations of the Red Shirt movement. Figuration here is a theoretical tool that can help explain how dissent was conceived, communicated, and eventually understood. But meanwhile, the ethnography of protest also feeds back into the theory of figuration, demonstrating how figures are embodied epideictically (that is, out loud) in performance. Protesters, when figuring their movements and conjuring worlds, *perform* those figurations. Sonic figuration differs from literary figuration because it unfolds through a different temporality. Sonic performance, as its contingencies and relations emerge in time, adds a wrinkle to how figuration might be theorized. It requires us to think of figuration in a layered fashion—language upon accent upon reverberation upon music upon noise. Its stories are not only told, but acted out.

Sonic and aural cultures operate in layered figurative terms. Acousticians and other physical scientists typically regard sound as merely wavelike, as described in the introduction. Even many sound studies scholars tacitly assume that acoustics offers a neutral, primary definition of sound, which may explain the familiar trope of a list of noises, in neatly ascending decibel order, found in many writings on the

2. Donna Haraway, *The Haraway Reader* (New York: Routledge, 2004), 223.
3. Stefan Helmreich, *Sounding the Limits of Life: Essays in the Anthropology of Life and Beyond* (Princeton, NJ: Princeton University Press, 2016), 48–61.
4. Helmreich, *Sounding the Limits of Life*, 56.
5. Ibid.

subject.[6] This list is generally given to explain what sound *is*. The flaw in this assumption is not that sound should never be explained acoustically, but that it asserts the universality of a narrow scientific discourse. Following Ochoa Gautier, I resist the notion that sound has any "inherent ontology," political, scientific, or otherwise, even though sound may have specific ontological potential in specific cases.[7] But listening with an anthropological ear, it becomes clear that sound can be figured in many ways, folded into many possible stories about being and experience, which will furthermore be layered upon one another in a resonant performance.

At Red Shirt rallies, the sound of the megaphone was figured through a story about self-actualization, reflected in one of the movement's most important slogans, mentioned first in Chapter 2: "I came by my goddamn self" (*kuu maa'eeng*). This story begins with authentic volition, and moves toward a resolution of political equality. The megaphone as a media object, its sound, and its mode of operation were together figured as more than themselves. They became, instead, a story about authentic volition and where it leads. Megaphone oration was figured as powerfully *kuu maa'eeng*. Person, device, and sound in combination figured authentic volition, the act of protesting without being hired or otherwise compelled to do so.

The megaphone was both tool and symbol for Red Shirt street lecturers. It was used for a type of demonstration called *hyde parking* in Thai, a term derived from English that refers to the London gathering place famous for displays of political oratory. In Thailand, *hyde parking* means standing on a crate or the ground in a public area and delivering an unscripted didactic address, usually on a political topic. The megaphones used for *hyde parking*, emblazoned with technoscientific brand names like NASA and Sonar, were sold cheaply at discount shopping centers. Many protesters clipped them to their belts. They were convenient and accessible, and they connected protesters to a fragmented, global symbology of protest. Their story linked Bangkok to London's political rituals, to Argentinian horizontalism, and to the American labor movement, among others.

The voice as it issues from the megaphone is clipped, terse, curt, and cut up by speech. Its tone wells up with a quick attack, summoned by a thumb's pressure or the click of a cheap ribbed plastic switch. The buzzing of the mouth-machine is a *megaphonic* timbre. Megaphones barely amplify the voice at all, and they reduce its clarity. (Writing about a similar broadcast technology, the loudspeaker, Brian Larkin asks why one would "use a machine at all when its main effect seems to prevent the clear comprehension of language rather than facilitate it?"[8]) But despite being noisy, megaphones increase a speaker's legitimacy. Their operator assumes the tenor of an administrator, an agent. The megaphonic voice promises to

---

6. See, for example, R. Murray Schafer, *The Soundscape: Our Sonic Environment and the Tuning of the World* (Rochester, VT: Destiny Books, 1993), 77.

7. Ochoa Gautier, "Acoustic Multinaturalism," 107–41.

8. Brian Larkin, "Techniques of Inattention: The Mediality of Loudspeakers in Nigeria," *Anthropological Quarterly* 87, no. 4 (Fall 2014): 989–1015.

speak beyond the point that its operator grows hoarse. The machine pre-amplifies any sound, even a strained whisper after the voice is lost. Straining in that case announces the voice's intention to speak sacrificially, beyond exhaustion.

The megaphonic voice may also announce authority. Its sound does not envelop an audience, does not overwhelm them like loudspeakers overhead might. Nor does it produce the kind of unlocatable sovereignty that Michel Chion hears in the acousmatic voice.[9] The holder of the megaphone is visible and engaged face-to-face with listeners. Megaphonic sound projects in a nearly straight line, and such direct-ness helps enact authority. As the speaker's head turns, the sound moves in tandem. It is often impossible, in a crowded place, to hear megaphonic speech from behind a speaker's back. The listeners are those that the speaker addresses linearly.

The megaphone has long been used in Thai dissident movements. Giles Ungpakorn, narrating an incident of unrest at a Thai factory in the 1990s, figures the megaphone as a Marxist tool of labor solidarity.[10] For Giles, megaphonic sound does not suggest "reasoned discussion," though it may bring about such discussion later. Rather, listening to the megaphone collects up the people by disciplining and uniting them, and by embodying a story of shared meanings. The lyrics of the song quoted within this excerpt summarize what the workers were already feeling:

It appeared that a labour dispute over end of year bonus payments had erupted in the factory. The union was, however, very badly organised, having been initially set up by a "stinking water" trade union leader. The workers, most of whom were men, were arguing among one another and some had been drinking alcohol. Such drinking is a major problem among male dominated mobs, because it can lead to disorganisation and rash behaviour, which weakens the dispute. On seeing the chaotic situation, an experienced lay trade union representative from Rangsit, who had been traveling in the bus, immediately took the megaphone and started to lead the mob in a well-known song called "Factory Gate," originally written and sung by the popular group "Carabow." The song is all about poverty among workers and in the original recording it contains a fictional "dialogue" between someone who accuses workers of having too many children and spending all their money on gambling and drinking, and a worker who replies to these accusations. Soon all members of the mob were joining in with the singing, some banging plastic water bottles on the ground in time to the music. In this particular situation, singing had the effect of uniting the crowd behind their original aims. After the song was over, a more organised and reasoned discussion of tactics took place.[11]

9. Michael Chion, Claudio Gorbman, and Walter Murch, *Audio Vision: Sound on Screen* (New York: Columbia University Press, 1994).

10. Giles Ji Ungpakorn, *Thailand: Class Struggle in an Era of Economic Crisis* (Hong Kong: Asia Monitor Resource Center, 1999).

11. Ibid., 64.

Figure 6.1 Somsak Sangkaparicha with his handheld megaphone. His hat reads "I wasn't hired" or "no one hired me." Photograph by the author.

Red Shirt street lecturers who wanted to find an audience but lacked a large broadcasting platform could use megaphones much as the labor leader in Giles' example did—immediately, to figure unity and self-organization. The megaphone figured the *kuu maa'eeng* narrative that the Red Shirts had adopted. Megaphones were cheap, portable, and deployable by one's goddamn self, bespeaking authentic volition.

Somsak Sangkaparicha is one Red Shirt street lecturer who favors the megaphone. Orating through it, he embodied a layered sonic figure of *kuu maa'eeng*. Somsak spoke at most large Red Shirt rallies in 2010 and 2011, as he had been doing at post-coup events since 2006.[12] Although he lacked the appeal or influence to address thousands of people from the main stage, he was precisely the sort of *hyde parking* orator who could routinely collect up a small crowd.

Somsak wore, almost as a uniform, slacks and a sport coat over a collared shirt, as in Figure 6.1. He often added a *Truth Today* bandana, a shiny gold belt buckle, and a laminated badge with a picture of Thaksin Shinawatra posing in a white

12. เสื้อแดงโคราชแห่ให้กำลังใจ"บุญจง "หลังนั่งรมช.มหาดไทย" ("Red Shirts Flock to Khorat to Show Unity: Doing Good, Followed by a Sit-in in Front of the Office of the Minister of Interior"), *Matichon Online*, December 21, 2007, http://www.matichon.co.th/news_detail. php?newsid=1229862263&grpid=03&catid=01. Somsak gave speeches on a very small stage against the government. He has consistently stressed, as the article explains, the importance of a do-it-yourself approach.

police uniform.[13] Somsak's clothing and demeanor were self-assured. He could be described as *phûuyày*—meaning mature, but also proudly dedicated to duty. Standing upright, gesturing firmly with his palm, and now and then walking briskly across the sidewalk, Somsak specialized in concise, partisan lectures. These were typically between two and five minutes, and covered topics of general interest to the Red Shirts, such as the likelihood that the military would illegally intervene in future elections or impede the democratic rights of Thai citizens. (A portion of one of Somsak's speeches is reproduced below.) He stood and spoke for hours, gripping a handheld microphone attached by a coiled cable to a megaphone on his belt, accepting applause from the small crowds that gathered before taking a short break and then launching straightaway into his next homily. He was not widely known, but never failed to attract listeners when he spoke.

Somsak's message corroborated his mode of presentation. His political ideas were explained in packets of photocopied essays that he sold for roughly the price of their printing, as didactic aids. The packets included writings from Dr. Chumpon Sangkaparicha's "thought of the day" series, published in 1993, which asks for instance "With whom does democracy begin, the leaders or the people?"[14] Chumpon's writing historicizes the power of the unelected military bureaucracy, explaining how such power is at odds with a democratic political system in which leaders are accountable to citizens. Another set of essays, written in September 2010, were written by a policymaker and ex-politician named Kanin Bunsuwaan.[15] Kanin's essays included one titled "When the Law Becomes an Instrument for Driving out Your Opponents" and another titled "The Thai courts and Cycles of Political Evil." On the back of the last page are five photocopied pictures of Somsak himself, speaking through his megaphone at dissident events since Thaksin's ouster, each captioned and dated. Somsak thus positioned himself within a history of dissident thought that, for twenty years or more, had aimed to challenge hierarchies of leadership, the law, and the courts. The heirs to their power would be the *pràchaachon* (people).

Somsak urged his listeners to assume responsibility for political change. Institutions such as the government, military, and partisan political groups that promised to do good had proven untrustworthy, he stressed. He invoked no word with more suspicion than *phûunam* (leader), and none with more reverence than *pràchaachon*. On January 9, 2011, Somsak made a speech on the periphery of the

13. *Truth Today* is a defunct Red Shirt television program hosted by core leaders Veera Musikapong, Jatuporn Promphan, and Nattawut Saikua. Its theme song and logo remain popular at rallies.

14. Chumpon's essays from the same year also address the effort to reform the constitution. A Facebook user named Kaew Nartrapee (https://www.facebook.com/profile.php?id=608298972) runs a group dedicated to creating a library for Chomporn's works. Translated from the original Thai.

15. "คณิน บุญสุวรรณ" ("Kanin Bunsuwaan"), http://www.thairath.co.th/people/view/pol/6339, accessed January 29, 2013. Translated from the original Thai.

inner circle of Democracy Monument in the early afternoon, about ninety minutes before the rally began in earnest. As he spoke, trucks filled with protesters drove past him in the roundabout. The traffic left him on an island, where roughly ten people listened with patient focus. He spoke through his megaphone:

> "There is no showing of opinion, there is no showing of anything political when the people are bullied *nákhráp*. But today, brothers and sisters, there is nothing like that *nákhráp*. My brothers and sisters can show their opinions about politics *nákhráp*. We can do this on the basis of the principles of the constitution. Therefore, may I say that when the people cannot be silenced, that showing opinion, speaking, and being vocal politically are rights within the democratic system. These are our rights absolutely *nákhráp*. I invite you, brothers and sisters, to speak comfortably today. Show your beliefs together, brothers and sisters of the Red Shirts *nákhráp*! May I please say this? You need not be afraid of offending people (*kreengjay*). You do not need to be afraid of anyone *nákhráp*. There is no fear anymore, brothers and sisters!!"[16]

The noise nearby was intermittent and impulsive. A song played from someone's car stereo, a man let out a jubilant shout from twenty meters away, the brakes of a red truck squeaked gently under the weight of a dozen passengers. There was growing excitement that had not yet opened into the full flower of the rally. Somsak's voice was the most energetic in the area, for now. He finished his speech with a long, drawn-out *phîi nɔ́ɔɔɔnggggg!* ("brothers and sisterrrrrrs!"), raising his voice dramatically on the final syllable.[17] An audience member handed him a bottle of water, and he chuckled with appreciation at the smattering of hearty applause.

Somsak's words might seem innocuous, like the language of a partisan pep rally, when read as text alone. But political speech of any kind in Thailand is risky. Consensus and submission to authority govern public discourse powerfully. Democratic expression is not an empty cliché. Frankness, in many cases, undermines conceptions of status that define people's roles in school, home, work, and polity. Inciting others to speak aloud, without regard for their own status or the status of those they criticize, is a seditious refiguring of social relations. The megaphone affords this: not only by the words spoken through it, but by its layered sonic figuration of an independent-minded, *kuu maa'eeng* actor.

But the megaphone was constraining, too. In calling for the overthrow of elites, Somsak and other megaphone lecturers relied on vocal gestures that manufactured

---

16. Speech translated from the original Thai. In another speech, Somsak referred to "the bullies in green." He announced: "The army has 80, 90 percent of the power. We must ask if these elections will be rigged by the military. The military are afraid. Of what? Only of one thing. Of Thaksin."

17. *Phîinɔ́ong*, or พี่น้อง in Thai, translates literally as "older and younger people," but in context is used much like "brothers and sisters" would be within an ideologically affiliated community of English speakers. For a detailed exegesis of this phrase and its uses, see Herzfeld, *Siege of the Spirits*.

hierarchical status for themselves.[18] For example, as he spoke Somsak made liberal use of the final particles *khráp* and *nákhráp*, which may be used in Thai to give directions or announce prohibitions. The authority figure who makes such announcements is, generally, an orderly person, who might be called *phûuyày* or *rîapróoy* (well-mannered and refined). Within the speech quoted above, twelve sentences ended with *khráp* or *nákhráp*, roughly one instance every five seconds. Somsak used this particle to sound authoritative. Thai studies scholar Craig Reynolds has described the quintessential Thai leader as someone "much admired for his personal discipline and powers of self-control" who "rest(s) his claim to authority on performance, not on lineage."[19] The way that Somsak used *khráp* and *nákhráp* performed his personal discipline and strengthened the authority of his proclamations.

A rhythmic consequence of ending almost every sentence with *nákhráp* was that most of Somsak's sentences, brief already, ended with abrupt, audible punctuation marks. Points were made, and then stamped with a firm *nákhráp*. Extending the effect of bluntness, the final *p* consonant in Thai produces a dead stop, an unaspirated tone with no plosive and no decay. The lips close with finality, as if mouth and thought were joining in a tight tandem, building into jagged rhythms of discrete, uncompromising conclusions. Somsak's voice conveyed clear *dètkhàat* (decisiveness), which Reynolds elsewhere calls "one of the keywords in Thai political culture."[20] Somsak pronounces, as opposed to conversing, through the megaphone.

The aural spaces of megaphone lectures at Red Shirt protests were, finally, fleeting. They were evanescent sonic figures, persisting only until the speech ended, rising and dying as abruptly as Somsak's sentences. And even while they lasted, these spaces were intimate, their audibility limited to those within close range. Off to the sides and behind, the voice was muffled, and ten meters away it was totally obscured by other sounds. One could not eavesdrop without being noticed. Megaphone oration lent itself to accidental discovery, because it was nearly impossible to hear from more than a few meters away. If a truck stereo system played music nearby, listeners had to huddle to catch the words of the megaphone operator. Geometrically, megaphone niches were shaped like tiny wedges, and were easily overwhelmed.

But they were common. Red Sunday's Sombat addressed his listeners with a megaphone, which his volunteer staff brought everywhere. The device figured *kuu maa'eeng* for his group, too. Some Red Shirts carried megaphones purely as a contingency. With a megaphone one could, with no prior planning, lead a chant or

---

18. For a study of the tension between egalitarian and authoritarian impulses in Thai leadership, see Herzfeld, *Siege of the Spirits*.

19. Craig J. Reynolds, "The Social Bases of Autocratic Rule in Thailand," in Montesano, Michael John, Pavin Chachavalpongpun, and Aekapol Chongvilaivan, eds., *Bangkok May 2010: Perspectives on a Divided Thailand* (Singapore: Institute of Southeast Asian Studies, 2012), 271.

20. Craig J. Reynolds, "Autocratic Rule in Thailand and Its Neighbours," http://prachatai.com/english/node/2720, August 23, 2011.

make an announcement, for any reason and at any time. Megaphones create a field of communication that instills the speaker with power over addressees, whether or not they elect to listen. I once watched, for example, as a protester in front of Bangkok Remand Prison at an event in December 2010 pulled out his megaphone and pointed it toward the oncoming traffic. "We demand freedom!" he shouted several times, as the cars flew past with a Dopplerized whoosh of indifference. The drivers did not necessarily hear him, but they were brought into a figurative fold nevertheless by being addressed, and by being seen as addressees within a refigured field of political communication.

The megaphone was among the simplest, cheapest, and most accessible broadcasting devices available to the Red Shirts. Its weakness limited the physical scope and penetration of the niches it produced, but by this limitation also imbued the megaphonic voice with an authority that told a story about the heightened autonomy and efficacy of the self-motivated political subject. Megaphonic sound spaces figured *kuu maa'eeng.*

CHAPTER 7

A Quiet Mourning

The Poetry of Dynamics

A s performances, Red Shirt protests were governed by a poetry of volume. Or, more precisely, a poetry of dynamics, which is to say inventive relativities rather than phenomenal absolutes. Here, I amplify a point from the previous chapter: sound's ontological potential should not be conflated with its inherent nature. Physical explanations alone cannot account for sound's meaning. Michael Heller notes astutely that an acoustical paradigm, at times favored by humanities scholars, may suggest that loudness is equal to power. In practice, however, "low loudness can exert a power that rivals, if not mirrors, that of high loudness."[1] Beyond this direct inversion lie myriad possibilities for reorganizing the links between acoustics and local assignations of power, intensity, and meaning. Amplitude must therefore be considered alongside other dynamics (both sonic and non-sonic) that matter in a given political field, in order to understand how sound functions there.

Among the Red Shirts, attention to common keywords will help in examining how sonic dynamics were linked with power. Chief among these was the figure of pity (*nâasŏngsăan*) which was sounded to produce affects and effects. Red Shirts registered their presence most intensely not through "high loudness"—the largest amplifiers, say—but through a poetry of dynamics that hailed listeners to feel pity. The word *nâasŏngsăan* recurs throughout this chapter; it was used by many Red Shirts to explain the appeal of the movement. *Nâasŏngsăan* has a subtly different meaning from the English word "pity," and this difference should be noted. *Nâasŏngsăan* lacks the potentially shameful or reprehensible sense

---

1. Michael C. Heller, "Between Silence and Pain: Loudness and the Affective Encounter," *Sound Studies* 1, no. 1 (2015): 40–58.

that "pity" can carry in English. In English, pitifulness and power can scarcely coexist. Thus *nâasŏngsăan* as a Thai idiom might be understood as "pity-worthy" rather than pitiful. That which is *nâasŏngsăan* deserves the pity that it hails others to feel.

This chapter is an ethnography of *nâasŏngsăan* quiet. It highlights three producers of powerful, and yet not high-volume dependent, sonic performance. The first of these is a man named Kittisak Janpeng, who meditated silently for many hours at a time in tribute to a slain Japanese photojournalist; second are young girls who survived dead or maimed guardians and then begged for donations on the street during gatherings; third is the *luk thung* and *mor lam* singer Pom Krongthong, who lost her livelihood and suffered a serious illness before joining the Red Shirt movement full-time. Each of these embodied figures of pity in their sonic performances.

The claim that volume does not correlate with political intensity maps onto a related point about "protest music" that hovers in the background of this chapter. "Protest music," as explained in the introduction, is a historically contingent term, steeped in twentieth-century North American and European political struggles, and not applicable to all cultures or contexts of dissent.[2] "Protest music," as many scholars and journalists have used the term, is freighted with expectations about how politics should be conducted. The scholarly and popular study of such music thus often centers on putatively noisy performers—say, Jimi Hendrix playing the "Star-Spangled Banner," or on musicians who strive for solidarity.[3] But noisy disruption and solidarity are not markers of dissent everywhere, as Heather MacLachlan notes in her ethnography of Burmese popular music.[4] Much as different poetics of volume complicate the acoustical paradigm in sound studies, different figurations of sonic dissent limit the analytical scope of the term "protest music." The three figures below engage in political dissent through sound and the poetry of dynamics, although they are unlikely to be legible as "protest musicians." This chapter explores their quiet poiesis.

2. Tausig, "Sound and Movement."
3. The introduction to Peddie, *The Resisting Muse*, for example, calls the 1960s "the heyday of social protest," and the figure of the singer/songwriter one of an "archetypical troubadour" (xix). Most of the essays in the volume deal with American or Western European musicians, including Billy Bragg, Woody Guthrie, and Bono, and with genres like straight edge punk, heavy metal, hip-hop, and American indie music. The two essays situated outside of the United States, on reggae and Australian aboriginal music, both look to theoretical work on protest music by scholars like Eyerman and Jamison, who are concerned primarily with Western protest music in the 1960s. The dissident music of non-Western political contexts is rarely theorized in English-language literature, and as a result may be framed in terms that distort or disregard its own terms.
4. MacLachlan, *Burma's Pop Music Industry*.

On April 10, 2010, a 43-year-old Japanese photojournalist named Hiroyuki Muramoto was killed while covering the Red Shirt protests for Reuters. Shot in the chest, Hiro died on the way to the hospital from Khok Wua intersection, where he had been filming the conflict.[5] That night, the bursting of firecrackers merged so seamlessly with the popping of automatic rifle shots that many protesters, for a time, continued dancing to joyous music even as live ammunition flew past their bodies. Hiro was one of twenty-five people who died in the dark confusion of April 10, amid the acousmata of gunfire and the terrified pleas of would-be medics and peacemakers. While much was unknown about Hiro's death, including who fired the fatal bullet and whether it was aimed deliberately, evidence suggests that it came from a Thai soldier's weapon. Witnesses claimed to see and hear shots from where the military's tanks were stationed, an impression confirmed by video. Later, the English-language daily newspaper *The Nation* published a leaked internal document from Thailand's Department of Special Investigations in which military officials admitted that Hiro had probably been killed by a soldier.[6]

Publicly, however, the military and government equivocated. Deputy prime minister Suthep Thaugsuban told several newspapers that "we didn't mean to kill people. We never used the power and duty of the police and military to crack down on the protests. Those who died ran into [it]."[7] Many people wondered what the "it" was that the victims were supposed to have run into. The ending of Suthep's quote is actively silent, obfuscating the fact that soldiers had fired at length into a crowd of civilians, wounding 800 people and killing 20. In Thai, the object can be omitted if the referent of a sentence is obvious. But the referent in this case was uncertain. Many English and Thai media sources thus interpreted Suthep's silent object as "bullets," and his quote was thereafter rendered "Those who died ran into [the bullets]."[8] In the months that followed, Red Shirt protesters dressed themselves as murdered corpses and carried grim, sarcastic signs such as "a protester ran into a bullet here."[9]

5. วีรชน 10 เมษา: คนที่ตายมีใบหน้า คนที่ถูกฆ่ามีชีวิต (*Heroes of April 10: The Dead Have Faces; The Murdered Have Lives*) (Bangkok: The Institute for the Heroes of Democracy, 2010).

6. "'Leaked' reports blame military for some crackdown deaths," *Prachatai*. https://prachatai. com/english/node/2209.

7. "'ชัย'เป็นห่วงปชป. ซักฟอก'ปาล์ม'" ("'Chai' is Afraid of the Democrats Interrogating 'Palm.'"), *Khao Sot*, March 6, 2011. Translated from the original Thai.

8. Saksith Saiyasombut & Siam Voices, "Thai Deputy PM: Protesters Died Because They Ran Into Bullets," http://asiancorrespondent.com/49822/thai-deputy-pm-protesters-died-because-they-ran into-bullets/, accessed February 5, 2013.

9. I observed this on April 10, 2011, at a rally marking the one-year anniversary of the deaths at Phan Fa bridge. Several actors dressed in white corpse makeup lay on the pavement, fake blood and brains spilled around their heads, with signs taped to their bodies reading "A Japanese reporter ran into a bullet here" and "Hiroyuki still alive!" Passersby tossed twenty- and one-hundred-baht bills on the ground nearby.

Figure 7.1 Diew in character on April 10, 2011, the one-year anniversary of Hiroyuki Muramoto's death. Photograph by the author.

One of these protesters, Kittisak Janpeng, developed a theatrical protest mode, centered on a poetry of dynamics, around the symbols of Hiro's death. Kittisak, who goes by the nickname Diew, was in Khok Wua intersection on April 10 when Hiro was killed. "I sat and meditated in front of the tanks for five or six hours [that day]," he told me.[10] Silent meditation had been part of his protesting for some time, but after that evening Diew created a protest character specifically to memorialize Hiro. For more than a year afterwards, Diew dressed as Hiro's ghost at protests. He painted his face and arms with white acrylic body paint, with a red circle representing both the sun of the Japanese flag and Hiro's bullet wound between his eyes. He sat near different props that he had prepared for the events, such as a cardboard blowup of Hiro behind a large camera or a rubber mace with a spiked animal skull attached to the chain. At one rally, a hand-painted sign (see Figure 7.1) to his side read "Who killed Hiroyuki? What cursed creature? We close our ears, close our eyes, close our mouths, close off the media, close off the people of the world, in order to kill people! Are we comfortable with this?"[11] That day, Diew kept his eyes closed and his lips pursed for hours as a friend carried him on a chair along the road. Meditating, Diew created a striking visual and sonic contrast with the busy event around him.

10. Kittisak Janpeng, interview with the author. Translated from the original Thai.
11. Translated from the original Thai.

Diew did not accept donations. At one of his earliest appearances as the Hiro character, other protesters thought he was begging, and placed a total of nearly 5,000 baht ($167) near where he sat. But Diew's aim was not to earn money. "I started thinking about what I could do out of the box," he said. "I started working with polyester, made a fake gun, fake tanks, things like that. I started telling a story about the incident that the people underwent, when they were teargassed by the military."[12] Diew told this story visually, through his costume and iconography. But he also told it through sonic figuration, with quiet and silence as dynamic poetic resources. It is possible that his silence achieved a political mobility that no sound could have matched.

Some protesters regarded him quizzically, or tried to provoke him into breaking character. I once watched a woman tickle his ribs and stomach, and as her fingers touched the fabric of his shirt, the muscles of his abdomen contracted involuntarily. He stared straight ahead. The woman approached him lightheartedly, amusing a companion by taunting the human statue, but Diew's persistent stillness defused the joke. The woman's face turned stony. The main stage one hundred meters away sent recorded music wafting from speakers high above, and a nearby CD vendor played a popular ballad from his stereo. The rhythms of the two songs tangled at a blistering volume. The road behind Diew was the jammed central artery for protesters walking between exhibits and events. Amidst the din, Diew sat on a small pillow, the most emphatic presence in the area, with his shallow breathing apparent in the rising and falling of his chest. Next to him was a plastic arm, covered in fake blood and tied to an umbrella stand, hanging disembodied. The woman who had earlier teased Diew paused and left respectfully, her eyes trained on him as she walked away. He did not react.

According to Diew, in situations like this, the noise is not a distraction. Instead, his character creates a shared affective space in relation to the sound, however loud. "I just meditate. . . . Sometimes someone sees me sitting, and her husband died, so she sits for a long time. I think that the Red Shirts are unusual. We feel pity (sŏngsăan) for each other. We feel sympathy for our brothers and sisters who died. Sometimes we have to meditate as our tears run."[13] Especially worth noting in this quote is how Diew's silence generated a social space of pain, sympathetic feeling, and suffering, qualities typically linked to experiencing sound at *loud* volumes. Here, these effects were produced explicitly by *low* or *no* volume. This was a poetic play with the dynamic possibilities of the gathering, and with the performance of being nâasŏngsăan.

Diew's character embodied multiple figures, including one that he hoped would inhabit a singularly powerful audience—the sitting prime minister, Abhisit Vejjajiva, who had presided over the military action of April 10. Diew's character sought to

12. Interview with the author.
13. Interview with the author.

model or tell a story about Abhisit's redemption. In addition to referencing Hiro, Diew drew on a Theravada Buddhist sutra about a murderer-turned-saint named Angulimala. Born with the name Ahimsaka, this saint was initially a talented young student whose teacher became jealous of him and demanded a gruesome gift of one thousand pinkies from one thousand different people's right hands. In the story, Ahimsaka complies, moving to a remote forest and taking the name Angulimala as he robs and kills every person he meets. After collecting 999 fingers, Angulimala's mother as well as the Buddha set out separately to confront him, realizing that by committing one more murder, he will be reborn in the lowest order of hell. Angulimala then sets out to murder his mother, but the Buddha intercepts him, and although Angulimala violently pursues the Buddha, he cannot catch him. The Buddha, while still moving, tells Angulimala that he has stopped, and the murderer says, "while you are walking monk, you tell me you have stopped; But now, when I have stopped, you say I have not stopped. I ask you now, O monk what is the meaning of it; How is it you have stopped and I have not?" [14] The Buddha answers, "Angulimala, I have stopped forever, foreswearing violence to every living being; but you have no restraint towards things that breathe; So that is why I have stopped and you have not." [15] On hearing the essential truth of the Buddha's words, Angulimala undergoes a spiritual rebirth, thereafter living as a gentle monk in the forest, eventually becoming a saint and a paragon of nonviolence. Even when attacked with stones thrown by his former schoolmates, who resent him for his past actions, he bears their assaults without reprisal:

> O let my enemies give ear from time to time
> And hear the Doctrine as told by men who preach forbearance,
> By men who speak as well in praise of peacefulness,
> And suit the while their actions to their words [16]

The story of Angulimala is about forgiveness and redemption, and suggests the piercing nature of spoken truth. It narrates a story in which a wicked person is so moved by a heard revelation that he transforms his actions immediately. Although prime minister Abhisit was never (to my knowledge) transformed through an encounter with Diew's character, Diew's poetics dramatized the problem of injustice and the value of restraint for Red Shirt observers. Diew explained:

> I [did this] to change minds. Why hasn't Abhisit changed his mind? Why did he kill all these people? Why did he send people to kill us as the head of the government? Why didn't he apologize to the people? Apologize even once? I wanted a character

---

14. Hellmuth Hecker, *Angulimala: A Murderer's Road to Sainthood* (Kandy, Sri Lanka: Buddhist Publication Society, 1984), 11.
15. Ibid.
16. Ibid, 18.

from literature like Angulimala who could provide a point of comparison, at the point when he hadn't yet changed his mind. Abhisit is like a non-person. He's never apologized to the people. He just trampled over them for his own benefit and his allies.[17]

I observed Diew many times before finally speaking with him. I thought often about ways to interview this person, whose low-volume interventions were so powerful. (Leave a business card when he was meditating? Find someone who knew his phone number?) As it turned out, interviewing Diew and his character were two different propositions. Speaking to the man required only that I pursue a few of the right social connections. But how does one interview a body that is resolutely silent? A surrogate corpse? It is macabre but possible; however, the terms of engagement are contorted. Questions reflect off a mute surface, like a neutral analyst, doubling back to the interviewer. This is what happened when the Red Shirt woman tickled Diew's ribs. Her provocation was neither affirmed nor denied by Diew's character. It became the woman's turn to answer, and she, like most others, became contemplative in an affective encounter with the silent presence of a murdered body (or its representation). Diew's silent memorial to Hiro made victimhood and pity politically instrumental.

When we finally spoke, by Skype in 2012, I was interviewing the forty-seven-year-old Kittisak Janpeng rather than his character. I learned that Diew was born in the small northern city of Phitsanulok, where he studied through the US equivalent of tenth grade. He is estranged from his family, who shunned him when he joined the Red Shirts, and has spent his life working odd jobs, including contracting and sales. He now lives in Bangkok. As Diew told me about his approach to protest, "the atmosphere when I sit silently is loud. There is some sound of gunfire. But the Red Shirts are an unusual protest group in the world. They hear the sound of bullets and dance with joy. . . . the Red Shirts are pitiful (nâasŏngsăan). They come to fight for their children and grandchildren."[18]

As noted above, to be nâasŏngsăan is to be worthy of others' pity, without the sense of shameful weakness that the word "pitiful" can carry in English. People with debilitating injuries or illnesses, for example, are often described as nâasŏngsăan, and donating money to them can yield karmic merit, no small benefit for even a casual Thai Buddhist. Diew's silent protest, with remarkable efficacy and poetic flourish, embodied a figure of noble pity and redemption. His silence was not of a universal type; rather, it was conceived in relation to nearby sounds and to a locally operative ethics. And it was therefore politically powerful.

17. Interview with the author.
18. Kittisak Janpeng, interview with the author.

At most large Red Shirt gatherings, sometimes just a few steps from Diew, the young daughters of slain protesters sat begging for money, sounding pity and victimhood. Although there were often many of these girls begging at a given protest event, they each invariably sat alone, and beseeched passersby to help them pay for basic expenses after losing a breadwinning parent, usually a father. They sat in abject places—behind garbage cans, under the stairway to the elevated train, or on the cement rims of ground-level planters surrounding trees, where food vendors stored plastic bags stuffed with fish scraps and burnt vegetable oil. Red Shirts prayed in front of them as if at a shrine, placing sometimes very large sums in their donation boxes. People bowed, cupping their hands for minutes at a time in deep and extended *wâi*. Every few minutes, the Skytrain rumbled above, shaking the concrete pillars and compelling the girls to raise their voices.

Protesters were keenly aware of, and could even be critical toward, the poetry of dynamics in the orphans' voices. The girls strained at the edge of small larynxes, and punctuated the end of each sentence with a sweetly inflected, falling *khâ*, the polite feminine particle in Thai. They narrated what happened to their fathers and with whom they were now living. Typically, a portrait of the father, including his name and dates of birth and death (the latter usually within the past year), was propped on a chair or tree nearby. But even girls who had experienced such tragedy were scrutinized. "Central Thai builds gendered identification into speech," Deborah Wong writes. "A proper Thai woman should speak softly and her voice should be rather high-pitched."[19] As an ethnographer, Wong benefitted by adapting to local conventions of feminized speech, but these conventions also subjected her to the constraints of middle-class womanhood. For Thai women, "proper" speech produces awareness of one's own supposed modesty, passivity, and humility. This, Wong argues, is an obstacle to social and political mobility, even as it affords the speaker something like an insider status. Constraint offers opportunities as well as limits. The orphans were likewise constrained in speech, and rendered immobile in the act of begging. To the ears of some Red Shirt protesters, the girls had to perform not only femininity but pity and affliction in order to earn their donations. A friend of mine, an active middle-class Red Shirt woman in her fifties named Pat, explained her reaction to the begging voices. Pat and I typically hung out at protest events informally, and debriefed later. For one such debriefing, I sent Pat a recording of one of the orphans who had begged at a protest in December 2010. Pat's initial response to the voice on the recording was sympathetic, and she was unsurprised that this particular girl had received a steady stream of donations. After hearing the recording, she said: "[The voice is] *nâasŏngsăan, nâasŏngsăan, nâasŏngsăan*. She's an orphan, right? Her mom left her, that's what she said. She lives with her grandma.

19. Wong, *Sounding the Center*, 220.

And now her father left her. So she is *nâasǒngsǎan, nâasǒngsǎan*. Did you give her money?"[20] As we continued listening to the recording, however, Pat began to express doubt about the authenticity of the girl's voice. She believed the story, but was troubled by what she perceived as a false or trained vocal affectation.

"The meaning of what she said is *nâasǒngsǎan*," said Pat. "But the voice, I don't like it much. The voice. . . see, that's what I said, some people, because she's young, some people can teach her to do this and take benefits or advantage of her. What she lost, you know. To make the benefits." "So she sounded trained to you?" I asked. Pat paused thoughtfully. "Yeah. A little bit, not one hundred percent. At one point I felt like that. And then the meaning pulled me out, the *nâasǒngsǎan*. But of course she had to make a loud noise, not like soft-spoken. Because you can't, because it's a huge group of people, right?" For Pat, the problem was not that the girl was loud, but that she seemed to be shouting, which suggested inauthenticity, undermining her capacity to sound believably pitiful.

Heller writes of "imagined loudness," meaning "listeners' ability to re-interpret the level of perceived sounds in order to meet certain requirements or expectations that are not fulfilled by a sound's physical characteristics."[21] Imagined loudness is an audile technique associated with high-volume listening, but it is equally applicable to quiet sound, as in the ontologically soft (even when loudly amplified) muted trumpet of Miles Davis, in Heller's example. Pat expected the girl to meet her halfway by staging an imagined quiet. High volume would not contravene this, but straining would. "Do you think that she would have been quite so *nâasǒngsǎan* if she had an amplifier and a microphone?" I asked. "Yeah!" exclaimed Pat. "Because she shouldn't be screaming that loud for me. Of course, it's a lot of people, it's noisy. You have to make it loud enough that people can hear you. That's why it came out negative a little bit, from screaming that loud. She has to do that! But sometimes when you talk too loud, it doesn't get to you much, to sympathize. But the way she talked, the meaning is so *nâasǒngsǎan*."

Pat partitions the orphan's voice into several interpretive registers. There is, first, content, which for Mladen Dolar is carried by the voice as a "vehicle of meaning."[22] Pat is repeatedly pulled back to sympathy by what she likewise calls "the meaning"—in this case, the orphan's story of grieving and penury. Second, there is the voice as a fetish object. Dolar offers an anecdote about Italian soldiers admiring the lovely voice of an officer while ignoring the content of his belligerent commands. Certainly, the voice in Thai speech is an equally common subject of aesthetic judgment, its minutest subtleties categorized, debated, and linked to ethics and identity in various ways. However, while Dolar pivots in the remainder of his monograph to a psychoanalytic dimension of the voice that bypasses empirical

---

20. "Pat," interview with the author, February, 2012. Real name withheld by interviewee request. The interview was in English, with Thai words, as they were used, italicized.
21. Heller, "Between Silence and Pain," 46.
22. Mladen Dolar, *A Voice and Nothing More* (Cambridge, MA: The MIT Press, 2006), 4.

questions in favor of philosophy, my concern here is how vocal aesthetics persist and adapt in tandem with technology, politics, and ethics. This creates idiosyncratic understandings of sound and volume. The quiet voice of a Red Shirt orphan, for example, would remain for Pat essentially quiet even if amplified, as long as the speaker comported herself humbly.

Pat's observation about how amplification can enable imagined quiet also recalls Susan Schmidt Horning's history of microphone use by twentieth century vocalists: "Frank Sinatra is widely regarded as the first to master microphone technique. Mitch Miller, who worked with Sinatra in the studio, said 'Sinatra couldn't be heard from here to ten feet away. . . . None of them. In fact, it's part of the art,' he emphasized, 'part of the art of recording. That's why Pinza sounds so ridiculous, "Sohm enchaahnted eve-e-ning," you know?' "[23] Sinatra and the Red Shirt girls dealt with similar poetics of quiet and restraint, even though Sinatra's gesture (offered in a different dynamic field) made him sound self-assured rather than pitiful.

Pat then turned to the girl's posture and comportment. She decided she could not fully evaluate the voice without visual information. This suggests, again, that the definition of quiet is contextual, dependent not only on sonic dynamics but on non-sonic factors as well. "From listening only, sometimes it's hard to tell you, because we can get bias from voice only. . . . How does her face look when she's speaking up?" she asked. "She looks serious," I answered, riffling through a series of photographs and videos of the girl on my hard drive (See Figure 7.2). "She doesn't smile, she doesn't frown, she just looks very straight ahead, kind of has no expression." "Well that changes my attitude a little," replied Pat. "See that's *nâasŏngsăan* more. *nâasŏngsăan mâak khûn* [more pitiful]. I wish I were there. I would give her money no matter what. Sitting is more *nâasŏngsăan*. The posture changes your mind a little bit. The smile is no good. Absolutely. If she smiles, turn the other way."[24]

The sympathetic voice sounded out narratives of victimization, and performed pitiful victimhood. It opened channels of social welfare for the bereaved, and of merit-making. But to move through the constraints of sympathetic networks, the orphan voice had to be quiet, as that concept is understood in a local field of dynamic poetics.

PEACE AND ORDER AS CONSTRAINTS

Expectations of quiet can impose difficult constraints on political movements. For example, many observers demanded that the Red Shirts conform to ideals of *sàngòp* (peace) and *rîapróoy* (order). These restricted how they could speak or sound. In Thai political discourse, peace and order are palliatives for political tension. During

23. Susan Schmidt Horning, "Engineering the Performance: Recording Engineers, Tacit Knowledge and the Art of Controlling Sound," *Social Studies of Science* 34 (2004): 711.
24. "Pat," interview with the author.

Figure 7.2 A young girl begs for donations next to a framed photograph of her deceased father at a Red Shirt protest. Photograph by the author.

the Red Shirt protests, the specter of disagreement that the movement raised was, for some observers, more threatening than poverty, inequality, corruption, or violence. Some even understood disagreement in itself to be the root of all other political problems. In fact the prime minister's first major project after the crackdown was billed as a "reconciliation," a return to an imaginary nationalist unity that barely mentioned policy; his highest priority, in other words, was unity. Tellingly, the Red Shirts were more often accused of sowing division than of advancing undesirable political ideas. The need to avoid division constrained dissent in many ways.

Tyrell Haberkorn has analyzed the 2008 arrest and eventual conviction of a woman named Daranee Charnchoengsilpakul, nicknamed Da Torpedo, who was an orator in the early days of the Red Shirt movement.[25] Daranee's activism was constrained on gendered sonic grounds. In 2008, she gave a *hyde parking* speech near Sanam Luang that did not name or directly allude to any member of the royal family. However, during her trial, the prosecution made a convoluted argument that her speech was full of covert references that harmed the monarchy. Haberkorn surmises that it could not have been the content of her oratory that had so offended the police, prosecutor, and ultimately the judge. No reasonable interpretation of her words could have resulted in her guilt. Rather, Haberkorn argues, it was Daranee's

25. Tyrell Haberkorn, "Engendering Sedition: Ethel Rosenberg, Daranee Charnchoengsilpakul, and the Courage of Refusal," *positions: east asia cultures critique* 24, no. 3 (August 2016): 621–51.

performed refusal of hierarchy, specifically as a woman daring to speak politically so close to the royal palace, that caused this reaction. Her use of what the court called "coarse language" and "shouts" made her a threat to peace and order, which is to say a threat to gendered norms of public speech. Not only were Daranee's words relatively benign, but her voice was *not very loud* as a matter of volume. Nevertheless, her breach of imagined quiet was heard as an insult to unity, which carried severe consequences.

The government and the Red Shirt movement fought a prolonged public relations battle over who was most committed to unity and its precepts. "Peace" and "order," as well as the compound phrase "the peace and order of the people," are not only invoked in everyday political discourse, but are used in legislation and agency titles as well.[26] The terms are even legally actionable. "Protecting public order or good morals," for example, appears throughout the Constitution of Thailand as an imperative that can merit a state of emergency if threatened.[27] Under the Emergency Decree of 2010, the government organized a quasi-military unit called the Centre for the Administration of Peace and Order, which includes the word *rîaprɔ́ɔy* in its Thai name. There were therefore real political stakes in conforming to ideals of "peace" and "order."

However, precise legal explications of "the peace and order of the people" are scarce.[28] Their definition emerged instead as an informal public consensus. The actions of the Red Shirt movement as well as the government during the protests were thus geared toward making a convincing case that each was, respectively, more peaceful and orderly. Chayanit Poonyarat notes that during the protests, "'peaceful methods' became a term of broad interest in Thai society, but this interest came with uncertainty and confusion over what these methods were, and what actions they involved."[29] Chayanit identifies pitiful appeals to "feeling" and "mood" as among the most important orderly and peaceful tools available to dissidents.[30] "The theory of nonviolent action," he writes, "specifies that the pain of those using

26. Si Klayonsut, "ความสงบเรียบร้อยของประชาชน" ("The Peace and Order of the People"), *Dulaphan*, book 1, year 3, January, 1956. Judge Si discusses the ambiguity in terms like "peace and order" and "good morals," noting in particular the religious nature of the particular term used for morality in multiple articles of the Thai criminal code.

27. See, for example, Constitution of Thailand, Chapter III, Part 7: "Liberty of Expression of Individuals and Media: A person shall enjoy the liberty to express his or her opinion, make speeches, write, print, publicise, and make expression by other means. The restriction on the liberty under paragraph one shall not be imposed except by virtue of the provisions of the law specifically enacted for the purpose of maintaining the security of the State, safeguarding the rights, liberties, dignity, reputation, family or privacy rights of other persons, *maintaining public order or good morals* or preventing the deterioration of the mind or health of the public." (Emphasis mine).

28. Manot Joramat, "Laws About the Peace and Order of the People," *Dulaphan*, book 5, year 12, May 1965. This piece, the most recent I could find, is almost fifty years old.

29. Chayanit Poonyarat, "The '13 Secrets', and Nonviolence in Thai Society," *King Prajadhipok's Institute Journal*. 8, no. 1 (2010): 16–27. Translated from the original Thai.

30. Ibid.

peaceful methods can have great influence on the viewpoint of the opposition by reaching their moods and feelings. This is a strategy that closes a social gap between two factions. It causes the opposition to feel bound to peaceful people who are experiencing pain, and to regard those using peaceful methods as human beings and friends."[31] Although Chayanit uses the word "pain" rather than "pity," his analysis suggests the importance of being nâasŏngsăan for the Red Shirts.

The tension over unity that gnawed at so many observers during the Red Shirt protests could only be avoided if the protesters were seen and heard to be behaving in a peaceful and orderly fashion. But, as in Daranee's case, this constraint had the potential to immobilize dissent. The demand for imagined quiet, mediated by ideals of peace and order, greatly restricted the performance of protest sound. At times, no degree of poetic cleverness could evade these limits.

POM

The third case study in this chapter is a musician who succeeded commercially by figuring pity. Pom Krongthong came to Bangkok in 2007, around the same time as Daranee, also to perform at Sanam Luang in the Red Shirt movement's nascent phase in support of the exiled Thaksin Shinawatra. Pom had worked on a cattle farm since her youth in Udon Thani, a province in the northeast, but business declined soon after the coup against Thaksin in 2006. Pom then left her farm for Bangkok, where she joined the protests. Within a year of arriving, however, a blood clot in her leg necessitated a lengthy hospital stay and an indefinite regimen of treatment. Her husband left her soon after, and the illness and lack of regular income quickly exhausted her remaining savings. She suddenly had little left except the Red Shirts. Pom had tried unsuccessfully, years earlier, to make a career as a singer. But just as she was recovering from her blood clot in 2009, the Red Shirt movement began to grow, and the demand for music at its events was great enough to revive her dream of performing professionally. By late 2009, Pom sang onstage as a regular gig, and by early 2010 she was performing every day. The movement became a platform for her career, and it functioned like an extended family as well.

Pom's medical history helped make her and her music nâasŏngsăan. In December 2010, she recorded a widely-viewed video from the hospital where she was being treated. In the brief video, which was addressed to her fans, she described her condition and explained that she was taking a temporary break from performing. She also announced the release of a new album. rûam phlang máhăapràchaachon ("The United Power of the Mighty People") would be available for 100 baht ($3), and feature ten songs, six of which had been written for her by Red Shirt leader and musician Adisorn Piangket. She noted that 30,000 ($1,000) baht remained to be

31. Ibid.

raised to cover the expenses of producing the album, including studio rental, the producer's time, and Adisorn's fees at a special discount rate of 5,000 baht ($167) per song. Pom wrote in a press release for the album, "I humbly ask to impose on all of the Red Shirts who want to aid with a project that will help pay for this album in advance as a New Year's present."[32] Pom delivered her hospital video address from a wheelchair; she would again perform in a wheelchair two weeks later at a concert in Chiang Mai. An online discussion board that linked to the video showed images of other people afflicted with Pom's same condition, deep vein thrombosis. One commenter wrote that "Pom is releasing a new album to raise money for her care and support her own survival. But because Pom doesn't want to bother anyone by asking for donations, please give her aid by buying this CD. This will be considered an act of great kindness."[33] Another posted in reply, "whoever is capable of helping, please do so continuously." Pom's suffering became an important part of how and why the Red Shirts supported her. The capacity to feel and respond to pity, to meditate as one's tears run, was an oft-noted dimension of Red Shirt identity.

On February 13, 2011, just two months after the hospital video was released, I spent most of a large rally in Bangkok with Pom's brother and one UDD volunteer who managed a CD-vending table on the ailing singer's behalf. The table was set up beneath a white canvas tent, with a large backdrop reading "Pom Krongthong is seriously ill—she is not pretending," accompanied by photographs of Pom with a feeding tube in a hospital bed.[34] (Concerns about the perception of inauthenticity were never far from the surface.) Tall stacks of her CDs were arranged atop a red blanket on a table, available for between 50 and 100 baht (about $2–3), in addition to VCDs with atrocity footage and a variety of CDs by other musicians. A donation box was set up for those who wanted to pitch in extra to help cover medical bills. Pom's brother had hooked up a gas-powered generator, which rumbled so loudly that the music needed to be turned up. Conversation inside the tent was nearly impossible. The generator periodically sputtered and stalled out, until someone fed it another quart of gas. The device powered a small television and stereo that filled the tent with clashing timbres and cadences. An orange-robed monk sat in a folding chair, placidly sipping bottled water through a straw and watching the protesters after his morning alms rounds. The tent remained busy throughout the day, usually with at least a few shoppers browsing within. Most customers whom I observed spent a moment looking at the posters of Pom, and then flipped through the CDs before purchasing one or several. From the stereo, which was cranked as loud as possible to be audible over the generator, Pom's voice sang a sweet, sad *luk thung*

32. "ด่วน คุณป้อม กรองทอง CD ยังเหลืออีกบาน ช่วยกันสั่งซื้อหน่อยนะครับ" ("Announcement: Miss Pom Krongthong's CD Still Needs Some Funding—Please Help by Buying a Copy"), http://nopeter.org/forum/index.php?topic=2138.0, accessed February 8, 2013. Translated from the original Thai.

33. Ibid.

34. The wording of the sign is translated from the original Thai.

piece. She sang that the *khɛɛn*, the free-reed wind instrument linked to provincial Thailand, sounded out the "heaven" of rural Isan. The music, at an earsplitting volume, evoked quiet and rurality. Its imagined quiet overwhelmed my conversation with her brother.

Pom first endeared herself to the Red Shirts in the spring of 2010, before her most recent hospital stay, through sheer persistence. Because protesters were camped out around the clock near the stage at Ratchaprasong and Phan Fa bridge during the March-May occupation, the UDD offered a steady stream of entertainment to fend off boredom. Among the entertainers who came to perform, Pom was not the liveliest or the youngest or the most extraordinary vocalist, but she was willing and able to sing onstage every day. The crowds quickly warmed to her. She performed in the daytime, hours before the best-known UDD orators took the stage at night, at mundane moments when members of the occupation were finishing lunch or huddling under umbrellas as a flash rain passed over. No superstar, Pom strode onto the stage in ordinary clothing—a large checked button-down shirt one day, a flower-pattern blouse the next—with a red beret at times the only color-coded mark of her solidarity with the movement. After a brief, rote introduction by an emcee, Pom took the stage each day with no instrumentalists behind her, no video display, and no other fanfare. At most, she brought one or two other dancers, depending on the genre she decided to perform on a given day. *Mor lam*, especially at a faster pace, was accompanied by dancers, but her singing of *luk thung* ballads was not. Regardless of the genre, she looked tiny on a full-sized stage that later at night would be used by bands, large dance troupes, and passionate orators. Her performances suggested intimacy and smallness.

In front of banners that read, in one instance, "our friends did not die in vain—dissolve the parliament," and that showed coffins draped in red cloth, each day Pom first told the crowd which genre she would play. For example, in front of a large crowd on March 27, 2010 at Phan Fa bridge, she began with an invocation to fate—*ailanoooooo*—making clear that she would sing a *mor lam* set, for which this invocation is part of the *kâɔrn*, or introduction. In contemporary popular *mor lam*, which has branched into various subgenres, the *kâɔrn* can be omitted, but here it proudly announced the music's distance from the country's geographic and political center. (Pai Pongsatorn's enormously popular 2010 *luk thung* single *khon bâan diawkan* ["People of the Same House"], which is about Isan pride, also begins with an invocation to fate.) Regional marginality and political marginality are often paired, as I discuss in Chapter 13. These twinned forms of marginality harness a "power of the powerless" agency.

Rather than aiming to be *thansàmǎy* (fashionably modern), as musicians in the subgenre of *mor lam sing* may do, Pom's gloss on *mor lam* was quite traditionalist. Instrumentally, her Red Shirt stage music foregrounded *phin* and *khɛɛn*, anchored by a deep, syncopated groove. Many of her songs, performed live, ran ten minutes or longer. She sang in rapid improvisations, followed by the instruments taking solos in turn. Her music was not so old-fashioned as to resemble *lam klɔɔn* (lam poetry), which is usually accompanied only by *khɛɛn*. She sang along with electrified instruments, often through a prerecorded backing track rather than a live band. On days when she played *luk thung*, this backing track consisted of songs from her own albums, including vocals. She was in essence singing a karaoke duet with herself. Other times, Pom was backed by *phleeng lênkan* (sometimes called *lên tam phleeng*), a widely available type of MP3 featuring uncredited musicians jamming with electric keyboards, cowbell-laden drums, *phin*, and *khɛɛn* for extended periods. *Phleeng lênkan* are designed as practice tools, but may also be used by solo musicians as accompaniment. Street musicians who busk in Bangkok commonly play a single instrument over a *phleeng lênkan*. Pom's audience did not seem to mind the digital component of the performance.

For nearly two minutes after the invocation to fate, Pom offered a long poetic dedication to the Red Shirts who died on April 10. Her introduction was sung over a recording of an electric *phin* soloing slowly, with a phase effect thickly applied. Pom stood nearly motionless, raising the microphone as she sang and then lowering it along with her eyes during dramatic silences. She used bits of Isan dialect like *khíthɔ̀ɔt*, meaning that she missed those protesters who had been killed, again reminding listeners of their regional and political marginality. The audience swayed in anticipation of the coming change in the music, a few waving their arms. Her voice soared to dramatic heights, cracked soulfully on the way down, and resolved nearly two octaves below its peak. The change came, as it typically does in *phleeng lênkan*, when a tuned drum fill descended for one measure, followed by the return of the *phin* and a propulsive bassline. All at once, the audience rose to their feet, as the *phin* busily navigated a major scale before ecstatically foraying to the upper reaches of the top string. The combination of funk-inflected bass, an active lead *phin*, and drum machine created a texturally rich and melodically crowded sound into which live playing or singing might slip inconspicuously. As with the heavy echo of a tiled shower or a karaoke setup with gobs of reverb, the density of a *phleeng lênkan* recording does wonders for covering up a musician's imperfections.[35] Every few minutes, the key of the song modulated a half step up. Pom's vocals were percussive—*mor lam* singing is frequently compared to rapping, although hip-hop, while well-known in Thailand, is rarely if ever cited as an influence on the genre. Singers like Pom do not draw out phrases or build melodies except during instrumental breaks, when "la-la-la-la" syllables may be improvised. Pom continued in this manner for several minutes, as she and a lone dancer brought the crowd to a much-appreciated midday emotional crescendo on March 27, in the early days of the Ratchaprasong occupation.

More than a year later, long after the occupation had been dispersed by the crackdown and the Red Shirt movement had embraced horizontality, Pom agreed to an interview at her home in Bangkok. Anti-clotting medicines and an array of her

---

35. When performing, I am often grateful for this affordance.

own CDs were spread on the kitchen table. She told me that her musical career was at its core dutiful, that she and the movement fulfilled a mutual obligation to one another. "They [listeners] want to give us money so we can maintain our lives," she said when I asked why crowds supported her.[36] "I'm not a normal singer. I'm a singer for democracy." Her music was an ethical project, not an effort to enrich herself. She recounted having been on stage when the death of Seh Daeng was announced to the camped-out crowd in mid-May 2010. She stressed that this moment helped connect her status as a performer to the collective pathos of the movement, and that it left her with a responsibility.

Pom's mother sat with us. Now retired, her mother had spent her career teaching Thai classical music in elementary schools, and had been Pom's first vocal teacher. Although her mother had earned a decent income for decades as a public employee, Pom felt that a government job was now insufficient, or at least limiting. The possibility of earning money as a Red Shirt musician was not at odds with authentic motivation for Pom. In fact, profiting as an artist might allow her to avoid certain constraints. "Working a government job is OK," she said, "because you get benefits and welfare. But there are limits to the salary. Singing with the Red Shirts, there are no limits, so it's better." Pom herself had only a sixth-grade education, not uncommon for people from the northeast. She resented that the Thai government failed to help the poor (though she made a clear exception for Thaksin Shinawatra and his sister, Yingluck, who had recently been elected prime minister, even at one point in the interview singing me a laudatory song she had written about her.) Pom contrasted the pity and love among the Red Shirts with the callousness of the military and the previous government. "I sang in Ratchaprasong every day, until the military came and shot us," she said. "The military doesn't negotiate. They just blast us with noise."

Pity was a threat to the military during the March-May Red Shirt occupation. Many low-level soldiers—precisely those tasked with containing and eventually dismantling the protests—were themselves poor northern and northeastern Thais. They were likely to be sympathetic to the concerns of the Red Shirts, having experienced the same indignities and political disenfranchisement themselves. I have elsewhere referred to this pity as "insurgent sympathy," or a tendency for class-inflected regional comradeship to supersede loyalty to the Thai state, as in the case of the "watermelon soldiers" described in the Introduction.[37] One former general told the media that "the military is completely red, excluding the top commanders. The army could disintegrate at any moment, but chain of command and military discipline is holding it together for now. But [rank-and-file soldiers] see their parents are in the protest, so their loyalty to the military

---

36. Pom Krongthong, interview with the author, December, 2011. Translated from the original Thai.
37. Benjamin Tausig, "A Division of Listening: Insurgent Sympathy and the Sonic Broadcasts of the Thai Military," *positions: asia critique* 24, no. 2 (2016): 403–33.

is in question."[38] Soldiers were reminded by their superiors that they should not pity the protesters, but must obey orders without hesitation. Pity of the kind that Pom utilized in her protest, her artistry, her marketing, and her ethics thus had political efficacy. As with the watermelon soldiers, pity could destabilize military and elite power.

Pom sang on March 31, 2010 at Phan Fa bridge in front of a massive banner that used the term "peaceful methods." She began this time with a *mor lam* recitation that she dedicated to Thaksin. With no backing track or accompaniment of any kind, the delay of her voice issuing from separate banks of speakers near the stage evidenced the incredible size of the performance space. Each phrase she sang echoed for several seconds along the imperial asphalt of Ratchadamneorn Avenue, exposing massive dissonant sheets of sound that washed along for hundreds of meters during each pause. Her volume was undoubtedly off the charts. And yet it seemed quiet, intimate, *nâasŏngsăan*. Pom addressed the protesters as *chaawnaa*—farmers, or people of the farm—pitiful figures of rural labor who Haberkorn notes were once propagandistically called "the backbone of the nation," and yet who have been repeatedly and violently attacked for protesting.[39] The term *chaawnaa* percolates with pride and history and martyrdom, with the imagined power of the powerless.[40] After the song ended, Pom asked the crowd a series of questions. "Brothers and sisters, do you miss prime minister Thaksin *nákhâ*? Do you miss him a lot *nákhâ*? Do you want him to come back *nákhâ*?" Their approval echoed in bright collective reply.

A *phleeng lênkan* kicked in loudly through the giant speakers, with the pitiful sound of a solo accordion, staple of mid-twentieth century *luk thung*, keystone of so many famous songs in the tragic mold that narrate lives full of hardship, wandering disconsolately up and down a scale. Then came a thunderous, tender invocation to fate: "*Ailanooooo. . . .*"

The poetry of sonic protest among the Red Shirts entailed a play of dynamics that could cast high-volume sound as quiet and silence as resonant, among other departures from an acoustical framework. The definition of quiet in the Red Shirt movement was emergent, contested, and highly inventive. Acoustical intensity was secondary to these processes of meaning-making. Acoustics thus serves as a weak explanation for sound's operation in the context of this movement. Instead, through the sonic figuration of *nâasŏngsăan*, which hails listeners to care for victims, the Red Shirts created politically effective gestures in their performed

38. "'Watermelon soldiers' increasingly dangerous for Thai military," http://www.channelnewsasia.com/stories/afp_asiapacific/view/1050561/1/.html, April 16, 2010.

39. Tyrell Haberkorn, *Revolution Interrupted: Farmers, Students, Law, and Violence in Northern Thailand* (Madison: University of Wisconsin Press, 2011).

40. City pillars in Thailand, such as Bangkok's famous one near the protests in the old city where Pom sang, were frequently constructed in conjunction with human sacrifice. An email that circulated after the Red Shirt protests also claimed that the Ratchaprasong area was the site of the live burials of slaves in the late eighteenth century, when the city was founded.

dissent. Sonorous intensity was determined not by decibel-level alone, nor by psychoacoustics, but by the discursive, expressive fields in which all politics take place. Diew, the orphan girls, and Pom each worked astutely with a sonic poetics of protest to create a sonority that was *nâasŏngsǎan*, that was in fact both pitiful and powerful at once.

CHAPTER 8
Whistles

The Red Shirts' *kuu maa'eeng* ethos drew on broadly familiar tropes of the performance of authority in Thailand, in settings ranging from protest to street traffic control. By repeating these tropes of hierarchy and control, the Red Shirt movement positioned itself not as a structural alternative to the current state, but as a contender to its control.

Consider whistles. Pea whistles, worn on necklaces, are standard issue for Bangkok's nattily attired, straight-standing parking lot guards, expressway traffic police, and mass transit station agents. Each of these is famously assertive. Especially in business districts, parking attendants supervise small, back-to-back lots, producing chains of abrupt exhalations nearly unbroken in space or time across long stretches of road. With little sonic competition at such a high frequency, the sound is hard to tune out. But constancy diminishes coherence. Drivers and pedestrians fail to understand whatever commands might be indexed by the guards' whistling.

Listeners thus tend to describe the metallic bleats as noise pollution. One group of Bangkok businesspeople organized a campaign called the Whistle-Free Zone project in 2010, in an effort to persuade the owners of downtown malls and office buildings to quiet their parking lot attendants. The Whistle-Free Zone project drew on a survey by professor Win Liawarin, who studied whistles using acoustic measurements. He found that "from the mouth of Silom Road to its end during rush hour, one passes 207 guards. One in three of these guards has the duty to signal cars coming in and out of various office buildings. The whistle sounds at 120 decibels, tweeting in a place close to your ears that is loud enough to make your heart shake. Your eardrums echo to the point of danger." It also cited the work of Professor Sujitra Prasansuk, an expert in hearing at Siriraj Hospital, who suggests that whistles contribute to drivers' stress by confusing them. Nevertheless, guards clearly feel empowered by their whistles, and the Whistle-Free Zone project remains a nascent effort.

The other major context for whistles in Bangkok is as a form of maritime signaling along the city's active waterways, including commuter traffic on Saen

Saep canal and the Chao Phraya river. One crew member on each craft (usually a motor-powered variant on the classic longboat type) is responsible for signaling to both dockworkers and passengers about the vessel's actions. From limited observation, these signals seem to be quasi-standard. Above the low groan of the motor and the fat slosh of wake against aft, the whistler releases a single whooping tone some ten seconds before the small ship reaches the dock. He follows this with several repetitions of a three-syllable call with an accent on the third, highest-pitched syllable, given at the moment that the vessel stops accelerating and begins maneuvering around the edge of the pier. Once the motor quiets, the whistler produces a five-note sequence—four identical notes in quick succession followed by a final one a few steps lower, indicating that the boat has stopped. As the boat briefly moors, a three-syllable call is whistled several times, only now with a sustained, urgent final note. This call means "all aboard!" and is repeated, with slight variation, a few times while the boat remains docked. Finally, a single long, loud note followed by two alternating notes tells the dockworker who handles the rope that the boat is ready to be untied. The motor engages once more and the sound of voices on land fades away under the noise of the motor, until the boat approaches the next station and the cycle begins again.

The use of whistles in Thai naval communication retains symbols from the southeast Asian seafaring Champa Kingdom, dating back more than one thousand years. The Royal Thai Navy continues to use obscure terminology from the Cham language, including *habaet* (to weigh anchor), a command that once involved blowing a whistle to coordinate the rhythm of rope-pulling by a crew. While the pragmatic necessity of whistling has diminished in the past century, decorative whistles are still presented to naval officers as tokens of honor and respect in formal ceremonies. As in traffic management, naval whistles remain important largely as symbolic rather than communicative objects (commuter vessels excepted) that mark, above all, power and rank.

There is, however, a crucial difference between the silver-plated silence of military whistles and the penetrating din of traffic whistles. While both are emblems of power, the sounding of the latter more actively invites the possibility of contest, both in the field of listening and in disputes over the right to broadcast. Whistles, freighted with histories of power relations, sound in public space as bids for sovereignty, in addition to any instructions they might convey. The whistling of parking lot guards and traffic directors make loud bids for sovereignty, but they are famously and often frustratingly non-semantic. Traffic whistles do not give specific commands, as commuter boat signals do. As a result, parking lot whistling is flat and repetitive, more alarm than tune. The guards wield the penetrating urgency of their instrument's high pitch, in tandem with its historical power as a tool of command, to convey that they are the arbiters of movement in space. The fact that this legitimacy is disputed by groups like the Whistle-Free Zone project is clear evidence of the ambition to power involved in the blowing of whistles in traffic scenarios. The debate between businesspeople who want to travel in quiet and parking lot attendants equipped with whistles is in truth a debate over who has the right to space, and on what sonic terms.

Whistles were common not only in traffic scenarios, but at protests as well. Red Shirts, as early as March 2010, blew them to make claims to public space, especially near traffic. The semi-permanent occupation of Ratchaprasong intersection in downtown Bangkok did not block vehicle movement altogether. Rather, Red Shirt citizen-guards stationed at either end of the kilometer-long tent city became traffic cops who managed the occupied zone as an artery. These guards dressed in hybrid outfits that combined the bright iconography of the movement—oversized *Truth Today* flags and bright red hats—with uniform-like pieces such as embroidered jackets and laminated ID badges. They gestured extravagantly at cars passing through the intersection, blowing their whistles without pause, just like parking lot attendants.

Given the Red Shirts' precarious ability to remain in these areas, and the need to perform "peace" and "order," the movement claimed legitimacy through gestures that ordered public activity in a conciliatory fashion. At stake was the patience of the government, the general public, and the owners of upscale malls and hotels nearby. This was a demanding constraint indeed. The delicate balancing act for the Red Shirts involved continuing their occupation of a central public space *to which they did not have a legitimate claim* without pushing the targets of their critique to the point of stopping the occupation. The Red Shirts thus needed to demonstrate that they were making an effort to maintain order, especially on behalf of drivers and shoppers. This strategy bought a little bit of time (though the crackdown eventually came anyway), but ultimately sacrificed what might have been a sharper, more confrontational affront to the political system. The protests faced down a critical response that, especially during the occupation phase in spring 2010, couched its political opposition in a language of concern about sanitation, traffic flow, disease, and chaos. The Red Shirts worked to address these critiques, rather than risk political marginalization or annihilation. They worked to show that they were trying to maintain order. And so they blew their whistles with alacrity.

The audible production of spatial order, however, was also a bid for sovereignty, which conflicted in certain ways with existing sovereignties. Dolar, by way of Agamben's *Homo Sacer*, describes the verbal shout as an event capable of initiating a state of emergency, and therefore a jealously guarded privilege of state sovereigns: "The voice is precisely at the unlocatable spot in the interior and exterior of the law at the same time, and hence a permanent threat of a state of emergency."[1] The question of who holds the right to announce emergencies, specifically through sound, is equivalent to the question of who holds the power to govern. Red Shirt guards used their whistles to announce dominion. The credibility of their announcements depended on the appearance of a good-faith effort to dictate order

1. Dolar, *A Voice and Nothing More*, 120.

for the benefit of the general public, achieved above all by whistling traffic along. This sounding, however, demonstrated that the Red Shirts were competing with the government for sovereignty, rather than contesting the ideological bases of sovereignty itself. Police officers, responsible for traffic direction in the areas where the Red Shirt guards were working, continued patrolling their normal intersections. Officers and protest guards often found themselves issuing the same commands in the very same places. Depending on the temperaments of the people involved, and on the circumstances, these encounters ranged from friendly and collaborative to annoyed and confrontational. At a September 19, 2010 Red Shirt rally, the southern end of the four-way intersection at Ratchaprasong was clogged with four officers and four Red Shirt guards (see Figure 8.1). Taxis and other vehicles edged their way through the reduced lanes, avoiding the fluid convexity of protesters who greatly outnumbered them. A protest guard in loose, knee-length jean shorts carrying a large flag approached a gray sedan, which he sent forward, directing the staccato blowing of his whistle at the level of the driver's head through the closed window. Across the intersection, a policeman stood nonchalantly with one arm pointed out, whistle balanced between his lips, whistling continually as he gestured. Although the verticality of pitch is a metaphor (in English as well as Thai), the high frequency of whistling in this case indeed cast it "above" the acoustic terrain of the rally. While the keynote sound of the protest, as with most mass gatherings, was

Figure 8.1 Officers in the foreground and Red Shirts in the background use whistles to direct traffic in Ratchaprasong intersection on September 19, 2010. Photograph by the author.

a low, expectant rumble punctuated by voice and musical bass, the contest over whistling happened at a high frequency. The sharp outbursts of the whistles, each producing nearly the same, uninflected note, mixed with each other in a restless, semantically fallow chorus.

However, for pedestrians and drivers who could trace the source of each sound, the question of who was whistling at them mattered enormously. For this reason, it became possible to assess patterns of control based on whether a specific whistler was convincing people to move. For example, on September 19, at a moment when the Red Shirt movement had grown more *kuu maa'eeng*, the four-month anniversary of the crackdown amidst the first large-scale return to Ratchaprasong intersection energized the crowd. As part of a reconfigured commitment to self-empowerment and organic cooperation, the protesters became more responsive to Red Shirt guards blowing whistles. As the crowd swelled and spilled from Ratchadamri Road, overwhelming the intersection, the police began to concede defeat, and pulled back. The Red Shirt guards remained, waving and whistling, announcing themselves, asserting their control and making audible claims to an existing form of sovereign control.

CHAPTER 9

Vehicular Stereo Systems

Bangkok's light industrial districts, along Rama IV road in Klong Toey and the Chalong Rat expressway in Bang Kapi, are lined with car audio installation shops. The shops offer bass boosts and trunk-mounted video systems from garages that often double as collision-repair centers. There are scores of them, "as many as 7-Elevens," one installer told me in reference to Bangkok's ubiquitous convenience store chain. In these shops, stylish global names appear behind glass cases: Alpine, mtx, Boston, Pioneer, ETON. Satisfied customers roll out of the garage slowly, windows up, ears tensed, merging into a higher tier of mobile listening.

Vehicular sound, video, and even laser lights are mostly unregulated in Thailand, and drivers indulge themselves. Bus companies install bulbs like stadium lights across the teeth of wrathful painted *yák* monsters on the bodies of their vehicles. Motor scooters become DJ booths with the addition of waterproof speakers and a subwoofer under the seat. Taxis double as listening spaces when the cheap, factory-installed speakers of a Toyota Corolla are torn out and replaced by a bevy of 91 dB Panasonics jacked into 950 watt amplifiers. The soft leather interior of a middle-class driver's Toyota Hilux gives a soft cushion to the brightly rendered bassline of the latest Usher single. Low-riding compact SUVs are augmented with $50,000 worth of stereo equipment, their trunks opening to vast external speakers illuminated by revolving pink and green lights from beneath the chassis, with colors shooting onto the pavement in wild patterns.

Red Shirt rallies, despite the movement's self-identification as a feudal peasant (*phrâya*) rebellion, were filled with vehicles that screamed of their own modern mobility, both upward and across town. Taxis with booming stereos were among the earliest options for ad hoc Red Shirt broadcasting, when drivers would simply swing open their doors and crank the volume. Rallies in March 2010 used cars and trucks as handy (and highly local) broadcasting sources, until in April semi-permanent overhead speaker systems and stages relegated them to a different role—as technologies for assembling impromptu musical crowds. Thereafter, drivers with loud systems parked in conspicuous places as the rallies filled in around them, spending the rest of the day feeding an insatiable desire for the generation and re-generation of musical events. Others invited friends and strangers into the beds of their trucks and drove slowly through Bangkok while their passengers danced to the familiar, cranked-up songs. These were roving advertisements for a charismatic politics that received, always, both honks of delight and silent condemnation.

CHAPTER 10

Developing Musical Economies I

CD Vendors

On May 19, 2011, at a rally marking the one-year anniversary of the military crackdown, I made a video of a woman walking through a temporary mall formed by vendors in Ratchaprasong intersection. She clutched several plastic bags and a purse to her stomach. Much as a bright red bandana or polo shirt could reveal someone as a political partisan, her cluster of bags revealed her as a consumer of Red Shirt products.

The woman browsed at a table of politically themed musical artifacts—CD compilations, karaoke albums, and concert footage. She appeared drawn to this table, instead of other tables nearby, by a video playing on a boxy grey television atop a tall black speaker cabinet. The video showed a Red Shirt fundraising concert from April 2009. Performing on the screen were the *mor lam* musicians Sombun Fachat and Kraison Saenmueang, he primarily a *khɛɛn* player and she a singer. Ordinary people of a certain age, the duo were unlikely pop stars. They were not well-known before the Red Shirt movement grew to prominence, but gained a small following once antigovernment concerts in Isan began apace in 2009. Onscreen, the couple was backed by a troupe of dancers wearing black bras and red feathered hats on a multi-tiered stage. Sombun blew a raspy, amplified *khɛɛn* in and out, in time with the sparse notes of the bass line, which leant a slow, heaving depth to the rhythm section. He and Kraison took turns improvising lyrics praising Red Shirt leader Adisorn Piangket for hosting the concert to spread democracy in Isan. Their lyrics affirmed the movement's opposition to dictatorship. Each improvised section was six measures long, beginning with an anacrusis (a few words such as "Thank you, brothers and sisters," rapidly delivered), which repeated before the second measure.[1] Then, four lyrically crammed lines filled out the subsequent four

---

1. All of Sombun and Kraison's lyrics were sung in Thai.

measures, elaborating the topic of the improvisation. The other singer responded with six more measures of lyrics, entering on the second half of the final measure of the previous segment, which chained the improvisations together. The tone of their banter was playfully competitive. In addition to the frenetic invention of lyrics, the show was a spectacle, with long lines of dancers, an ornately decorated stage, and a sound system large enough for an audience of thousands.

The shopper paused briefly to watch all of this, and made up her mind within seconds. Turning toward the vendor, she leaned forward over the table, shouting above the music, and asked where she could find the album that was playing on the television. The vendor, idly thumbing a wad of twenty-baht bills in one hand, jabbed a finger toward his colleague, who worked a part of the table where four different VCD albums were neatly arrayed, including three different selections by Sombun and Kraison. The second vendor stood up from his red plastic stool and placed the VCD in a translucent pink bag, barely larger than the album itself. The woman handed him several bills totaling eighty baht, and added the bag to the cluster she already held. She disappeared back into the rally. The browsing and purchase took about two minutes.

From a certain vantage, this exchange was banal. Like nearly all human affairs in the twenty-first century, political protests are mediated by commercial exchange. But in the Red Shirt movement, the scale of commerce was unusual and structurally significant. Collectively, small transactions like the one described above were an important economic engine of the movement. The profits of informal retailing made it easier for sellers to come to rallies habitually, and in this way helped the events grow. Spaces of commercialized public listening also helped protesters locate themselves within a sprawling national movement. Finding a table to patronize, and then an album to buy, were everyday political choices within the rallies. Shopping was a means of finding one's own ideological niche in a sonic niche. For the Red Shirts, vending was an economically sustaining practice, and shopping was a political act.

For many vendors, moreover, selling Red Shirt products was not only self-sustaining, but offered something gift-like to the movement. The Red Shirts, with rare exceptions, did not claim an opposition to capitalism. In fact, they hoped to build an alternative economic juggernaut that might eventually propel the movement to electoral success, mass participation, and other forms of political power. To be a vendor, then, was to become part of a developing musical economy, a new and idealistic industry. Selling music was not only a small business arrangement, but a way of joining in politics. My argument in this chapter, as it engages sound and listening, seeks to complicate one made by Michel de Certeau in *The Practice of Everyday Life*. There, de Certeau argues that *strategic* action (that which is conceived as broad-ranging and long-term) is the province of the dominant classes, while *tactical* action (that which is impulsive and short-term) is the only mode available to the proletariat. According to de Certeau, conservative forces produce place as a set of rigid, ahistorical, and strategic regulations. Dissent in these places is thus constrained; it can only be opportunistic.[2] For Red Shirt music sellers, however, vending was a political strategy, as evidenced by their own language. Vendors hoped that their entrepreneurialism would coalesce into a challenge to the elite political establishment. They were not constrained by an inability to act strategically, but by the imperative to think and act through financial logics.

THE MALL AS A MIRROR

The Red Shirts were routinely constrained by the need to strategize economically. From one political side, they were judged by the press and by middle-class witnesses according to how their actions affected the national economy. From another side, the movement was compelled to maintain a flow of money that could sustain its members and pay for all kinds of mobilization activities. Most protesters had no savings, and could not afford to leave their jobs unless food, shelter, and transportation were covered. For the Red Shirt leadership, therefore, money was an existential concern. As will be described in this and the next several chapters, individual protesters assimilated these concerns about money into their own political thinking, and into their own habits of exchange at rallies. Earning and spending money became central to Red Shirt life, often as a kind of moral act. The grammar of protest was, in many ways, a grammar of commerce.

This was equally true of my fieldwork. At each rally, I browsed the vending stalls looking for new recordings. I took note of anything I hadn't seen before, and assessed political trends by being an astute shopper. I usually left rallies with a significant (and sometimes expensive) haul of new albums, which I then went home and excitedly put on the stereo. The experience became, unwittingly, a lot like boutique music shopping in non-political contexts, in which one hopes to unearth rarities and build complete collections. After a time, it was unclear whether I was an ethnographer shopping, or a shopper doing ethnography. As I wrote in field notes after a rally in January 2011:

> There were easily a hundred vendors throughout the grounds. I lingered at one stand, where I bought an album by Dr. สุทินคลังแสง, a member of parliament from Maha Sarakham. At the same table was at least one album by a young Arisman Pongruangrong. I noticed some other unusual selections. But the most interesting release of this particular rally was, apparently, a new album by Jatuporn Promphan that the UDD was selling for 20 baht. Being well below the usual purchase price, the meaning in that gesture is clearly "we're not trying to make money here." And that's undoubtedly true. However, if one assumes that the point of acquiring political power is to gain capital in one form or

---

2. Michel de Certeau, *The Practice of Everyday Life* (Berkeley: University of California Press, 1984).

another, the product is certainly a kind of advertisement. Orn told me about the album, but at every table I asked they either didn't have it or were sold out. Orn promised she would buy one for me, and said not to bother asking anymore since the UDD were the only ones able to sell it. I am anxious to find out what is on the album, and to see how the new songs circulate in the coming months.

Capital loomed. Aptly, given its scope and hubris, the mall that towered above the Ratchaprasong protests is called Central World. This compound, at 550,000 square meters, is the largest mall in Thailand, and as of 2011 was the fifth-largest mall on Earth. It is the heart of a national cosmology of consumption. The health of the Thai economy allegedly requires that Central World and other high-end commercial nodes remain profitable. And the Red Shirt protests could hardly avoid the mall's gravitational pull. Central World was badly damaged by fire during the military crackdown, after being besieged by the protest encampments. The financial damage was tremendous. But these assaults on the mall spoke to a double bind that the protesters faced: although the grandest monuments of inequality could be besieged or even destroyed, they remained the central subjects of political reference, the targets of all political attention, positive or negative. As political protest turned toward the mall, capitalism thus closed the loop upon itself.

But what was the alternative? Without economic strategizing, the Red Shirt movement would have risked both backlash and stagnation. Daily news articles noted that the protests were hurting tourism and GDP, often before or instead of offering political analysis.[3] For many journalists, it was evidently difficult to judge the movement apart from its effects on tourism and economic growth. Protesters were sensitive to the charge that they were damaging the economy. One CD vendor near Democracy Monument defended his own right to protest on the basis of financial entitlement. "People who pay their taxes are not terrorists," he told me. Yet politically moderate observers, whose sympathy the protesters sought, were skeptical of claims like this. Many saw prolonged blockades of commercial areas as selfish political ploys that took Thailand's collective financial interests hostage. Moderates and conservatives repeated tirelessly that all Thais had a stake in the health of the national economy. Even at protests, the sale of music (among other goods) was part of a strategic effort to create an amended economic order, and it was clear that the movement's capacity to move depended on its success in this regard.[4]

3. "Economy and Jobs Are Also Victims," *The Straits Times,* May 24, 2010; "Thailand Tourism Devastated by Political Unrest," *Time,* April 18, 2010.
4. On the topic of music and commercial space in sound studies, see Jonathan Sterne, "Sounds Like the Mall of America: Programmed Music and the Architectonics of Public Space," *Ethnomusicology* 41, no. 1 (Winter 1997): 22–50; Goodman, *Sonic Warfare*; Karin Bijsterveld, "Acoustic Cocooning: How the Car Became a Place to Unwind," *The Senses & Society* 5, no. 2 (2011): 189–211.

VENDORS AND VENDING

It is difficult to know how many albums Red Shirt music vendors sold over the course of several years, let alone their margins of profit. The industry was informal and decentralized, and no trade group or other organization represented it. No cumulative sales figures or even estimates were ever published or collected by the UDD, to my knowledge. It is possible, however, to offer a few general details about the size and finances of the vending operations. In this section, I describe the informal economy of music vendors, their distribution networks, the vendors as laborers, and the products that they sold.

Throughout 2010 and 2011, every rally attended by a few hundred or more protesters included at least a few vendors of musical recordings. Small rallies typically had five or ten tables or tents; large rallies had forty or more. Vendors selling audiovisual material were interspersed among others selling T-shirts, food, haircuts, massages, plastic clappers, and books and magazines. The music vendors did not necessarily cluster together. The spaces they staked out were available to whoever claimed them first. These vendors would set up in any place that a protest was unfolding. Whether an event was in Bangkok, Chiang Mai, Khon Kaen, Ayuthaya, or Sukhothai, whether in an upscale commercial area or an untended public park, more or less the same musical material was sold. However, the stock changed over time as new albums were released, different concert footage became available, or simply as purchasing trends shifted. At rallies, the spatial organization of vending tables was at least somewhat improvised. But in semi-permanent areas such as the tent cities of Ratchaprasong in early 2010 or the markets of the fifth and sixth floors of the shopping mall called Big C Lad Phrao (discussed in Chapter 2, and in-depth later in this chapter), the same vendors came routinely, usually occupying the same spaces each time. For many people, Red Shirt vending was—for a period that briefly seemed indefinite—full-time work.

The most common audiovisual format sold at Red Shirt protests was re-recordable discs, with content burned onto them either by the vendors or by middlemen with access to bulk reproduction technology. Only the most successful musicians could afford to manufacture their own CDs and VCDs, and then sell them wholesale to vendors. Much more often, small vendors bought packs of blank CDs, VCDs, or DVDs, almost always made by a brand called Princo. Princo blanks could be purchased at 7-Eleven for about 10 baht ($0.33) per disc. The vendors or middlemen would then photocopy small squares of paper with the singer's name and face to insert in the CD's jewel case as cover art. Even some of the most popular merchandise was made in this unceremonious fashion. For example, at the May 19, 2011 rally, I sat with a vendor named Not for an hour to observe what was moving well that day.[5] I asked Not what

---

5. In this chapter, vendor names are withheld, or nicknames used, except when permission was explicitly granted, because revelations of their protest vending could imperil other employment.

his best-selling album was, and he handed me a Princo karaoke VCD (with this format, each song was accompanied by a video with lyrics onscreen) featuring a pixelated, apparently homemade design printed and glued directly onto the disc. Democracy Monument appeared in the background of the cover art, and Thaksin Shinawatra's head was superimposed onto Superman's body in the foreground. In the image, Thaksin/Superman flew past the words of the title: *khít hôot* ("Miss You"). The music on the album was an unthematic collection of MP3s, with sixteen songs ranging from recent major label releases to home recordings to dusty mid-twentieth century ballads. Among these was a contemporary hit by Wanchana Koetdi, a popular independent singer as well as a UDD leader, a cover of Saksayarm Petchompoo's *luk thung* oldie *khít hôot nóong dɛɛng* ("Miss You, Red Girl") which was accompanied by a video tribute to Thaksin, and Takkaten Chonlada's mainstream 2009 *luk thung* single *pròot chûay ráksǎa khon dii* ("Please Take Care of Good People"). The word "red" in Saksayarm's song has nothing to do with twenty-first century politics. In fact, it was written and recorded in the 1970s. And although Takkaten's popular single was rumored among Red Shirts to be a secret ode to Thaksin, she does not mention him directly in the song, and she has never said publicly that she meant to refer to him. As a major label recording artist, in fact, Takkaten was tacitly barred from speaking politically at all, but especially in a way that might have favored the controversial former prime minister. In other words, no one really knows what "Please Take Care of Good People" was meant to be about. Nevertheless, such vaguely political songs became part of the Red Shirt canon, just as much as the music of Wanchana, which was politically explicit. The vendors, compiling and burning these collections by hand, helped generate the canon of Red Shirt music one disc and one sale at a time.

By the vendors' own admission, compilation albums like these were made without permission. Unauthorized reproduction was widespread. Although some Red Shirts characterized this as piracy, others celebrated it. For example, Tata, an active young volunteer with the Red Sunday group, described the relationship between recording, online distribution, and retail as usefully unburdened by intellectual property law. "The seller downloads the song from the internet, and copies the song to sell," she explained with a note of indignant pride before a rally in October 2010. We had just gotten off a chartered bus after a long drive, and were walking along a row of CD vendors setting up near the road where that evening's rally would take place.[6] "No copyrights," she said. Thailand does in fact have copyright laws, but Tata was correct that the vendors almost always ignored them. In the view of Tata, who has worked as an assistant to Red Shirt musicians including Pae Bangsanan (see Chapter 11), copyright laws interfere with rather than protect a political musician's work. But others, such as Om Khaphatsadi (see Chapter 11),

---

6. Tata, interview with the author, October 2010. Nickname used at interviewee request.

rolled their eyes in annoyance when discussing the vendors, charging that they illegally cut into artists' sales.

The output of some musicians was conscripted into the Red Shirt movement not only without copyright, but also without other forms of express permission, at times controversially. As with Saksayarm's "Miss You, Red Girl," many songs became resonant by circumstance rather than intention. For some observers, this raised the ethical question of whether the Red Shirts had the right to play their music at all. Consider the case of Opat Fakumkrawng's upbeat, goofy *phûakkhray phûakman* ("People and Things"), which I estimate was one of the five or ten most ubiquitous Red Shirt songs in 2010–11. The piece was featured on many greatest-hits albums, including Not's compilation. With a heavy lead electric guitar riff and an anthemic refrain in the singer's off-kilter, nasal voice, the song is resolutely modern, if something of a novelty. "People and Things" is a litany of complaints about thoughtless people that was originally released on a thematic album with a title that translates as "Annoying Problems." Red Shirts, including my friend Pat (see Chapter 7), cited this song as a poignant expression of the movement's core beliefs. In its chorus, the song contrasts an imagined community of "us" with a collective "them," using the impolite pronouns (*kuu* and *mʉng*) that the Red Shirt movement adopted in so many of its slogans.[7] Pat identified the piece as a "UDD song" and liked that the singer condemned the elites for a failure to "think before they act."[8] However, Pat did not know that Opat had in fact died in the early 2000s, several years before even the first inkling of the Red Shirt movement.[9] The song was therefore, of course, not written for or about the Red Shirts. Pat was surprised by this, but stuck to her interpretation anyway. Others challenged the ethics of the adoption of "People and Things" as a Red Shirt anthem. One user on the Facebook page of Thailand's communist party, for example, posted that "when people die they cannot speak. We can only mourn them. This man's rights are violated by the use of this song."[10] The accretion of the Red Shirt musical canon was, like all canons, disjointed and fiercely debated.

Most vendors were blue-collar laborers by day, selling Red Shirt music and other goods as the opportunity arose. Often, both of their jobs involved vending. The two income sources paralleled one another; the first was formalized (in the sense that shops or stalls are licensed and subject to rents), while the second was more spontaneous and insecure. However, while the economy of protest events was even more tenuous than regular work, it had the benefit of flexibility. As peddlers in the formal economy, vendors' lives are hardscrabble, and their labor is alienated.[11] By

---

7. The pronominal *kuu* here is the same as that which appears in the slogan *kuu maa'eeng*.
8. Pat, interview with the author, April 25, 2011.
9. He was, moreover, thought to be politically neutral.
10. "พรรคคอมมิวนิสต์คนเสื้อแดงภายใต้สันตืนเรา" ("Our Own Fucking Red Shirt Communist Party"), October 28, 2010, https://www.facebook.com/permalink.php?story_fbi d=165796460114541&id=134530939932969). Translated from the original Thai.
11. This class-inflected language about work is present in musical representations of labor in Thailand, especially *luk thung*. Consider Tai Orathai's *naangbɛ̀ɛpngaanbun* ("Woman of the Merit Festival," discussed in Chapter 13), as well as Mike Pirompon's *yaajaykhonjon* ("The Darling Poor"), the latter of which describes the unfulfilling nature and tediousness of the

Figure 10.1 Customers and a vendor deliberate over a purchase. A VCD of a rally plays on a small screen on the table. Photograph by the author.

contrast, Red Shirt vending put far more money in their pockets, while giving them a central role in a political movement that they expected would benefit them in the long term. Investment is not a word that vendors generally used to describe their motives but, to a person, the purpose of selling albums at protests was said to be the promotion of the movement as a political force that could improve their own lives.

For the urban poor, money from Red Shirt vending was a windfall. I knew one older woman who sold CDs from a small table at every rally she could attend since the Ratchaprasong occupation. She worked by day in Bangkok as a vegetable seller, a common low-wage occupation with minimal profit margins and volatile swings in the price and availability of goods. She estimated that a single protest was likely to gross about 5,000 baht ($167) for her.[12] Even accounting for the costs of printing covers and buying blank CDs, that figure dwarfed her daily take as a vegetable seller. CD vending thus modeled how an equitable economy might operate: nearly all of the money she earned went into her pocket.

Music vending tables offered between ten and one hundred different albums or videos, roughly speaking, which protesters browsed studiously (see Figure 10.1). In considering these selections, it becomes clear how Red Shirt consumers located themselves ideologically within the movement. The stock at a given table varied

---

singer's job. Such descriptions of labor as exploitative drudgery are extremely common within the genre.

12. Vendor, interview with the author, May 20, 2011. Name withheld at interviewee request.

Figure 10.2 A table selling a combination of CDs, VCDs, and DVDs. Photograph by the author.

depending on the personal preferences of the vendor, the audience he or she hoped to bring in, the current popularity of various musicians and speakers, and the availability of new releases. As seen in Figure 10.2, a table set up at a February 2011 rally featured a mixture of speeches by UDD leaders, republican figures, and even one album with a cover that subtly called for the overthrow of the monarchy.[13] Many vendors also sold videos, including of concerts and notable speeches. And nearly every vendor had at least one VCD or DVD that showcased the military's amorality and bloodlust. As described in Chapter 3, these showed footage, usually shot by cell phone, of (for example) protesters being hit by army bullets, and their bodies being dragged away by comrades. Such material, described at length in the context of Bangkok's 1992 antigovernment protests by Klima, returned forcefully in 2010. Its presence may even have expanded because of the decreased cost of reproduction. Some of the atrocity videos were so common that vendors gave them away free with the purchase of any other item. Most people I spoke to in 2010 and 2011 suggested that the footage they watched served as evidence, an unfiltered alternative to the news. Certain tables specialized in these videos, and even hosted daylong viewing sessions. Watching them offered a chance for self-education.

In Figure 10.3, below, a man photographs an array of violent images inside of a CD vending tent. Behind him, in the same tent, several tables were set up, selling

---

13. The seditious album is the one in the near bottom-left of the image, with a dancing figure and a dragon on its cover. The vowel over the first letter suggests a double-entendre that, in one of its senses, translates as "overthrow the king."

Figure 10.3 A man takes a cellphone photo of images of death and violence mounted on a poster within a CD vending tent. Photograph by the author.

both CDs and VCDs. The images on the poster were not so much contemplated as documented, or assessed briefly before the purchase of Red Shirt recordings. Much as the woman at the beginning of this chapter paused to watch a video before purchasing a VCD of concert footage, atrocity videos drew spectators in. They heightened outrage or, in the language of the viewer in Chapter 3, allowed people to "learn more about the truth." In other words, the atrocity images framed politics differently than state-approved news.[14] This framing was then immediately linked (by a distance of just a few feet) to the opportunity to buy the products of this ethical, putatively transparent media.

The variety of musical selections on offer spanned much of what is heard on the radio in Thailand, with the exception of jazz and "classical" ensembles like *mahori*, *piphat*, and *khrueang sai*, which were not part of the Red Shirt repertoire. Popular genres, including *luk thung*, string, and "songs for life" were each well-represented. Certain vendors bore strong allegiances to a particular musician or leader figure in the movement, and consequently stocked their tables with content related to that individual.

Among politicians or leaders, Thaksin Shinawatra was the figure most commonly depicted on cover art, whether or not the music on an album referred to him directly. The charismatic paramilitary martyr Seh Daeng, killed by a sniper in

14. On frames in this sense, see Erving Goffman, *Frame Analysis: An Essay on the Organization of Experience* (Boston, MA: Northeastern University Press, 1986).

Figure 10.4 The stock at a vending table at one Red Shirt rally. Photograph by the author.

spring 2010, was often memorialized through the sale of videos of his speeches. As an orator, Seh Daeng spoke with an appealing bluntness, befitting a former military general who still wore fatigues onstage. Other popular figures included Jatuporn Promphan, the hyper-masculine Nattawut Saikua, and the older, outspoken Surachai Danwattananusorn. In Figure 10.4, above, roughly one-third of the material consists of DVDs of Jatuporn's speeches. Seh Daeng and Thaksin are also featured, in addition to recordings that claim to prove that "the prime minister [Abhisit] ordering the killings [at Ratchaprasong]." The content of this particular table affirmed the UDD's leadership hierarchy and discourses. Other vendors had different emphases. For example, a table stocked with Nattawut's speeches and music was considered a draw for women, while Surachai's material appealed to republicans.[15] One vendor who worked exclusively on the fifth floor of Big C Lad Phrao rotated her stock so that, for example, when Jatuporn gave a speech at the mall, his albums and videos were on display concurrently.

VENDING AS STRATEGY

Scholarship on sound and music in public spaces of capitalist consumption has often echoed de Certeau's binary of control and dissent, with auditory regimes of

---

15. As of this writing, Surachai, now in his mid-seventies, is serving a seven-and-a-half-year sentence for purportedly insulting the royal family in his speeches.

order on the side of control and heterodoxies of noise on the side of dissent. Sterne, for instance, writes in his work on the Mall of America that "what disrupts the Mall environment is noise, the voicing of differences. The signs prohibiting 'loud, bois-terous behavior' located at the entrances and exits to the roaring amusement park are reminders that the Mall is attempting to construct a very specific kind of con-sumerism, and interference with that goal is grounds for ejection."[16] Resistance is anonymous and decentered, like that of de Certeau's itinerant walker, whose de-fiance is always and necessarily ad hoc. But must dissenting sound always be im-pulsive sound? Red Shirt music vendors helped produce a spatial order that was not only tactical. Their vending mirrored the commercial logic of the malls near which they worked. They thought demographically, and effectively linked con-sumer identity with music and sound. The stylistic diversity of their wares helped the movement maintain a big tent under which people of different class, political, and regional backgrounds could gather. This strategy enabled the sprawling Red Shirt movement, which claimed millions of members, to speak to a mass audience with heightened individual sensitivity. A stage speech by then-UDD chairperson Thida Thavornseth at a 2011 Red Shirt event in Khao Yai alluded to the stakes of the movement's musical diversity:

> This is not just regular entertainment at the concert. It is the battle guidelines for Thai culture. . . . The Red Shirt group has a lot of music and its importance is high. We have many melodies. We have international and local and village music. And *luk thung,* which is a real hit with the grassroots. We have *luk krung* (city music). We use this music to reach the people (the poor). And we use it to get the response from the middle class. We use the music *strategically.* . . . The group that has music that is on the side of the people will grow very big.[17] (emphasis mine)

For Thida, musical pluralism not only reflects but invites demographic pluralism ("we use this music to reach the people"). A movement only becomes a *mass* move-ment by being internally diverse. To that end, "international music" (*phleeng sǎakon*) and "local music" (*phleeng phʉʉnbâan*) are code words for cosmopolitanism and its opposite, respectively, while the genres *luk thung* and *luk krung* are clear sig-nals for rural and urban tastes in turn. Both extremes are welcome among the Red Shirts, Thida explains. Listening to *phleeng sǎakon* reflects a middle-class aspiration toward global citizenship and mobility, while *phleeng phʉʉnbâan* connotes fixity. The breadth of the Red Shirt musical canon, which could in Thida's view harbor both, helped produce a political faction representative of "the people," in all of that category's proportional scope.

16. Sterne, "Sounds Like the Mall of America."
17. *Mahachon,* April 21–27, 2010, 14. Translation from the original Thai provided by Michael Volpe.

The Yellow Shirts, by contrast, rarely strayed from a small subset of musical styles. Thida had a clear interest in implying as much, but my own observations at numerous Yellow Shirt events substantiated her claim. Yellow Shirt protests (or protests politically aligned with them) were rarer and smaller in 2010–11 than they had been in 2008, but their aesthetics were internally consistent. The commonest Yellow Shirt genre by a wide margin was "songs for life," which originated in the 1960s and 1970s, first in close imitation of American folk music and later as a unique and politically incisive leftist style. The best-known "songs for life" group from the 1970s is called Caravan.[18] Caravan was started by student activists in Bangkok. Their music was deeply cosmopolitan, equally reflective of *mor lam* and of the fingerpicked guitar and vocal harmonies of international musicians like Simon and Garfunkel. But songs such as *khon kàp khwaay* ("Man and Buffalo") and *khon phuukhǎw* ("Mountain People") do not address student life or global politics. Instead they are romantic homages to farming and rurality. From the 1980s onward, "songs for life" came to be dominated by a group called Carabao, who were less expressly political (and certainly less leftist) than Caravan, but who similarly romanticized rural life. The lead singer, Aed Carabao, popularized a cowboy-hippie pastiche style of dress that was marked by long hair, torn shirts, sunglasses, and buffalo skull symbols. Rather than a student-farmer proletarian alliance, Carabao's version of "songs for life" suggested a by-the-bootstraps rural masculinity. Today, Carabao is a highly successful energy drink magnate.

The Yellow Shirts adopted "songs for life" despite how awkwardly their own politics fit with the music's leftist history. Contrary to Caravan and Carabao in the 1960s and '70s, the Yellow Shirts were neither leftist nor especially interested in the aesthetics or moral consciousness of rural life. Nevertheless, "songs for life" had become linked with Thainess as a national mythology, and a handful of twenty-first century artists had utilized this link to support a latter-day conservative nationalism. In a somewhat surprising gesture, Caravan co-founder Surachai Chantimatorn even joined the anti-Thaksin movement, buttressing the Yellow Shirts' claim to the use of his music. But this example notwithstanding, the Yellow Shirts simply did not attract as many musicians as the Red Shirts. Popular genres like *luk thung* and *mor lam* were almost entirely absent from Yellow Shirt concerts and recordings. Yellow Shirt music vendors sold "songs for life" albums, Western classic rock (most often, pirated copies of music by the Eagles), and older recordings of royalist songs and militant right-wing music. But they could not match the sales or scope of the Red Shirt vendors.

Thida noted later in her Khao Yai speech that "there used to be Yellow Shirt musicians. Now the interest is not there and they are not producing new songs any more . . . .Yellow Shirts musicians need to go back to playing the old music of the

---

18. Today, one "songs for life"-themed bar in Bangkok has a line-drawn portrait of Caravan, similar to the cover of the Beatles' *"Revolver,"* hanging reverently above its stage.

ammat (elites) to persuade people to feel loyalty to the monarchy. They must use the old songs like the *ammat* once used."[19] For Thida, musical variety explained the vast difference in the size of Red and Yellow Shirt protests. And it was in part the informal economy of Red Shirt music vending that had made this possible at the rallies. Vendors were central agents in carrying out a program that the UDD's chairperson described explicitly as "strategic."

VENDING AS A SONIC NICHE

The sound of vending was advertorial. As in the anecdote at the beginning of this chapter, vendors reached protesters by putting songs on the speaker as people browsed nearby, like in a record store. Some vendors brought small, handheld stereos, while others set up complex component systems and provided seating and shade for fifty or more people to sit and listen as long as they wished.

At the May 19 rally, a short walk from where the woman had purchased a VCD of Sombun and Kraison, a different vendor moved busily behind her own table. Her small speakers, clipping at maximum volume, played a medium-tempo *lam* with a whining organ line and lyrics that recounted recent political events. The singer narrated how Red Shirts had gathered at Phan Fa bridge in April of the previous year to fight for democracy in Thailand, without firing weapons, only to be "attacked until they could no longer stand it." As I stood near the speakers, I heard the song at about an equal volume with an orator standing on a truck nearby, which served as a mobile stage. He told a small assembled crowd about the special guests who would appear on the main stage that very evening. The slow pace of the song, and its historical emphasis, contrasted with the orator's rapidity, and his focus on the near future. The sonic niche around the music vending table jumbled these two different rhythms and temporal perspectives.

With a sweat rag draped over her shoulders and a hip pouch packed with small bills around her waist, the table's lone vendor juggled conversations with one older man and two younger female customers as they each browsed. One of the women wore a bright red shirt with several photographs of Thaksin's face surrounded by white hearts. She and her friend were particularly interested in an album by Wanchana Koetdi, the Red Shirt leader and singer affiliated with the UDD. Wanchana is marketed, in his musical merchandise, as a heartthrob. Like quite a few other male Red Shirt musicians, including former boy band singer Arisman Pongruangrong, he is presented as simultaneously tender and virile. The cover art of the album that the two women browsed shows Wanchana looking directly at the viewer with a warm smile, his lips touched up with an artificially bright red tone. A colorful geodesic shape and a flurry of stars frame his handsome face. The artwork

---

19. *Mahachon.*

draws from a half-century of *luk thung* record covers, on which singers are often photographed from the front and cropped a few inches below the neckline—just enough to reveal that they are well-dressed, while keeping the focus on their dapper, modest visage. This album included songs like "Concern for Red Shirt Girls," on which Wanchana extols the brave women who come to rallies despite the risks.[20] Odes to women by male singers were something of a cliché, albeit a successful one. Nattawut Saikua's "Love the Red Shirt Girls," for example, was by far his biggest hit. Moreover, many Red Shirt songs presented relationships between protesters—whether the rank-and-file, the leaders, or Thaksin himself—as intimate and even subtly romantic. Slow ballads with titles such as "Miss You Badly" and "Waiting for the Day You Return" were typical. Love was an important force in Red Shirt politics, and was often said to account for the movement's power. Thaksin's policies, for example, were described by many supporters as an expression of authentic love and concern for the people. Love was a constitutive element of Red Shirt identity, often expressed through tropes of heteronormative intimacy. This mode of love staged a contrast with the indifference of careerist politicians and military bureaucrats. Singers like Wanchana flourished as professional musicians by writing songs that brought love thematically to the fore.

The two women turned Wanchana's CD over and back again. The customer with the hearts on her shirt asked the vendor for two copies, and then bought them.

"WE HAVE OUR OWN FINANCES"

The selection on the table pictured in Figure 10.5 is unusually diverse. This table was run by the vendor mentioned earlier, who rotated her stock when Jatuporn spoke. In the upper lefthand corner of the image are identical, adjacent copies of a karaoke VCD by Pae Bangsanan (see Chapter 11), next to an atrocity video and an album with Mahatma Gandhi on the cover in the top right. Also pictured are a VCD featuring a television program about the Burmese dissident (later president) Aung San Suu Kyi, an album of speeches by Surachai Danwattananusorn, a dubbed History Channel episode about the French Revolution, and two musical albums featuring the work of then-imprisoned leader Nattawut Saikua. The high number of VCDs valorizing figures of the international left suggests that the vendor held potentially dangerous political views, or catered to an audience that did.

This music vendor was one of a handful who set up almost every day on the sixth floor of the Big C shopping mall in Lad Phrao, Bangkok, quite far from the commercial and touristic center of the city. The fifth and sixth floors of this mall had, since late 2010, been leased almost exclusively to Red Shirt businesses. Nearly every store

---

20. This song title, along with all others cited in this chapter, is a translation from the original Thai.

Figure 10.5 An array of albums for sale on the table of a Red Shirt CD vendor at Big C Lad Phrao shopping mall. Photograph by the author.

was occupied by a Red Shirt retailer or organization, and vendors also gathered socially on the floor of a mezzanine overlooking an ice rink.[21] There were coffee shops, booksellers, an office of medical resources (called "Red nurse"), a satellite TV station (People Channel), food stalls, a publishing office, and a knickknack store ("The Red Shop by People Channel") selling Red Shirt stuffed bears, coffee mugs, and T-shirts. One of the larger stores became the headquarters for the Red Sunday group in 2011. Sombat, Red Sunday's organizer, once held a happening on the ground floor of Big C Lad Phrao, at which one hundred Red Shirts gathered on the sixth floor, and marched down to a large supermarket. Wearing red clothing, the mass of shopper/protesters walked through the aisles selecting only red-colored groceries, which they then took to the checkout line and dramatically purchased, as cameras flashed all around. Sombat's shopping event was conciliatory, very much a part of his effort to play along with the government's "political game." Like the CD vendors, he was joining a strategic operation to transform the Red Shirts into a long-term, economically stable movement.

I sat down with the music vendor who set up routinely in Big C one afternoon in December 2011, for a conversation and a plate of *phàt phàk ruammít*, bought from a Red Shirt food stall immediately next to us, at the vendor's suggestion. I had come to follow up with her, and with the general scene at Big C Lad Phrao, five months after the election of Yingluck Shinawatra, the new Red Shirt-friendly prime minister.

21. The ice rink was apolitical.

Now that the largest protests had subsided, how were the Red Shirts (at that point still plenty active) thinking about economic strategy? As it turned out, little had changed. The vendor described the same channels of distribution that had existed during the height of the protests. Her CDs and VCDs were purchased from Asia Update, a Red Shirt news outlet, which acted as a manufacturer and middleman. And she described a system of pricing and retailing that was nearly identical to the active period of the protests. Setting up in Big C Lad Phrao, for her, routinized an economic strategy that had been in development for the previous two years.

A man named Phong, an attorney, was browsing at the same table, and he joined our conversation. Phong supported but was not formally affiliated with the Red Shirt movement. However, he was eager to offer his perspective, especially about capitalism. He insisted that the Red Shirts could eventually become a financially independent state-within-a-state in Thailand. This very vending table, he suggested, could be an exemplary unit within such a state. He hoped the movement would standardize its commercial operations and begin to think bigger—vending tables at protests earned money, but the movement needed to scale up and build even larger institutions. He hoped the movement would eventually reduce government to a weak facilitating mechanism:

"Like her, she's doing this, it's a good thing," said Phong, gesturing to the vendor.[22] "She's trying to make a living supporting her family, supporting the party."

"By selling these [CDs]?" I asked.

"Exactly. . . . I really support them. Do you know what I mean? A hundred baht a month, it's not so bad. How much is that, three dollars? If I may say. I'm willing to do that, maybe a thousand times to help them without getting anything back. Do that for two years, alright? You take that one hundred baht times two years, should be twenty-four months. How much is that per person? Twenty-four hundred baht, right? It's about sixty, seventy bucks. For two years! You take that money, multiply it by fifteen million. How much is that? Can you own a bank yourself? Can this Red party own a bank? They can own, right? Can they own manufacturing? They can, right? Can they own a better hospital? Can they? They can, right? They have to be able to build their own better schools. You cannot rely on the government. Government will do their part to bring the country along. But us, as a group? Fifteen million people. We have our own finances. We have our empire. We have our standard. We have our quality of education. We have a way of living," he said.

"Bypassing the government?" I asked, suddenly aware of how closely his language hewed to neoliberal or at least libertarian discourses.

"We are not anti-them [government]," he responded. "But we are not taking anything from them. . . . Us as a people, we should do our own."

---

22. Interview with the author, December 2011. The interview took place in a combination of English and Thai.

"So the job of the government is to give people the freedom to lift themselves up?" I replied.

"Exactly," said Phong.

"Through what? What kinds of policies?" I asked.

"The policy of the government should be to set up a standard for how to provide security for the people, for the country overall, the law, changes to the constitution. All these things will take time for the government. I'm talking about the current government. . . . People, like the Red Shirts, should stay together and educate each other. Not take over the government, no. But compete economically." Phong explained.

"Be independent economically, autonomous?" I asked.

"Right," offered Phong with an open palm upturned on the CD table, as if offering his plan for approval, as the vendor and I listened. "If you look at the whole world right now, the war is between economies. It's nothing with the technology, with the weapons, none of those. Whoever is better financially, those people will survive, those people dictate, those people will have power. What I'm saying to you is, if the Red Shirts don't build this empire, financial stability for themselves, they'll be waiting for charity only. Someone to help them, give them equal opportunity, giving them free speech, giving them a better life. There's no such thing gonna happen."

CHAPTER 11

Developing Musical Economies II

Stage Musicians

The informal industry described in the previous chapter involved not only vendors and shoppers but also musicians. Some of these musicians pursued celebrity, a level of recognition beyond the usual intimacy and intersubjectivity among Red Shirts. Protest events gave aspiring professional Red Shirt musicians a chance to play on an elevated platform in front of large, attentive crowds, to sell albums, and perhaps even to jumpstart a career beyond the spaces of dissent. The movement gave rise to a (temporarily) stable musical economy that could generate income and express discontent at once. This economy in turn depended on celebrity musicians, including their live performances and their active fan networks, which were maintained online and through radio and television. Disconnected from corporate infrastructures of recording and distribution, which denied them a platform on political grounds, a handful of Red Shirt musicians became the stars of a new network of fans and performers based almost entirely on shared political sentiment. The faces and sounds of these musicians became recognizable to hundreds of thousands of people around the country, and their art was decently compensated. The scope of their recognition raises important questions about the communicative structure of Red Shirt protests, and about the relationship between that structure and capitalism. The Red Shirt musical economy was key to the movement's existence, and thus to its mobility as well.

This chapter examines the intersection of entrepreneurialism, celebrity, and political protest within the Red Shirt movement through the burgeoning careers of two stage musicians, *luk thung* pop singer Pae Bangsanan and "songs for life" singer-songwriter Om Khaphatsadi.[1] Although these two performers played for crowds

---

1. These case studies are far from exhaustive. For a more complete list of Red Shirt musicians, including those who might qualify as professionals, see Mitchell, "Red and Yellow Songs."

in a manner similar to that of less famous musicians like Mii (see Chapter 13) and Pom (see Chapter 7), the fact of their stardom demands a distinct accounting. The difference here is primarily one of degree. Small protest concerts could help amateur musicians earn a better wage in difficult economic times. But top Red Shirt performers on the main stage, en route to possible long-term careers, reorganized how other dissidents could relate to them as well as how the Red Shirt movement would be witnessed as a spectacle. The previous chapter describes the complexity and constraints that arise when rank-and-file members of political movements are driven to think in economic terms. A study of Red Shirt stage musicians will illustrate another dimension of this issue—stardom.

This analysis will, I hope and in part, show more clearly how entrepreneurialism was linked to dissent. In the Introduction, I noted that "contradictions around money" were among the major constraints that the Red Shirts faced in their pursuit of becoming a movement that moved things. These constraints mostly arose because of outside judgment, as I detail below, because witnesses to the movement considered profit inauthentic. The Red Shirts did not recognize their own income-generating enterprises as incompatible with dissent, but they were aware of the fact that others did. Stage musicians were therefore greeted warmly as exceptional economic beneficiaries, but their stardom was in certain respects muted. Professional Red Shirt musicians were unique figures within the movement. Even those protesters, such as vendors, who had an economic stake in the protests were generally content to make ends meet or to pay for non-luxury expenses like medical bills. Nevertheless, the opportunity for a sustained windfall came to a fortunate few, whose experiences reveal how the movement could, in some cases, catalyze full-time careers. The aim of this chapter is to show how Red Shirts incorporated stardom while managing the spectacular problem (one might say the poor optics) of the irony of celebrity dissidence.

THE STRUCTURE AND RESEMBLANCES OF RED SHIRT STAGE PERFORMANCE

Red Shirt musical economies depended on a resemblance between Red Shirt events and similar recent happenings in Thailand. This section provides some important details about these resemblances, before proceeding to the question of celebrity and its publics. By 2010, live stage concerts had for the past several years already been a fixture of large rallies across the political spectrum. These earlier concerts, and their modes of presentation, were honed long before the Red Shirts cohered as a mass movement. By the time of the anti-Abhisit protests and the Ratchaprasong encampments of spring 2010, Red Shirt protesters were accustomed to regular patterns of stage performance. Rally organizers, having had several years to practice, could quickly and expertly put on large concerts in the style of rural variety shows. Much of what made long stage shows tolerable for crowds was a rapid-fire mixture of comedy, music, and political speech, including overlapping segments of each. During these stage shows, political oration and entertainment were not especially distinct. For example, Jatuporn Promphan and Adisorn Piangket, both high-ranking members of the UDD, each routinely broke into song at emotional moments during their own speeches. Such moments underscored the proximity between music and political oration, even their mutual dependence. Musicality and political leadership were closely connected. Comedic bits were also scheduled between speeches and music, in a fashion borrowed directly from stage shows in genres like *phleeng khûu* and *mor lam sing*. The UDD stage presentations thus often felt like politicized stage revues. Performance modes flowed into each other, just as the roles of musician, organizer, and political orator often bled together. Many high-ranking UDD officials in fact had prior or ongoing careers as entertainers, including 1990s boy band singer Arisman Pongruangrong, *luk thung* crooner Wanchana Koetdi, and comedian Yossawarit Chuklom. There was a thin line, always, between dissent and entertainment. Red Shirt performance was marked by this performative fluidity.

Prefiguring the semi-permanent stages of 2010, the UDD held a number of daylong events at Sanam Luang and Ratchamankala Stadium in 2008–9, often in front of audiences of tens of thousands. These shows turned out to be test-runs for the relatively sophisticated audio and video displays that would be installed in the encampments two years later. Mixing boards and speakers were loaned by temples or procured through networks of contacts. Temples use sound equipment to broadcast monastic chanting from within the *cheedii*, to host evening concerts (often *mor lam*), to amplify music during merit-making ceremonies, or to place atop sound trucks that drive around town advertising upcoming religious ceremonies.[2] Politically supportive temples often loaned such equipment for large rallies. Over time, the UDD also purchased its own broadcast equipment using money donated by members. Amplifiers and subwoofers stamped with the Thai letters *nor por chor* (UDD) were a common sight. Meanwhile, any protest volunteer who happened to work in a job relevant to performance or broadcasting, such as installing car audio equipment or setting up promotional concerts in malls, could pitch in by loaning gear or volunteering to assist with setup. This might include lending line-array speaker columns, amplifiers, rigging, or even industrial cranes for lifting heavy equipment into place.

Red Shirt organizers also drew from the organizational approaches of their political rivals the Yellow Shirts, who were especially active between 2006 and 2008.

2. Miller makes reference in *Traditional Music of the Lao* to the use of sound trucks to advertise *mor lam* performances as early as 1946, noting that before one performance in Bangkok, "Migrant Northeasterners, upon hearing [the music from the sound trucks], followed the trucks to the stadium where nearly three thousand people heard the performance." (40). Mobile sound trucks remain an important means of advertisement for concerts and festivals in the twenty-first century, and continue to play a major role in political campaigns.

Their most effective event was called (oddly, and not so substantively) "Operation Hiroshima," a two-week occupation of Bangkok's Suvarnabhumi Airport that stalled nearly all commercial air traffic in and out of Thailand's capital. The Red Shirts modeled their own protests after those held by the Yellow Shirts, and not only by strategically occupying spaces vital to the national economy.[3] For example, the Red Shirts hung large banners across their stages with English slogans like "peaceful protesters not terrorists," mirroring the PAD's own awkwardly translated signs, such as "Neo-Protest: Non-violence, Integrity, Purity, Profundity, Straightness." And during Red Shirt concerts, protesters could sound their approval by waving red, foot-shaped plastic clappers, much as the PAD had used yellow, hand-shaped clappers. Whereas the PAD's hand-shaped clappers were not especially symbolic—in fact, they were said to be surplus stock from the 2008 Olympics in Beijing, purchased merely because they were cheap, yellow, and loud—the UDD's foot-shaped clappers were deliberately chosen to represent the group's low status in Thai society. Feet are considered dirty and even taboo in Thailand. By wielding foot-shaped objects the Red Shirts implied that they were stuck at the bottom of a constraining social hierarchy. Despite the symbolic difference, the use of clappers was otherwise identical. In many ways, the Red Shirt rallies resembled the earlier Yellow Shirt protests.

James Mitchell has catalogued and explained some generic differences between Red and Yellow Shirt music.[4] Mitchell notes that while the Yellow Shirts enjoyed the direct support of pop and "songs for life" artists who were signed to major record labels, the Red Shirts benefitted from their constituents' passion for *mor lam* and *luk thung*. Mitchell argues that these latter genres are historically steeped in political critique.[5] *Mor lam* and *luk thung* thus symbolized the strong political sentiment of the Red Shirt movement, as opposed to its links with capitalism or nationalist power. The Yellow Shirts, in deliberate contrast, relied less on the symbolic utility of music, as described in the previous chapter. Mitchell suggests that both factions were reasonably diverse in their musical tastes, but that certain stylistic preferences emerged anyway, including the Yellow Shirts' emphasis on genres linked with "ancient" Thai culture such as the courting style *lamtat*, and the Red Shirts' interest in Cambodian-influenced regional forms like *kantrum*. In this regard, Yellow Shirt music could index ethnonationalism and political power, as opposed to the Red Shirts' efforts to signal authenticity and political marginality.

But even these distinctions become muddled to some extent when considering musicians who performed on smaller stages or at the level of the street, and who typified the Red Shirts' aesthetic transformations after the Ratchaprasong crackdown. For instance, as Red Shirt rallies increasingly centered around Democracy Monument rather than Ratchaprasong in 2011, "songs for life" musicians were in ever greater demand, perhaps as a result of nostalgia for the kind of music heard at

3. Mitchell, "Red and Yellow Songs."
4. Ibid.
5. Ibid.

protest events held in the very same place in 1992 and 1976. A different symbolic register was evoked. Thus even "songs for life," the closest thing to a signature genre for the Yellow Shirts, was at certain points quite popular among the Red Shirts. While Red and Yellow music were far from identical, the performative habits of the two movements often overlapped. And the Red Shirt stage shows were indebted to recent histories of protest performance that crossed partisan divides. Red Shirt stage music was nested within these histories, even nurtured by them.

PAE

Red Shirt stage music was part of a well-developed informal economy as early as spring 2010. By this time, singers like Pae Bangsanan had become de facto celebrities. Pae became perhaps the most popular and financially successful Red Shirt musician, with the possible exception of some of the leaders. His musical career had been fledgling for some time beforehand. He began recording semi-professionally in 2003, after quitting the army, where he had advanced to the rank of sergeant as a bureaucrat in the Ministry of Defense. Thirty-five years old at the time, Pae left his position in order to record an album with a friend who was a professional producer. For several years, Pae busked under the Skytrain. His music was not yet politically oriented. It was only around the time of the coup against Thaksin and the emergence of the PAD in the mid-2000s that Pae (like many Thai people) first grew interested in questions of governance and citizenship, rather than feeling alienated by them. Unlike a significant number of Red Shirts, however, Pae was at no prior point a member of the PAD. As his belief in the Red Shirt movement grew stronger, he explained, he began to recognize himself as having a duty, in accordance with his musical skill, to compose and perform political songs. Specifically, he began to address the accusations and doubts of anti-Red Shirt observers in his lyrics. This impulse led him to write a number of pieces, including *rákkhonsûadɛɛng* ("Love the Red Shirts"), a song that he told me he wrote to summarize the essence of Red Shirt political identity. The piece explicitly rejected the notion that the group was terroristic or even socially divisive. "Love the Red Shirts" (discussed at length below) soon became wildly popular, and was played at rallies perhaps more often than any other song in the movement's canon. As a stage performer, Pae's lean build and boyish face, along with his signature red bandana, sunglasses, and wristband, helped make him a fan favorite. His personal history as a lower-middle class laborer estranged from state institutions like the military also made him a symbolically resonant figure. These factors facilitated his stardom.

As Pae became a celebrity, he began performing above the crowd. The position of the main stage contributed to a performer-audience relationship that was quite different from the kind found at the level of the street. At the massive outdoor rallies of late 2010 and 2011, which overwhelmed major intersections, the main stage was given overtly as the central attraction. It was high, loud, and stood in the middle of everything. At Democracy Monument, this stage was invariably set up at the base of the monument, which made for a dramatic and highly symbolic backdrop. In Ratchaprasong, the stage was usually in the middle of the intersection, at the head of the largest open space in which crowds could gather. Above, billboards for Toyota and Prada lent a powerful if somewhat ironic grandeur. The fact that this same space was usually the junction of multilane vehicle traffic also made the stage more imposing. It stood in a place that demanded attention. The stage was central, in fact, to multiple publics at once, to those standing nearby as well as to the media forms bearing witness. The eye and ear of the video camera were drawn to the spectacle of a platform that sought to speak for an entire movement far more readily than they were drawn to the heterogeneous niches sounding down below. Pae sang on the higher platform.

The arrival of higher stages at Red Shirt protests resembled similar recent transformations. Miller describes the mid-to-late twentieth century as a period when stage performance transformed genres like *mor lam*. Stages began to rise, which altered how musicians and audiences related to one another. New media technologies were introduced to bridge the spatial and social gap that taller stages produced. As Miller writes in reference to the 1970s:

> During the past ten to fifteen years two significant changes have occurred. First, mawlum glawn began performing on small wooden stages erected for the occasion probably in response to mawlum moo's practice. Though these platforms raised the singers above the audience making them easier to see, they also eliminated the close rapport between audience and singer. The inability to hear from a distance was corrected by the second change, the advent of electrical generators to run both amplifiers and lights. Lacking training in vocal techniques, few mawlum know how to project their voices properly, and many cannot be heard at all in the open air. Since competing forms of entertainment at fairs and tumboon also have amplifiers, such equipment has become necessary for survival.[6]

At Red Shirt rallies, the main stage was of course not the only source of entertainment or communication (indeed, small and heterogeneous sonic niches were crucial). Nor was the main stage heard in the same way by all protesters. In a telling example, once at Ratchaprasong I was straining to hear an orator whose words were distorted through a nearby loudspeaker. I asked a man and woman who were clapping and cheering excitedly if they could summarize what the speaker was saying. They admitted that they could not hear, either; they were responding only to the energy of the performance. Thus, while it may be tempting to interpret the content of the main stage, on which Pae sang, as the broadest and therefore most representative source of ideas and discourses within the movement, its content was not

6. Miller, *Traditional Music of the Lao.*

always clear. Nevertheless, the main stage required many things of performers that the street did not. Conventional markers of stardom, including good looks, youth, and charisma, were tacitly mandatory, except for performers who foregrounded amateurism, or wounds incurred during acts of protest. In either case, main stage performers had to be visually striking. Pae looked the part of a star singer, and his skills onstage were polished. He was booked for performances not only by the UDD but by Pheu Thai, the national political party linked with the Red Shirts, and one of the two largest parties in the country.

After singing during the Ratchaprasong occupation in 2010 and at events later in the year, Pae became famous enough to play stand-alone concerts. One of these, held on April 12, 2011 in Chiang Mai, charged an admission price of 100 baht (a little over $3), the typical cover for live concerts given by Thailand's biggest *luk thung* and *mor lam* stars. Though the event was billed as a benefit event for "healing the Red Shirt family," the high price of admission reflected Pae's outstanding drawing power (see Figure 11.1). His albums were sold in professional packaging, with CDs and VCDs mastered and reproduced in bulk quantities rather than in small runs of recordable discs copied on a home computer, as the majority of vendors did (see Chapter 10). The vending tables that sold his music, in contrast to most vendors' more diverse selection of merchandise, often featured *only* Pae's albums (see Figure 11.2). Sturdy, full-color posters advertised the price of his CDs—100 baht, about

Figure 11.1 A concert flyer for Pae Bangsanan, organized by a Chiang Mai-based Red Shirt pirate radio station. The text reads, in part, "For the healing of the Red Shirt family." Photograph by the author.

Figure 11.2 A vendor manages a CD table selling recordings by Pae Bangsanan, who is pictured on the large poster behind her. Single-artist tables were very rare at Red Shirt protests, and the degree of professional production reflected in the poster design, album art, and audio mastering of the recording is unusually high. Photograph by the author.

as much as a Red Shirt merchant could charge for any good or service, and two or three times the average price for a CD.

Pae's celebrity owed a great deal to the aforementioned hit single, "Love the Red Shirts." This recording played from cars, trucks, buses, trains, personal stereos, and the mouths of children and adults at nearly every Red Shirt gathering from 2009 onward. Reviewing sound recordings that I made at various Red Shirt rallies, the song can be heard in a striking number of them, if not at the center of my recording then playing somewhere distantly or being hummed idly nearby. "Love the Red Shirts" was exceptionally popular and replayed exceptionally often. The album version is four-and-a-half minutes long, and features a heavy guitar riff, as well as a chorus consisting entirely of a melodic repetition of the word *dɛɛng* (red). The recording opens with a clean electric guitar playing a punchy, eight-bar introduction, and floor toms hitting in sync with each guitar chord while an arpeggiated keyboard line plays underneath. The guitar then moves to a soaring chorus as cowbells enter on the off beats. Pae then sings the hook, which is a full eight bars of the word *dɛɛng* and *rák khon sʉ̂a dɛɛng* ("love the red shirts").

"Love the Red Shirts" does not fit neatly into any particular contemporary Thai genre, nor is it typical within the Red Shirt musical canon. The song falls generically between modern *luk thung* and international rock, with a tempo faster than most *luk thung* ballads, which themselves bear only a passing resemblance to the more somber, classic form of *luk thung*. The lone signifier of Thai musical aesthetics in

"Love the Red Shirts," aside from being sung in Thai, is the playing of cowbells on the twos and fours, a percussive flourish heard in all but the most overtly Korean- or American-inspired pop music. Pae told me that, overall, he intended the song to sound "contemporary, not rustic."[7] Pae clearly hit a commercial sweet spot with his production and songwriting decisions. The lyrics to "Love the Red Shirts" summarize a common attitude of defiance among rural Thais: "We won't wait because we are people khráp, not buffalo / We don't need anyone to think for us, we can think for ourselves." The term "buffalo" is an extreme insult, often leveled at people from agrarian areas where water buffalo are used as beasts of burden. The slur implies ignorance, gullibility, and a lack of worldly knowledge. During the Red Shirt protests, critics used it as a shorthand for political naiveté. But protesters also coopted it in self-reference.

"Love the Red Shirts" is frank in its demands for political change. But Pae's stage manner was non-confrontational, a mode of engagement greatly valorized in Thai political life.[8] Not only does he use the word khráp within the song, a gesture that in this case conveys politeness, but he also phrases other demands tactfully. For instance, after posing the question "where is the justice?" in one lyric, he then asks khǒo nɔ́ɔy dây máy, roughly equivalent to "may we have some, please?" Pae carefully situated his performing identity between uncompromising insistence and civility. In the Thai public sphere, displaying such civility is a condition of possibility for political action, a constraint. Sutharin Koonphol notes that "displaying civility has always been at the heart of the modernizing process of the Thai authorities.... The Thai conceptualization of the public realm is therefore controlled by order; however, it is not so much a disciplinarian order in the modern European sense, but a duly aestheticized one."[9] The success of "Love the Red Shirts" as a political/aesthetic intervention, and of Pae as an artist, was predicated upon achieving the right balance of insistence and civility.

Finally, like most Thai musicians who become superstars, Pae is a singer primarily. Instrumental skill, especially on stage, is a less likely avenue to superstardom than vocal skill. In fact, few luk thung musicians are widely recognized for anything but their singing, mirroring genres like US country music. In front of Red Shirt crowds, Pae bowed diligently and exuded strength without aggression. His success as a dissident musician was premised, above all, on his resolute performance of civility while making political claims. Even as he became famous, even as his platform rose, he was compelled to demonstrate this civility.

7. Pae Bangsanan, interview with the author, August 2012. Translated from the original Thai.
8. Savitri Gadavanij, "Discursive Strategies for Political Survival: A Critical Discourse Analysis of Thai No Confidence Debates," (PhD diss., University of Leeds, 2002).
9. Sutharin Koonphol, "Concept and Practice of 'Public Space' in the City of Bangkok, Thailand: A Case Study based on Sanam Luang," (PhD diss., University of London, 2001), 294.

Though Pae was humble about his success, he was inarguably famous among the Red Shirts. Fans organized multiple online pages dedicated to his music, and most Red Shirt protesters knew him well, even if they did not regularly come to rallies. As a star whose presence at events could generate large donations, he was hired to perform and appear often, and was thereby deeply immersed in a system of financial exchange that operated like a parallel record industry. But the matter of money was delicate. Ethnographies of commercial music are notoriously difficult because of the strategic self-representations of performers, as David Pruett notes in a study of mainstream country musicians in the United States.[10] According to Pruett, the "complex web of interpersonal relationships" in which the careers of artists performing for large audiences are enmeshed means that these artists are especially circumspect when speaking to members of the media. Ethnographers and journalists probing commercial music industries must therefore be cautious in citing claims made by artists who have enormous financial stakes in their own public representation. For Red Shirt stage performers like Pae, questions about money required caution and even a degree of evasion. Artists who generated robust album sales were careful to avoid being seen as superstars, lest it compromise their reputations as activists.

The case of popular Red Shirt singer and political leader Wanchana Koetdi is instructive here. Wanchana's recordings were on many vending tables at rallies in 2010 and 2011, including the one purchased in the anecdote near the end of Chapter 10. Wanchana sang about politically safe topics, such as the mutual love and support shared by protesters at Ratchaprasong, or the ways that Thaksin compared favorably to Abhisit.[11] He likewise took few risks in production, showcasing his soft tenor high in the mix with *luk thung* ballad arrangements marked by a combination of electric guitar and classic Thai court ensemble instruments like the *ránâat* (a large wooden idiophone that plays three octaves of a seven-note scale). These musical choices matched the mildness of Wanchana's politics. Nevertheless, Wanchana was pursued in 2012 by Thailand's Department of Special Investigations (DSI) on suspicion of channeling money from the sale of musical cassette tapes into an account that funded parts of the spring 2010 protests. Among the purchases that the DSI claimed Wanchana made with money from his tape sales was an SUV driven by the UDD's leaders. Although the government was overtly prosecuting its own critics (it was never made clear which law Wanchana was supposed to have broken),

10. David Pruett, "When the Tribe Goes Triple Platinum: A Case Study Toward an Ethnomusicology of Mainstream Popular Music in the U.S.," *Ethnomusicology* 55, no. 1 (February 2011): 1–30.
11. One example is the single, "Please Return from Deceit," in which Wanchana expresses shock that anyone could call Thaksin deceitful when Thaksin, according to the singer, helped the poor, built an airport, repaid the IMF, and filled the national treasury. The piece is an ode, and comes across as a love song rather than political invective.

conservative-leaning media outlets had a field day with the story.[12] For critics of the Red Shirts, the specter of musicians who made passionate claims to political belief having links to hidden caches of money served as evidence of rampant insincerity. In addition to the risk of being sent to prison because of his financial participation in the protests, Wanchana's reputation was thus compromised by the revelations. The comingling of money and dissent could taint artists.

Perhaps partly for this reason, album sale details for Red Shirt musicians were very difficult to find. Pae and his peers had no affiliation with major record labels, and official sales figures were never released. Thailand's largest major record label is GMM Grammy, which dominates the market for mainstream *luk thung*, rock, and pop. A number of international labels also maintain subsidiaries in the country, and breakout stars like Tata Young, who are actively marketed outside the country, may sign with international companies like Sony. With the exception of a few moderate-sized "indie" and classic *luk thung* reissue labels, there is a wide gap between the majors and the vendors who sell unsanctioned CD copies in public outdoor markets and shopping malls. Pae claimed to have sold about 5,000 copies of his albums at rallies as of 2012, 60 percent of which were on CD compared to 40 percent on karaoke VCD.[13] But Pae had every incentive to avoid the appearance of bragging about his earnings. Although he acknowledged that he earned an adequate income as a musician, he routinely minimized the importance of money. Was he concealing something perverse, or gesturing toward an alternative notion of value? Or was he simply being careful to manage a loaded topic?

Pae routinely deflected questions about sales by drawing attention to the number of albums he had given away for free. He implied that he performed and recorded mainly to communicate political messages, not for personal gain. And he resisted the designation of "professional." Although he was a professional in the strictest sense of the term, he instead invoked duty whenever the word came up, as a substitute. When I asked directly whether he considered himself *muu aachiip* (professional), he replied bluntly: "Not at all. I'm just a person who likes to sing, and who sees it as my duty. . . . [Singing] gives me enough, but that's not where my heart is. It is my duty to make my brothers and sisters happy."[14] He stressed that the content of his music was a defense against the Yellow Shirt charge that the hidden goal of the Red Shirts was to sell the country to the highest international bidder, depriving Thailand of its autonomy. In Pae's words, his own songs were "a countermove against the accusations of the PAD leaders who try to stress that we

---

12. "วันชนะ เกิดดี อ้างใช้เงินจากขายเทปการชุมนุมถอยฟอร์จูนเนอร์ มีเงินเข้า-ออก10รายการช่วงม็อบแดงเคลือน," ("Wanchana Koetdi is Claimed to Use Money from the Sale of Protest Tapes for a Toyota Fortuner"), *Matichon*, July 13, 2010.

13. Pae Bangsanan, interview with the author, August 2012. This number refers only to the number of sanctioned albums Pae sold and received money from personally; the number of burned copies of his CDs sold at rallies by enterprising vendors was undoubtedly far greater.

14. Ibid.

are terrorists selling the country."[15] Claims of "selling the country" are common in Thai political mudslinging, and relate to a fear of the loss of territory that is far older even than the nation itself, dating back centuries in Southeast Asia. Such fear is routinely stoked by contemporary Thai politicians during moments of crisis to stir up reactionary political sentiments. This may result in, for example, deadly border skirmishes with the Cambodian military or threats against international bodies like UNESCO.[16] Prime minister Thaksin in particular was widely criticized (and even sued) for selling a majority of his telecom, Shin Corp., to a Singaporean concern in 2006, and the Red Shirt movement inherited much of the suspicion that arose from that sale.[17] Pae was keenly aware of this perception.

Pae's efforts to keep money at arm's length spoke to the dual status of entrepreneurial economies within the Red Shirt movement. The organization of dissident relations through commerce was on one hand vital to the Red Shirts' sustainability as a movement, and even created a laboratory for their experiments in political reform. The entire Ratchaprasong encampment was, arguably, an experiment of just this kind. The Red Shirts were not anti-capitalist, and their informal economies were a source of excitement as well as a site of utopian possibility. On the other hand, money was volatile because an excess of it could be read as bankrupting the authenticity of motivation. Financial relations, as exemplified by Wanchana's case, were grounds for public critique as well as legal sanction. Money was important, but showcasing it invited risk. Money and its appearance were constraints that had to be carefully managed. Profit could not be too visible or audible.

ECONOMIES AS SUPPORT SYSTEMS

Judith Butler writes about the complicated status of support systems in political movements. She offers that "the organic bodies that we are require a sustaining social world in order to persist"—while emphasizing the capacity of co-present bodies and their expressions to constitute space as such.[18] "As much as we must insist on there being material conditions for public assembly and public speech," she writes, "we have also to ask how it is that assembly and speech reconfigure the materiality of public space, and produce, or reproduce, the public character of that material environment."[19] Her first principal point is that the labor of the most basic

15. Ibid.

16. Daniel Schearf, "Thai Yellow Shirts Protest Against Leaders, UNESCO Temple Listing," *Voice of America*, June 16, 2011.

17. Wayne Arnold, "Court Will Hear Challenge to Thaksin's Telecom Sale," *New York Times*, October 5, 2006.

18. Judith Butler. "Bodies in Alliance and the Politics of the Street," *European Institute for Progressive Cultural Policies* (September, 2011), http://eipcp.net/transversal/1011/butler/en. This lecture was later adapted in her monograph, *Notes Toward a Performative Theory of Assembly.*

19. Ibid.

political change does not arise from the individual will, but from the character of relations among social beings. The second is that public space is not determined by architectural form, but by the reproduction of the relations mentioned above. This point recalls Louis Althusser's maxim that "the ultimate condition of production is therefore the reproduction of the conditions of production."[20] It also accords with scholars like Henri Lefebvre, who have stressed the contingency of space, including public space.[21] It follows from this that in order for a movement to sustain itself, to *move*, it must continually legitimize its right to be present in public spaces. This requires adequate supportive action, from being fed and clothed to enjoying protection from violence. If protesters cannot be physically sustained, then they enjoy no legitimacy, and the spaces where they gather will be precarious.

Butler therefore interprets movements throughout the Arab Spring (in Tunisia, Libya, Egypt, and Bahrain) as efforts to produce oppositional societies in miniature, as living rehearsals for how a better kind of public might be produced and sustained. The Red Shirt movement strove to become an oppositional society of this kind. Its mundane, sustaining institutions included volunteer-staffed laundry, toilets, and networks of donations for the needy or injured. The entire Red Shirt informal music industry was also, in a sense, a sustaining institution. Butler's remarks encourage a consideration of live stage performance as an apt form of mutually sustaining co-presence. Performance is rich with the production of gestural symbols that emerge from a position of physical vulnerability. Though all of the Red Shirts exposed themselves to the risk of state violence and legal sanction by dissenting in public, in the context of music and musical reception the bodies of participants served as public referents in a play of relations set in opposition to the order of the state. Pae's performances modeled relationality, as he sang and worked the crowd in what appeared to be a dialogue among dissidents. When audience members bestowed flowers and adulatory handshakes on him from the foot of the stage, as they often did, Pae would acknowledge them in return collectively as "Red Shirt brothers and sisters," the same form of address Somsak Sangkaparicha had used through his megaphone (see Chapter 6).[22] Performance seemed to be an act of collaborative labor between singers and listeners, with the ultimate beneficiary being the legitimacy and sustainability of the movement. Visible, audible bodies at protests, Butler argues, pose a "challenge (to the legitimacy of the state) in corporeal terms."[23]

At protest events in the current historical moment, Butler further suggests, human beings must appear and be vulnerable in the flesh in order to initiate direct

20. Louis Althusser, "Ideology and Ideological State Apparatuses," in *Lenin and Philosophy and Other Essays* (New York: Monthly Review Press, 2001), 85.
21. Henri Lefebvre, *The Production of Space* (Hoboken, NJ: Wiley-Blackwell, 1992).
22. Musicians in Thailand commonly address their audiences as "brothers and sisters." At Red Shirt events, this address was almost always extended to become "Red Shirt brothers and sisters."
23. Butler, "Bodies in Alliance."

political action.[24] This necessity invested Pae's stage persona with high stakes indeed, and largely explains why his live performance of civility mattered so much. He embodied political depth, but he also demonstrated how to behave without provoking a backlash. As Butler writes, "it is not that bodily action and gesture have to be translated into language, but that both action and gesture signify and speak, as action and claim, and that the one is not finally extricable from the other."[25] Musicians like Pae made claims by their presence, which modeled how participants could be at once visible as dissidents and yet at least somewhat physically safe. Stage music thus gave the Red Shirt movement vital sustenance.

However, the example of Pae's celebrity raises two important critiques of Butler's argument. The first is that the "corporeal challenge" posed by protesters, although spectacular, does not in itself constitute a public sphere. The corporeal presencing of bodies cannot ensure reciprocal communication. Musical celebrities on the main stage helped make the Red Shirt movement visible, but did not necessarily make it *audible*, either to outside witnesses or even to audiences within the movement. (Recall the two listeners who clapped supportively despite not understanding the orator's words.) Rosalind Morris describes this condition as "a displacement of the political value of 'having a voice' by that of 'being seen to speak.'"[26] Morris argues that this rending of visibility from audibility is a salient characteristic of protest in the contemporary medial moment. Dissidents act in order to be *seen speaking*, ideally in a manner that suggests massive proportions of support (such as Occupy Wall Street's claim to represent "the 99 percent"), but they do not or cannot hope to be heard. The split between audibility and visibility forecloses reciprocal *communication*, instead allowing only *connection*. Celebrity musicians such as Pae exemplify the creep toward specularity that ensues. While it is true, in Butler's framework, that the presencing of bodies is productive of dissident space, transforming that space into an intersubjective public sphere is a much more difficult challenge, especially within the constraints of global capital and its media. This is a problem that vexed the Red Shirts, Occupy Wall Street, and the Arab Spring, in each of their respective moments. These movements immediately became highly visible, but were blocked in multiple ways from audibly communicating their concerns. Morris's important critique is one that recent literature on media and dissent has mostly bypassed, in favor of a thinner debate about whether social media technologies are by their nature empowering or debilitating.[27]

This connects to a second critique of Butler's argument; namely, that Butler does not account for the primacy of economies as support systems. The "sustaining social world" of the Red Shirts necessarily included financial support. When examining

24. On this point, see also Chapter 2.
25. Butler, "Bodies in Alliance."
26. Rosalind Morris, "Theses on the New Öffentlichkeit," *Grey Room* 51, (Spring 2013), 98.
27. Zeynep Tufekci, *Twitter and Tear Gas: The Power and Fragility of Networked Protest* (New Haven: Yale University Press, 2017).

the economies of movements, public assembly is revealed to be nested within the very structures that limit its audibility. Butler identifies food, shelter, care, and protection from harm as nonnegotiable dimensions of a livable life, but does not deal at length with the vicissitudes of finance, income, or employment. The issue has certainly been debated in protest movements before. Bradford D. Martin, writing on political performance groups like the Living Theatre in the 1960s United States, observes that:

> The Paradise Now production notes explained (the phrase) 'You can't live if you don't have money,' by arguing that 'there is no way to sustain yourself on this planet without involvement in the monetary system.' 'The Rite of Guerrilla Theatre' criticizes this state of affairs; taken further, however, the critique implied by 'You can't live if you don't have money' was that it was morally and ethically inconsistent to make theater calling for social transformation in traditional venues with their high ticket prices.[28]

The Red Shirt movement took no such position. Its ambivalence toward anticapitalist critique set it apart from anti-austerity protests in Europe and Latin America as well as Occupy Wall Street. However, even Occupy Wall Street, with its core principle of opposition to an exploitative financial system, imagined thoughtful alternative banking methods; Occupy Wall Street's aim was not necessarily to opt out of financial relations, but to render them ethical. Although the majority of the Red Shirts, like the Arab Spring protesters on whom Butler's discussion centers, were chiefly opposed to repressive state regimes rather than global capitalism, they shared with Occupy Wall Street the mission of fostering ethical financial relations. At no point and in no subsection of the Red Shirt movement was an escape from capital proposed, even in utopian terms. To the contrary, economies such as those that fostered Red Shirt music were cast as utopian sites.

With the Red Shirts, then, the relational spaces of dissent that generated merit and modeled relationality in opposition to the state could not be disentangled from economies of productive, capitalist exchange. Pae was an economic asset, the function of which was to fund and make a spectacle of the Red Shirt movement. The participation of listeners in this economy as consumers became ethical to the extent that it helped to benefit not only an individual (Pae), but also the movement as such. After all, only an economically sustainable system could remain in place long enough to challenge the holders of power. But, ethical though this system may have been, it could not easily challenge the structures of power, a constraint about which Morris duly warns.

---

28. Bradford D. Martin, *The Theater is in The Street: Politics and Public Performance in Sixties America* (Amherst and Boston: University of Massachusetts Press, 2004), 11.

I was fortunate, on February 13, 2011, to get a photograph of the singer Om Khaphatsadi in which she was in the frame at all. By 5:00 p.m., the stage on the western end of Democracy Monument was the center of attention for a mob of listeners stretching toward the Pinklao bridge. I stood far back. Om, strumming her guitar, was a distant speck. I stood to the far left of the stage; rows of steel rigging and members of the sound crew blocked my sightline, forcing me onto tiptoes. The music was a warm-up for the speeches that would be delivered after sunset. At the climax of the protest, around 8:00 p.m., Thaksin Shinawatra would connect to the rally by videoconference to give a twenty-minute talk from one of his many residences abroad—London, Montenegro, or Dubai. Straddling the stage on either side were large white projection screens that, once darkness fell, would simulcast the performances for the benefit of those in the back. By late afternoon, the audience was already overflowing.

The musical portion of the program included multiple acts. After three songs by the "songs for life" singer Motkhanfai (Red Ant), Om, wearing moccasins, black T-shirt, jeans, and sunglasses, took the microphone. Her style of dress clearly situated her near "songs for life" and the aesthetics of Aed Carabao. Om's drummer counted off, and launched into a fast *kantrʉm* rock beat to which the audience immediately began clapping. *kantrʉm* is stylistically similar to *mor lam sing*, with its frenetic pace and extended minor pentatonic jamming, but uses a different array of instruments (including the oboe-like *pìi ɔ̀ɔ*, the stringed *sɔɔ*, *chàp* cymbals, and a pair of wooden clappers called *kràp*), with the *pìi ɔ̀ɔ* featured as the main reed accompaniment rather than the *khɛɛn*.[29] This instrumental arrangement owes to the genre's roots in Cambodia and the Thai provinces on the Cambodian border. In its contemporary, popular incarnation, however, *kantrʉm* relies mostly on electric keyboards for the melody and a full kit of rock drums (rather than a pair of calf- or goatskin *thoon*) for percussion; traditional instruments are typically quoted rather than acting as central parts of the arrangement.

The bass was mixed too high in the speakers on my side, while the lead guitar was panned the other way, and therefore audible only fleetingly between drum beats. Where I stood, the mix was badly out of balance; such are the perils of standing far away at an outdoor arena show. Democracy Monument is, furthermore, surrounded by broad avenues radiating in six directions, producing long echoes and making it exceptionally unfriendly to mixing audio for large crowds. Om's set was brief, just three or four songs, but I was intrigued, and asked a vendor if any of her albums were for sale. The vendor pointed to two CDs on her own table that cost 60 baht ($2). The first was by Motkhanfai and the other by Om. Both were similarly

---

29. "กันตรึม จ.สุรินทร์" ("Kantreum in Surin Province"), October 7, 2009, http://surin108. com/web/blog/2009/10/07/กันตรึม/.

packaged, with a single piece of white paper folded over the CD inside and a stylishly photocopied image of the musician to the left of the track names, which were typed in black. The font and other design features were similar enough to make it clear that they were produced by the same person or company. On the back of each album was the logo of a record label called *phleengphrây* (songs of the feudal serfs), which showed the red silhouette of a musician holding a guitar with a naga snake for a head. Naga heads have been common ornaments atop *phin* since the twentieth century in *mor lam*, and now serve to signify rurality.[30] The combination of guitar and *phin* on the label's logo was likely intended to demonstrate a marriage between modern and classical aesthetics, loosely defined. Below the logo was a phone number and the words "contact to arrange performances." I wondered if I could reach the label to find out more about their operations? Having experienced Om's performance at such a distance, I felt alienated from its details, and wanted a closer hearing.

It was only on my way home, after the rally, that I noticed Om's album was titled *khûu hǔu phleeng phrây*, or "Intimate Songs of the Feudal Serfs." In addition to "intimate," *khûuhǔu* translates literally as "a pair of ears." In fact, the Thai word for "ears" is part of many idiomatic phrases, such as *tìt hǔu* (trendy, as a slang word might be; literally, "stuck in the ear") and *ɔɔn hǔu* (bored). Intimacy and aural communication merge in the term *khûuhǔu*. Listening is often the sensory figure of choice in representations of dialogic ideals, of the overcoming of divisions, as Dyson has argued.[31] The intimacy of a pair of ears implies immediacy. But I could not help noticing the contrast between this figure of intimate listening and my experience at the concert that afternoon; I heard Om perform from a great spatial and social distance. The height of the stage, the specter of celebrity, and the mass mediation of the live event left me in a position where sound could not overcome the communicative divide between me and the musician. If the ideal listening subject, as suggested by the title of the album, was a person who entered into the intimate, immediate space of the music, I felt instead as one typically does at big concerts—like a cog in a system that functioned at a scale beyond me, within a crowd I could only know as an imagined community, entitled to hearing and experiencing at great remove.

The phone number on the back of the album connected me to an office inside the Red Shirt headquarters at Big C Lad Phrao, among the many other Red Shirts business and volunteer organizations housed there. I spoke to a man who invited me to stop by at any point during normal daily business hours, and the next day I made the familiar subway trip to Lad Phrao, where the subway station exit leads out to a divided highway and a bus stop. A tattered blue bus merely slows rather than stopping to pick up passengers. The ride from the subway station to the mall may be fifteen minutes or an hour, depending on traffic. It passes what seems like an

---

30. Miller, "From Country Hick to Rural Hip."
31. Dyson, *Sounding New Media.*

endless stream of fruit and vegetable vendors along the sidewalk. People mill about, carrying parasols to protect them from the sun, selecting the ripest mangosteens and durian, all day. The scope and ubiquity of these small-scale vending areas throughout and beyond Bangkok is stunning. Seeing the markets from the window of a bus, as they stretch for miles through the city, comprising its veins and arteries, is a reminder of how thoroughly markets envelop public life.

The bus arrived at Big C, whose big-box exterior conceals the fact that the inside is ordered much like the vending areas on the street. Individual proprietors set up stands wherever there is room, not only in storefronts but throughout hallways and lobbies. I took the elevator to the fifth floor, where every available space is leased to Red Shirts. The large office where the record label *phleeng phrây* operated was a shared office space, and no one from the label was there that day. I spoke with a man and woman who explained that the office was primarily a publishing house, specializing in the widely-read Red Shirt magazine *mahaprachachon*. Unused rooms, however, were offered to any Red Shirt who needed them. *Phleeng phrây*, it turned out, was the label name for material that Om released on her own, including her solo albums and compilations with titles like "Humble Lives—Artists of the Street." As a record label, *phleeng phrây* was fledgling at best. Om and her boyfriend burned each CD by hand, and hired no employees. The image of her superstardom was spectral.

Because she was out of the office, I had to call Om's cellphone to arrange an interview. She invited me to a café near Democracy Monument the following week, after a concert she was giving in the morning. Our meeting point, the Sidewalk Café, had been a major gathering place for dissidents during the 1992 antigovernment protests. To this day, when Red Shirt protests occur near Democracy Monument, the crowd at the Sidewalk Café mimics the aesthetics of the 1992 movement. This includes a healthy dose of acoustic "songs for life" musical performances (given live in the rear corner of the restaurant). Performers wear cowboy hats, sunglasses, and long hair in the style of Aed Carabao. The clientele during these events tends to be older people who participated in the 1992 movement, and who now gravitate toward the restaurant as a matter of habit or symbolic association. Others, who instead understand its symbolism as anachronistic, avoid it.

Our interview was both the inverse and complement of the performance I attended a week earlier. Mirroring Pae's balance between celebrity and humility, Om had a different persona when appearing at a spectacular distance (onstage) than when she was in a space of reciprocal contact (at the interview). The distance one experiences hearing her perform from half a mile away is precisely what generates the desire to engage with her in an intimate setting such as a personal interview, or in the hand-to-hand exchange of a wreath of flowers. This is inherent to the performance of Thai celebrity. Even as it also resonates with the general necessity of mass media celebrities to be, in part, reflections of the aspirations (and expectant potentialities) of fans, the Thai culture industries have a relatively unique set of rules. These draw upon merit-making, in which monks, who are designated adherents of the strictest practices of the dharma, receive gifts and reverent bows from lay people. Lay people receive religious merit in turn. Celebrity in Thailand works similarly. Superstar musicians perform beautiful acts that ordinary people cannot perform on their own. For this, the stars are given gifts, the receipt of which they must publicly acknowledge. According to Mitchell, "In the *luuk tung* concert scene the fans who attend most regularly and who are well known for their gifts achieve special status and receive special privileges. In the midst of performing singers will sometimes point out these fans by name, especially if given *malai* (wreaths of flowers), thus elevating the symbolic capital of both fan and singer."[32] Given the public character of these exchanges, celebrities must be careful to make both their time and their presence available nearly on-demand to their most supportive fans. When I asked Om about her relationship with her fans, and why they like her music, she answered that "they like it because the mood is good, it's creative, suitable to the situation, and because I myself am like them, just an ordinary person. I'm not a superstar. They prefer that."[33] I sat with her and her boyfriend at a long wooden table in the mid-afternoon, amid empty beer steins and plates left over from an earlier party. Like Pae, Om would not acknowledge her stardom, nor confirm her income. She told me only that the vendors are the ones who make the real profit by copying and selling albums (tens of thousands per rally, she estimates). She and her boyfriend both dismissed insinuations that her music and their label had a financial dimension at all. She said that *phleeng phrây* was "not yet a real business."

Indeed, Om and her boyfriend were not wealthy. They worked together as freelance photocopiers by day. Om framed music not as a side job but as activism, an endeavor that might benefit the Red Shirt movement by providing entertainment and moral support. She described the social injustices that precipitated the movement, as well as the personal histories of living with poverty that led them to become artists in its name. At every turn, she disavowed celebrity. The manner in which Om can be called a celebrity in fact depended on this disavowal. If the appearance of being a normal person had to be carefully tended by Red Shirt stage musicians, these same musicians were also called upon to help drive an informal economy that not only offered them material benefits, but that sustained an informal industry of CD vending, concert production, and the like. Their relationship to finance could not be disarticulated from their participation, their performance, and even their art.

Ultimately, the intersection of protest, money, and celebrity does not imply corruption or inauthenticity, but rather the tendency of spectacular dissent, dependent on capital and its contemporary media, to create a public sphere without reciprocal communication. As has been described, Red Shirt musicians avoided discussion of money largely because of the humility that is a condition of possibility for participation in public life. Even the most politically dedicated performer cannot sustain

---

32. Mitchell, "Kon Baan Diaokan."
33. Om Khaphatsadi, interview with the author, June 2011.

their work if the appearance of wealth undermines perceptions of their character. But money nevertheless structured how Red Shirt performers were made visible and audible. Om was constrained by being an entrepreneur, by being on a high stage. She and her boyfriend were running a business, even if that business wasn't "real yet." Her stage performances were spectacular appearances above audiences and in front of media that could see her speaking more readily than they could hear her. This was a dissidence that, in Morris's terms, "had the power. . . to displace political regimes but not political structures."[34]

34. Morris, "Theses on the New *Öffentlichkeit*"

CHAPTER 12

Spontaneous Chants

I t begins under the breath, a voice latching to a pneumatic rhythm. It synchronizes
with the song, playing or imagined, that triggered it. It is soon enriched by more
voices, diffuse affirmations.

Spontaneous chants are stochastic. They cannot be predicted or located. By
the time a crowd of several hundred is chanting something illegal, even unspeakable, there are no longer wrists on which to slap handcuffs. And the state is not
shy. In 2011, a member of parliament was arrested for saying about the crackdown
at Ratchaprasong only this: "I know who ordered the killings." The MP did not
specify the "who," but the mere possibility that he meant the monarchy could not
be abided. Then in 2013, protest leader Yossawarit Chuklom was arrested for covering his mouth with his hands. "By making a gesture of being muzzled—placing
his hands over his mouth—Mr. Yossawarit had insinuated that he was talking about
the king, the court ruled."[1] The ruling prosecuted words not yet (and perhaps
never to have been) spoken. But spontaneous chants may evade even this paranoid
disciplining.

Spontaneous chants are tactical maneuvers, to be sure, born of opportunity
rather than planning. They may include any words, any sentiments. *Âyhîa sàng
khâa!* ("the fucking lizard ordered the killings") was the most outrageous, disruptive phrase one could conceivably utter. It bluntly invited charges of *lèse-
majesté*. Huge crowds in Ratchaprasong in the late, dark, heady evenings of rallies
shouted these words in unison, while much of the country listened in horror
on television or the internet. *Âyhîa sàng khâa! Âyhîa sàng khâa!* The police and
military stationed all around these crowds could only frown in shock and dis-
approval at the lawlessness that spread through the air like a mist. Spontaneous

---

1. Thomas Fuller, "In Thailand, a Broader Definition of Insulting Royalty," *New York Times,*
January 18, 2013.

chants were a horizontal cloud of political feeling, impossible to locate but plainly present.

At other times, the chants were musical, the outpouring of welled-up sentiment by two friends together at a rally that had not quite started. Chants did not always result in massive expressions of univocal dissent, and they were not always vitriolic. They could also be short experiments, joined or not.

CHAPTER 13

Developing Musical Economies III

Mr. Bear

While some musicians played from the heights of the main stage, many others staked out space below, at the level of the audience.[1] The demand for live music at ground level was strong enough that any musician with some skill in the genres favored by the Red Shirts could find plenty of financial and emotional support there. Moreover, barriers to performance were low, and instruments and power sources were cheap and portable (see Figure 13.1). Thus music that was played on the ground, where musician and audience stood on the same plane, performed the sort of access and equality that Red Shirts were simultaneously calling for at the scale of national politics. This drama was imbued with a moral energy that drew on indices of rural space. Even where blacktop stretched in all directions, and truck fumes choked the urban air, *mor lam* heard in a crowd could still evoke a purified rural ideal. This evocation was powerful, but it revealed fractured logics within the movement, especially when money and morality became entangled.

As described in Chapter 11, musical performance was heard skeptically by the Red Shirts' political opponents. Music invited discussions of authenticity, and an insincere-seeming musical performance could seem especially profane. Critics of the Red Shirts found, in the confluence of music and money, a smoking gun for the movement's fundamental insincerity. For these critics, the sounds of rural life figured not morality but a mixture of gullibility and greed.

Impugning protests by suggesting that they are covertly financed, and thus insincere, is an ancient charge, as well as a very modern one. The Tea Party, the Movement for Black Lives, and Occupy Wall Street in the United States have each

---

1. A different version of this chapter was published as "Neoliberalism's Moral Overtones: Music, Money, and Morality at Thailand's Red Shirt Protests," *Culture, Theory and Critique* 55, no. 2 (2014): pp. 257–71. Adapted for republication with permission of Taylor & Francis Group.

Figure 13.1 A small *mor lam* band with *khɛɛn* (left), miniature drum set, and *phin* (right) plays between parked cars on Wireless Road during a Red Shirt protest in Bangkok. Photograph by the author.

been accused of having secret patrons, just as political crowds often were in imperial Rome. These claims are sometimes accurate, sometimes not, but they have power regardless of their veracity. My intention in this chapter is not to prove whether such charges are true in the case of the Red Shirts, but to continue examining how money—invariably present in mass movements—is a force that shapes and constrains those movements. I do not seek evidence of sincerity, nor of its lack. Rather, this analysis steers away from the question of sincerity, which I take to be both moot and reductive. More complex logics are at work, as the ethnography in this chapter will suggest.

Claims of insincerity, in any case, mostly reveal things about their claimants. William Mazzarella has argued that liberal subjects of the West, in seeing images of North Koreans mourning the death of Kim Jong-Il, perceived both the effects of total hegemony (something akin to brainwashing) *and* the likelihood of a privately felt dissent.[2] Naïve sincerity and self-preservationist insincerity were somehow copresent in the Western witnessing of North Koreans' mass mourning. These incommensurable perceptions, and the very impossibility of resolving them, Mazzarella claims, might gesture to the post–Cold War Western subject's desire for a foil to his or her own imagined political subjectivity. The figure of the ideologically dominated (and yet enlightenable) North Korean offered just such a foil. Mazzarella's analysis

2. William Mazzarella, "Totalitarian Tears: Does the Crowd Really Mean It?," *Cultural Anthropology* 30(1) (February 2015): 91–112.

Figure 13.2 Mii giving a lesson near his home in Bangkok. Photograph by the author.

usefully focuses on those who judge sincerity, and why, rather than adjudicating sincerity itself.

This chapter similarly avoids adjudicating sincerity. Rather than psychoanalyzing the critics of the Red Shirts who made claims about insincerity, however, it asks how money and morality acted as agents in protest. How did the intersection of money and morality constrain both dissidence and sound? My inquiry is skeptical of both rural moral utopianism (which claimed total sincerity) *and* charges of gullibility and greed (which claimed total *in*sincerity). Music at Red Shirt protests did not enact a utopia, nor a space of any kind, beyond capital, as the preceding chapters have argued. Money drew musicians in, and compelled the movement to think entrepreneurially. But money was also multivalent, tangled up with other systems of valuation. "The concept of value spans the registers of that which is technical, economic, moral, and political."[3] In the intersection of money and morality at Red Shirt events, musicians were moved to act in ways that obviated the question of political sincerity altogether.

To examine how money and morality together constrained dissent, this chapter attends to a musician named Mii, who played the three-stringed Isan *phin* at Red Shirt events throughout 2010 and 2011, and who taught me the instrument for much of that period (see Figure 13.2). Mii is in his 40s, was born in the Northeastern city of Ubon Ratchathani, and today lives on the outskirts of Bangkok with his wife,

---

3. Horacio Ortiz, "Financial Value: Economic, Moral, Political, Global," *Hau: Journal of Ethnographic Theory* 3, no. 1 (2013): 65.

two young sons, and college-aged daughter. He co-owns a small farm with his sister in the city of Lopburi, central Thailand, where he retreats for short vacations from Bangkok. Mii and I became close friends and frequent collaborators, hanging out for informal jam sessions and lessons, playing at temple events, and busking in non-political contexts. The question of money, and the imperative to act as an entrepreneur—to pursue uncertain but potentially lucrative opportunities—arose routinely for Mii. *Mor lam*, the genre that Mii plays, has frequently been described as part of a moral system. A *mor lam* musician, historically, was "teacher, entertainer, moral force, and preserver of tradition," as well as a kind of town crier.[4] Linked as it is to village life, *mor lam* sounds out what Keyes calls the "moral basis" of Isan identity.[5] At Red Shirt protests, this moral system coexisted with entrepreneurialism, suggesting multiple simultaneous modalities of value in Mii's playing.

Wherever an audience would hear him, Mii said, he had a duty to play, and then to keep playing. Even when his fingers throbbed, his clothes dripped with sweat, and his head drooped with exhaustion, an artist was obligated to continue. Mii revered duty (*nâathîi*), a term that (much like Pae in Chapter 11) he used to explain his respective roles as student, teacher, Thai, Buddhist, musician, and human being. He named his sons Fender and Marshall, after the American guitar and amplifier manufacturers, lading them with artistic duty from birth, before they could either accept or reject it. They were interpellated into these ideals.

"Everyone must have an aim," Mii said one day at his home, during a break from a long practice, as we took turns dipping sticky rice in an electric orange *tômyam plaa* broth. I had asked him to explain the meaning of Fender and Marshall's names. In naming them, Mii intended to transfer his own aims to his sons. Fender, five years old and doe-eyed, busked now and then alongside his father. He played the *phin* with a fearlessness that I admired, and wished I possessed. His small fingers quickly grew sore contending with the high action of the strings. Fender described the experience of playing for long periods as one that he *mây wǎy* (could not endure). But learning to endure, in the name of duty, was precisely the exercise his father meant for him. Mii was motivated by a commitment to his listeners. A receptive audience, not political sympathies, was the primary factor in convincing him to play at the Red Shirt protests. Indeed, Mii distrusted the movement for its confrontational language, and had little interest in its strategic political goals. He did consider the protests to be ethical in that they allowed weak actors to speak truth to influential and corrupt forces. But Mii regarded the Red Shirts' methods as improper, and their aims as unreachable. He found their behavior, including drinking alcohol at protests and using curse words, troubling. Simply put, he was not driven by party politics or sympathy for dissent, but by his musical "aim," including his duty to

4. Miller, *Traditional Music of the Lao*, 295.
5. Keyes, *Finding Their Voice*.

listeners. I once asked him why, in light of this, he bothered to wear red clothing at the protests. He answered with a sardonic laugh that he was "working undercover."

Wasn't he, then, insincere? In fact, Mii could not have worked (that is to say, played) any other way. While the Yellow Shirts dismissed the music of northeastern *mor lam* as low-class, the Red Shirts were enthralled by it. The Yellow Shirts preferred musical genres that marked nationalistic unity (such as *phleeng plùkjay*), or that carried a whiff of dissidence from the 1960s and 1970s, but evacuated of that period's leftism (such as "songs for life"). "Songs for life" had, in the 1980s and 1990s, grown into a popular radio style. *Mor lam* and *luk thung*, on the other hand, though not often explicitly politicized, sounded out a marginality that better suited the Red Shirts. This difference in reception described a constitutive divide between the two factions—less that the Reds were poor and the Yellows monied than that the groups identified, respectively, with periphery and center. Mii's *phin* sounded the morally-imbued identity of the powerless periphery. And Mii, despite his coolness to the Red Shirt movement qua political change, shared its moral identity. It was a sense of moral duty shaped by marginality, not political conviction, that led Mii to perform so often for the Red Shirts.

And what of entrepreneurialism, and Mii's relationship to money? By day, Mii works as a tailor along the sidewalk near his home, earning about 500 baht ($17) daily, which is a typical blue-collar income in Bangkok. As a musician, he plays gigs once a week or so, either by staking out a spot on a sidewalk, or being hired by an organization such as the Bangkok Metropolitan Police to entertain at a private party. Busking near the popular outdoor market Chatuchak on an ordinary Sunday might bring in 1,000 or 1,500 baht ($30–45), much more than his tailoring income, but not a huge sum considering the costs of transporting equipment and the exhausting labor of playing for eight or ten hours in a row in the searing heat. He and I played one such gig together at Chatuchak, nowhere near any protest. Mii deployed me so that he could take breaks (it was well over 100 degrees Fahrenheit), and to earn a little extra money, since visitors to the market found it so odd and interesting to hear a foreigner playing Thai music. We arrived early and found a prime spot along the sidewalk just a few meters from the main entrance to the market. But neither of us turned out to be a big draw. I watched thick streams of passersby as they watched and listened to me. I tried to meet their eyes (as Mii suggested). Most looked briefly bemused before continuing along through the crowd. The donations that came were the result of politeness or even just convenience; if someone had a small bill or coin, and it was reachable, they might decide to toss it in our bamboo steamer. But the labor of getting the steamer to fill up was long and hard; it took all day before the collection looked anywhere near robust.

At Red Shirt protests, by contrast, Mii made at least 3,000 baht ($100) for a day of playing. Even that low figure was more than double what he earned at a place like Chatuchak. At protests, the money just flowed. After one crowded rally, Mii went home with an incredible 7,000 baht ($233).[6] In the course of that single

---

6. Money was typically collected throughout the day, and in the evening divided among performers. As a student of Mii's, I was not entitled to a share, but any other musician who was still around at the end of the show could negotiate a small fee.

performance, Mii earned the equivalent of two weeks' salary, of which he gave some to the musicians who played with him, invested around 2,000 baht ($67) in a new car battery to provide power for future performances, and pocketed the remainder. The car battery glinted a proud blue-and-white at our next practice, alongside the weather-beaten, rust-pocked tin loudspeaker that it powered. The gap between what a street musician could earn at a protest event and what they made on a normal day was reflected in the contrast between the two pieces of equipment.

Mii and I first met on January 11, 2011 at a large rally of around eighty thousand people who traveled from the Ratchaprasong intersection to Democracy Monument, a trip of some five miles that I had taken by foot. Mii, whose nickname translates as "Bear," set up an impressive rig on the edge of the rally near the monument, a Modernist shrine to constitutionalism. I saw him there after the long walk, as the rally was just beginning. Attached by bungee cord to the seat of his parked motorcycle was a red plastic egg crate teeming with audio cables and effects boxes. Mii fixed a small amplifier on top of the wires, and a beaten-up gray loudspeaker cone made by a company called Accord. On two sides of this equipment tower, Mii tied framed collages of his son Marshall, his mentor *ajarn* Tongsai Taptanon (one of the best-known living *phin* players), and a few of his own students, each posed with instrument in hand.[7]

Mii played at this rally with a brooding expression that I quickly learned not to confuse with self-seriousness (see Figure 13.4). His instrument was a *phin* that he had built by hand, including the carved wooden body, ornate naga head, and internal electrical wiring for the pickups, as in Figure 13.3. The Isan version of the *phin* is a three-stringed plucked lute thought to have originated in Laos and the portion of northeastern Thailand that the Lao kingdom once encompassed. It is a crucial if relatively new staple of many Thai folk idioms, including *lam* from the lower Mekong, and in its electric form is a backbone instrument of *mor lam sing*, a fast-paced style associated with dancing, whisky, the temple, traveling stage shows, and other vital rural institutions. According to Miller, "while the [phin] repertory is severely limited to three or four pieces, players have nevertheless created a very distinctive style in which one drone string may parallel the melody in fifths while the remaining strings produce unstopped drones. [Phin] combined with kaen have become the standard accompaniment for [mor lam] plun theatre."[8] The *phin* repertoire has since diversified, especially as *mor lam* has joined *luk thung* as a popular form, and the two genres themselves have cross-fertilized. But mastery of a limited idiom is still more important than breadth of repertoire. A talented *phin* player may

7. See "ทองใส ทับถนน" ("Tongsai Taptanon"), (http://www.tlg.rmutt.ac.th/wp-content/uploads/2011/06/67—ครูทองใส-ทับถนน.pdf, accessed January 28, 2013 for more information about *ajarn* Tongsai.
8. Miller, *Traditional Music of the Lao*, 17.

Figure 13.3 Many *phin*, in various states of manufacture, near Mii's home in Bangkok. Mii carves each instrument from raw wood. Photograph by the author.

Figure 13.4 Mii (center-right, blue denim shirt) performs with an impromptu band at a rally on March 12, 2011 near Democracy Monument. Photograph by the author.

work with only ten or twelve melodies, but facility with these, as well as the ability to move fluidly between them, defines a *phin* player's craft.[9]

The physical form of the *phin* varies enormously, with electric and acoustic versions, different body and cavity sizes and pickup types, and various design extravagances. The most common type seen today has a crest-shaped body (as opposed to a more traditional teardrop shape, or sometimes a rectangle) attached to a long, slender, fretted neck. The head is carved like a naga, a type of mythical serpent (the more fearsome the better). The wood used to build a high-quality *phin* comes from the sturdy, heavy jackfruit or fig tree, while a cheaper version might be pine. An excellently crafted *phin* is far heavier than it appears. The body is rarely painted, but usually finished with a high-gloss coat of medium-dark varnish that highlights the grain of the wood. Most *phin* sold nowadays are not fully chromatic. There is no standard tuning, but often the lowest of the three strings is tuned to E, the middle string to A, and the highest string also to E. The available notes are restricted to an A minor scale with an added F♯. Many *phin* have unused frets, typically the first frets of each string. A small number of *phin* are fully chromatic, however, and some musicians use their own distinct tunings. Given this variety, an unfamiliar instrument is not always easy even for an expert to play.

When I saw Mii at the January rally, his playing seemed effortless. He had an ease and manner that can only be described as cool. Frowning behind black sunglasses under the mid-afternoon sun, his red shirt, red fisherman's hat, and red satchel nearly matched the cherry-toned pick guard on his instrument. He was playing undercover. Electrified, the *phin* is often treated with heavy echo, phase, or chorus, lending its rapid picking even greater density. This timbre was in full effect at the rally. The sound of the instrument is often described by casual Western listeners as "psychedelic," an adjective with some historical grounding (its contemporary tone is indeed influenced by 1960s psychedelic rock). However, this cluster of effects, when applied to the *phin*, does not suggest an ethos of altered consciousness. At that rally, I didn't yet know how to hear it. So I listened rapt for longer than Mii could ignore the gawking *farang* in his midst. After several minutes, he pulled the yellow canvas shoulder strap over his head and placed the instrument in my hands. I had often imagined such a moment, had even considered buying a *phin*, and was excited by the opportunity. I instinctively finger-picked the strings, like a guitar, and they responded with a vile, broken phrase. I did not anticipate the scale, nor the lack of chromaticism. I related to something in the sound of the *phin*, but was out of my depth when I tried to repeat it, as when you hear a voice clearly in your mind but sound absurd or offensive trying to reproduce it aloud. A crowd formed to behold the novelty, if not the tragedy. The *phin* was heavier than expected, its body narrow but made from strong wood. The naga head was delicately carved and painted gold.

---

9. *Phin* performance is dominated by men, both at protest events, among street buskers and bands, and in live concerts.

Despite the instrument's grandeur, in my hands the music came out listless and full of wrong-sounding notes. To the disappointment of those watching, I returned the *phin* to Mii after less than a minute. Embarrassed but intrigued, I asked Mii if I could pay him for lessons. He passed me a business card with his phone number, and offered to teach me for free at his home. Assuming the gesture was mere politeness, I insisted that I would pay him, but he declined. I tentatively agreed, expecting to revisit the matter of payment later. Mii not only refused to take money for lessons at any point, but bought meals, paid for part of my first acoustic *phin*, and eventually gave me several handmade electric instruments as gifts. This kind of arrangement was more or less standard between Mii and his students. It was an investment in his relationships with them, and thereby also in the continuity of *mor lam*, an outcome that he valued greatly.

Our first lesson, about two weeks after the rally, involved a communicative bungle that underscored his neighborhood's distance from Bangkok's cosmopolitan commercial heart. Mii lives in a peripheral area about forty minutes from downtown by car, near the King Rama IX bridge. The most notable features of his neighborhood are a large *wát* (Buddhist temple), a bustling afternoon food market, and a heavily polluting Japanese bra factory that employs many women from the neighborhood. Before our meeting, on the phone, Mii told me to meet him at the "Wacoal business." I relayed this instruction to the taxi driver, who dropped me off at the front door of the factory's administrative office. I went in, assuming I would meet Mii on his lunch break from work in the building. (I did not yet know what he did for a living.) The Wacoal business had an open-plan office area filled with women sitting at desks, who all looked up at once when I entered. As I approached the receptionist, and asked to see *khun mĭi* (Mr. Bear), she could not suppress a laugh. Did I know his real name? Or which department he worked in? She was aware of no Mr. Bear. I looked up at the young women sitting at their computers, who were glancing furtively in my direction. I dialed Mii's cell once more. He answered, and told me he was walking toward the factory just then. I stepped out and saw him coming, this time wearing a denim shirt with decorative patches sewn all over, along with shorts and flip-flops. It was a much more casual outfit than his natty red attire at the protest. He did not work at the bra factory, he clarified. The building was simply an orienting landmark; he mentioned it for no reason other than that it was nearby, and prominent. Like the protest rallies to which Mii was drawn *as a musician*, with politics secondary, the building logically suggested itself.

We walked down the road together for a few minutes, around a bend, past a 7-Eleven toward the bank of a canal that shimmered a stagnant black from industrial runoff. On the southern side, Mii showed me a few small, covered pavilions— one with a sewing machine and other tailoring equipment, and three or four more for his substantial collection of Thai instruments (in various stages of construction), including *phin*, *khɛɛn*, and *ching*, as well as his DVD player and other electronics. Many neighbors worked in view of Mii's sewing/music space, including his wife, Tong, who is also a tailor, a *som tam* vendor who set up next to her daily, two independent recycling collectors (and ardent Red Shirts) who drove up and down the street in a motor-powered cart throughout the day, and an older couple across the small canal who sold food from the kitchen of their shophouse. The couple in the shophouse also kept a brood of noisy chickens that ran freely about the area, noticed by humans only when someone's broth needed flavor. Their squawking, combined with the chatter of people, the hollow thud of cars driving slowly over the short concrete bridge that slopes over the narrow canal, and the lovely metallic tone of Mii's *phin*, were the keynote sounds of the neighborhood.

The *phin*, as it was heard in marginal neighborhoods, was an important sonic presence for the Red Shirts. It kept Bangkok at bay. The sensory environment of rural life is often framed as an idyllic antithesis to the chaos of the capital city.[10] Agrarian life is "epistemologically purified," and regarded as the essence of Thainess.[11] One might indeed still hear something like pastoral quiet in a rural Thai village, although many areas of the northeast have urbanized. Such purified referent environments exist in the city as well, and tend to be much noisier than their idealized representation would suggest. In other words, their sonority is not the same as the *representation* of their sonority. As my field recorder heard at one practice (but, initially, with my ears alone, I did not), the cries of the chickens were harsh, a police radio kept interrupting the music, and the sound of wheels on a nearby highway was jarring and constant. It was acoustically loud. But where Mii and Tong live, on the edge of the city, almost no one was born in Bangkok, and purified rural representations supersede acoustical totalities. The sound of *phin* is added to a sonorous field to announce the neighborhood as both regionally and politically peripheral. Mii's neighbors expect him to play the *phin* to help distinguish their space from the center of the metropolis. To be marginal is, in a sense, to be more Thai than is possible in the center. "*Krung Thep mai chai mueang Thai*— Bangkok is not Thailand—is a phrase one hears often in reference to Thailand's enduringly primate city, an uncompromising megalopolis convoluted in disposition as well as design."[12] In the case of Mii and Tong's neighborhood, where the *phin* sounds, this part of Bangkok is not Bangkok at all. Here, instead, Bangkok is created

10. Keyes, *Finding Their Voice*, describes this urban/rural binary as an important rhetorical construction in Thai politics. Among the great musical commentaries on the sonic distinction between the city and the provinces is singer Kwanchai Phetroiet's album *jòtmǎay pen mǎn*, on which the two lead singles, *jòtmǎay pen mǎn* and *lákhɔɔn mɯangthay*, use synthesizer effects to mimic, contrastingly, the pastoral sonority of birds in the country and the cacophony of car horns, emergency vehicle sirens, and other harsh tones that infest the city.

11. This term draws upon Ana María Ochoa Gautier, "Sonic Transculturation, Epistemologies of Purification and the Aural Public Sphere in Latin America," *Social Identities: Journal for the Study of Race, Nation and Culture*, 12, no. 6 (2006): 803–25. For a similar point made about Thailand, see Haberkorn, *Revolution Interrupted*. Haberkorn presents a history of the metaphorization of farmers as a purified, ahistorical "backbone of the nation," even as these laborers were exploited and marginalized by the state.

12. Sophorntavy Vorng, "Bangkok's Two Centers: Status, Space, and Consumption in a Millennial Southeast Asian City," *City & Society* 23, no. 1 (2011): 66–85.

in audition, but the sonic symbols of rural life can mask it. Like the psychoacoustic perception of a clanging bell as a single note, an imposition of order onto auditory chaos, here Bangkok and its antithesis are aural effects, a culling of an excess of overtones into reductions (notes, places) so profoundly false that they become meaningful. Bangkok is ringing; so too is its absence, its denial.

At protests, Mii was especially put off by the noise from two sources: the main stage and car stereos. Loud, drunken, and overly direct speech were un-Buddhist as well as un-Thai, he claimed. His performances fostered an aesthetic of rurality and religion in contrast to these sounds. Once I asked Mii if the outside noise at the rallies disturbed the mood of his performance space. He assured me it did not. In fact, the sonic niche of *phin* music could act on its hearer even in an area packed with amplified music and speeches. The relationship between the interior of this space and the sound beyond was not one of foreclosure, but of mindful incorporation. "How is it playing music in a chaotic environment like this?" I asked. "You have to focus. If you focus, it's not a problem," he answered, using a word, *sàmaathí* (focus, meditate), that was something of a mantra at our practices. "The atmospheric sound isn't important, then?" I followed up. "Not necessarily. It trains us," said Mii.[13] This "training" implicates auditory labor in the creation of sonic niches. There is work involved in purifying a sound environment so that it can be heard as meaningful. Mii suggests that some degree of sonic leakage is not only tolerable but productive as a foil or a kind of didactic challenge.

Our conversation took place on March 12, 2011, at a rally near Democracy Monument. I had been playing alongside Mii long enough by then that he routinely invited me to join him. A *farang* playing *mor lam* with him was a tremendous novelty. But unlike our shows at Chatuchak and elsewhere, this event was politically contentious and so I declined, citing conflicts with my research role. Mii set up on the periphery, outside the tall white walls of Pom Mahakan fortress, part of the original border of the city of Bangkok and, today, site of a land rights conflict between a small group of residents and the city administration.[14] Mii brought several different *phin*, a power generator, his Accord loudspeaker, and a crate of wires. He placed two large, laminated posters of his son Fender on the curb next to the sidewalk, along with two packets of drug store photo prints on top of the upturned crate (see Figure 13.5). The prints showed Mii and me playing together near the canal next to his house. We had been photographed since our earliest practices by Mii's childhood friend, a taxi driver named Daorung who is technologically savvy and who has appointed himself Mii's personal archivist. It is unusual for Thais outside the most cosmopolitan circles to have *farang* friends, except occasionally as husbands. Mii

13. I translate *man fùk raw* (มันฝึกเรา) directly as "it trains us." The assignation of agency to sound in this phrasing strikes me as relevant.
14. Herzfeld, *Siege of the Spirits*.

Figure 13.5 Mii plays next to a fort, a few hundred meters from Democracy Monument at a rally on March 12, 2011, with printed photographs on top of his red crate. Photograph by the author.

was as proud to have a non-Thai student as I was to have a master teacher. He was eager to show off our relationship as part of his teaching portfolio. While he played, a steady stream of audience members approached the crate and leafed curiously through the prints.

Mii was accompanied by two musicians, one a friend who plays percussion in a local marching band, and the other a metropolitan police officer whose daily beat takes him past Mii's home. The officer often invites himself over for quick lessons when no one in the neighborhood seems to be breaking the law. Mii is not fond of this person, who he describes as having the sort of bad manners common to those made arrogant by their high positions. "People with bad manners don't play music well," Mii assured me, in a half-joking aside after I tried in vain to teach the officer a simple melody once during practice. Still, Mii's lessons, like the bands he assembled at protests, were open to all, so he never turned him away. At the protests, the officer wore a face mask so that his colleagues or superiors would not spot him playing music at a partisan political event. During the eight-hour performance on March 12, a succession of musicians took turns playing drums, *phin*, and *ching*, some with great skill and others with almost none. There was an egalitarian spirit of participation in the performance.

The structure of the set was familiar to me from many weeks of discussion with Mii about how to develop audience involvement. Mii began by sitting on an overturned crate, his face turned down toward the pavement, playing almost exclusively on the top string, using the middle string as a drone. He played slow, descending intervals, punctuated with occasional rapidly picked notes high on the fretboard, a technique that he had stressed in practice could help build up the mood early in a show. This went on for half an hour as he carefully tweaked the chorus and echo pedals in response to the difficult acoustics of the street corner. He also retuned his *phin*, which had been jostled on the motorcycle ride over. The crowd parted on the pavement just wide enough for a single lane of vehicle traffic to pass through, and that lane limited the sound on one side of Mii's otherwise unmarked stage. The road graded steeply upward to the east, creating a sonic break between the valley where Mii played and the plateau above, where a Red Shirt satellite TV station had a small canvas exposition tent. Mii's setup was best heard on the downward slope to the west and the flat area directly in front of him. Behind the speakers, the sound was muddled. The audience, which at times swelled to a hundred or more, thus tended to settle in an L-shape in front of Mii's setup, where the sound was clearest. I briefly wondered how the music resonated inside the walls of the fort, which had been closed to the public during the protest. Some monks observed from nearby, watching and listening to the cramped rallies from within empty enclosures.

The drummer joined for a warmup around 2:30 p.m., and the set properly began just before 3:00, the drums and *phin* slowly advancing in tempo together. The crowd, anticipating something even faster to dance to, stood to the side, arms folded, waiting to be moved by the music. Mii began weaving together melodies. The fragments he used included tunes of obscure authorship, such as *pleeng lɔɔy kràthong* (Loy Krathong festival song) and *lam teuil*, Laotian melodies like *lam tangwai, lam phuthai*, and *lam phloen*, as well as others adapted from popular songs like Phipat Buribun's *phûuyày lii* ("Village Headman Lee") from the early 1960s and Siriporn Ampaipong's *bo rák sǐidam* ("Bo Loves Black") from the early 1990s. *Phin* players like Mii often weave melodic fragments together in this way. The fragments also may become motifs in wholly new compositions; for example, *lam teuil*, one of the first folk melodies Mii taught me, is the basis of Pimpa Ponsiri's 1993 single *plùuk man thúk pii* ("Plant Potatoes Every Year"), as well as many other songs. Standard *phin* melodies cross genre, region, and era, though they are largely drawn from Laotian religious, theatrical, and courting genres that until the twentieth century employed only *khεεn* and voice, with no stringed accompaniment at all. What unites these fragments, in a sense, is their marginality. The melodies are connected to either Laos, Isan, or rurality otherwise, with a strong moral undercurrent. "Village Headman Lee" is probably the clearest instance. Once a hit pop song, its lyrics satirically describe an encounter between savvy villagers and an inept civil servant from Bangkok who comes to announce the new and utterly misguided policies of the central government. This music engages a poetics of exclusion, and valorizes the margins as a site of dignity and morality, not backwardness.

Though the genre Mii plays is typically referred to as *mor lam*, the idiom is more precisely called *lam*. The practitioner of this poetry is called a *mor lam*, meaning a (typically northeastern) expert in *lam*. Especially in Isan, *mor lam* bear a moral authority and perform a role of community leadership, being historically among the better educated members of their villages. Their poetry is replete with fables and wisdom, of which they are standard-bearers. "The main poetic subjects developed in the *lam* and *khap* involve Buddhist morality, historical and mythological stories and the major themes of courtship. These songs, sung in a good-natured spirit, also have a didactic function. As holders of a tradition, they allow for a transmission of knowledge and cultural values."[15] Pattarawut Bunpraseri identifies *mor lam* as simultaneously philosophers, social critics, satirists, entertainers, and holy men who can improvise performances of moral folk tales set to song.[16] Before the spread of television and other mass media, *mor lam* linked their community to an awareness of the world beyond their immediate comprehension, whether spiritual or geopolitical. Facility with the *khɛɛn*, as well as a quick wit, were fundamentally necessary for *mor lam* in commanding the attention and respect of their listeners. "Most male [*mor lam*] singers, especially those of earlier generations, had served as monks for extended periods of time. In the temple they became deeply imbued with Buddhist morality and learning. They emerged from the temple as learned men and. . . were respected by their peers. As artist and entertainer, they were as much a part of Buddhist ceremonies as the monks who chanted."[17]

Even as *mor lam* as a genre has diversified, its moral dimensions remain an important part of its appeal. Numerous contemporary *luk thung* and *mor lam* songs that receive regular airplay in Bangkok make this clear. Tai Orathai's *naangbɛɛp ngaanbun* ("Woman of the Merit Festival"), for example, tells the story of a rural migrant in Bangkok who wears a degrading work uniform so she can save enough money to buy a beautiful dress for the event that *really* matters, a merit-making festival at the temple in her hometown. Tai herself is from Isan, and her music and persona trade in the symbols of rural life. "Woman of the Merit Festival" frames migrant work in Bangkok as a sacrifice that good people must make in order to maintain ties to their village, which is the putatively true moral center of their lives.

Morality structured Mii's performance in other ways, including through the duties of lineage. Part of Mii's artistic duty is to continually *buuchaakhruu*, or honor his teacher, *ajarn* Tongsai. Mii plays Tongsai's repertoire in order to sustain it. Wong writes about the *wây khruu* (honoring teacher) ceremony that "the ritual technologies that create performers are wielded by men who are not only exemplary teachers in the here-and-now but who are routinely collapsed with the first teacher of all time. They not only bring the past into the present but literally *become* the past in ritual contexts."[18] Although Mii did not use this language, his teacher Tongsai was ever present—his photograph was displayed at every practice and every performance where Mii played. Mii spoke about sustaining Thai music

15. "Molams and Mokhenes: Singing and Mouth Organ," Inedit, 2009. W 260137, compact disc. Liner notes.
16. Pattarawut Bunpraseri, "Local Media in Mass Media: The Case of Mor Lam" (Master's Thesis, Institute for the Development of Mass Media in Thailand, 2008).
17. Miller, *Traditional Music of the Lao*, 62.
18. Wong, *Sounding the Center*, 15.

in nostalgic and sometimes bitter terms. My status as his student underscored the failure, he said, of Thai people to learn "their own" musical lineage. If a *farang* could learn the *phin*, why couldn't Thai people? This supposed failure lent even greater urgency to Mii's effort to continue teaching *phin*, and explains in part why he offered lessons for free. Transmission was a moral necessity.

The importance of lineage at times made studying the *phin* a rigid exercise. Mii had me play melodic fragments ad nauseam. When we busked together on street corners far from the protests, he insisted that I not venture beyond the three or four parts I could execute most sharply, despite playing for several hours in a row.[19] The repetition was at times extremely boring and difficult on my hands and arms. More than once, exhausted by the lack of variety, I began improvising on a scale only to have Mii hurry over and bring me back in line. The goal of these lessons was to standardize my playing, not to help me develop a personal musical identity. "*Mor lam* must receive good training," notes Pattarawut. "*Mor lam* must have successful teachers. After that, they follow their teaching, memorize poems, rhythms, and cadences with precision until they are experts with the material."[20] Mii's emphasis on repetition seemed contradictory in the moment; after all, his own performances were full of improvisation. And, depending on the day, he might direct me to play freely, offering no direction at all. But when he asked for repetition, the request was firm.

The impulse to play repetitively seemed to stem from an anxiety about standardization in Thai music. In lengthy conversations at practice, Mii suggested that in contemporary Thailand, music was, like most things, insufficiently regulated. *Mây mii mâattràthǎan* ("there is no standard"), he explained when I asked how one melody should transition into another. He told me during one balmy afternoon practice that Thai music had no standards, with apparent embarrassment. "It's not like American music, which has known rules that people follow. Nowadays Thai people cannot abide rules." Mii's generalization about "American" music is extremely reductive. But it nevertheless revealed his anxiety that something had been lost not only in Thai musicality, but about Thainess broadly. Thailand had once, Mii felt, been governed by Buddhist wisdom. Now Thais were lazy, chaotic, and indifferent to their own history. The behavior of politicians, drunken Red Shirts, and self-important police officers were three of his favorite examples to support this point. When Mii cited lapsed facility with "traditional" Thai musical idioms, this claim was offered as proof that standards had bypassed the nation. He bemoaned that few people still knew how to play instruments like the *phin*. However one might assess these claims historically or comparatively, they point

19. In *Traditional Music of the Lao*, Miller describes a similar pedagogical practice for *mor lam phuen* poetry in the middle of the twentieth century: "Ajarn Gun. . . required [his student] Pao to learn the texts orally through imitation. Ajarn Gun divided each story into parts, and Pao practiced and mastered each part before going to the next." (42).

20. Pattarawut, "Local Media in Mass Media."

to the deep-seated motivations and valuations that drove Mii to perform at Red Shirt events.

Concern over a lack of standards also extended to Mii's opinions of instruments. The superiority of Japanese keyboards over their Thai counterparts, for example, was allegedly the result of Japan's superlative regularity in manufacturing. In Thailand, even *phin* were now made on the cheap, he complained. At our second lesson, I asked Mii to recommend a shop in the city where I might buy a *phin* of my own, and he immediately drove me across town on his motorcycle to the musical instrument section of Chinatown.[21] We visited several stores, including a tiny shop-house piled from floor to ceiling with plumbing equipment, drums, and a couple of *phin*. The elderly shop owner offered one dusty specimen for 1,200 baht ($40). Mii was appalled at the price, and did not think he could talk her down to something reasonable, so we left for the next shop. Mii explained that the *phin* she showed us was made from light wood liable to warp, that it would sound tinny and small, and that it was not at all worth the price. This was typical contemporary Thai workmanship, he scoffed. At the next shop, run by a husband and wife who peddled a variety of inexpensive instruments, Mii talked the vendor down to 600 baht ($20) for a *phin* almost identical to the one we saw before, made from similar wood and lacking an electric pickup. This one was poorly built as well, he said, but at least we had not been overcharged. It would do for now. As we walked back toward Mii's motorcycle, we came to a large store on the corner filled with American and Japanese instruments, similar to large corporate musical instrument stores in the United States. The shelves were stocked with digital effects boxes and MIDI keyboards, and resting in plastic stands were neat rows of guitars and amps manufactured by Fender and Marshall, his own children's namesakes. Mii was drawn in, and we chatted with the clerk for ten or fifteen minutes. The air in the store smelled like vacuumed carpet, in contrast to the musky, yellow odor of the shophouses where we had browsed earlier. Mii asked about one item after another, from guitars to pedals, and inevitably the conversation ended when the question of cost came up. In stores like this, which sell imported products from the United States, Europe, and Japan, there is no haggling, and the prices are as standardized (and high) as they would be anywhere in the world. I asked Mii if he wanted a guitar like the ones we were looking at, even though he didn't know how to play it. His answer was unequivocal: "Yes."

Standardization was also a key term for the Red Shirts, as it happened. Protesters complained that Thai society had an unfair system of "double standards" (*sǒong mâattràthǎan*). Elites held all power, and the poor held absolutely none. This inequality, they claimed, colored nearly everything about Thai political life. The government not only failed to provide social welfare or genuine democracy, but the

---

21. The musical instrument district was also the meat-grinder district and the handgun district.

poor were required to supplicate themselves in spite of this. Like Mii, the protesters described social inequality as a result of uneven standards. But Mii's desire for "standards" was not quite the same as that of most Red Shirts, even though he used the very same word as the movement in its slogans. Protest coalitions house divergent impulses. Even when words and symbols appear to converge, suggesting unanimity, they may drift apart on examination. People play undercover. Single words ring with many meanings, many overtones.

Another term that was important to Mii as well as to the Red Shirts—freedom— drifted apart as well. Mii values freedom. This is evident in the way that he sews his own clothing. The day we met at the Wacoal building, the denim jacket he wore was adorned with a bricolage of patches, most displaying the logos of Western fashion companies like Levi's and Wrangler. He also had a pair of jeans that he wore to more formal events such as temple ceremonies, which featured an array of jagged red threads shooting in different directions. The design was not planned, he said, but came from letting his imagination run free. Mii preferred to design his own clothes in an impulsive, personal way, following his instincts rather than any preformatted design. Despite skill in sewing other peoples' clothes in a standardized fashion, he generally wanted his own clothes to be made with a minimum of premeditation. Such a lack of planning, a trusting of the gut, was what Mii meant—and what he valorized—when he used the word "freedom."

During lessons, freedom was an important basis of instruction. It was our aim. Balancing the imperatives of freedom and standardization could be frustrating and a little confusing. Freedom became especially crucial when I was struggling. Mii addressed my struggles not by choosing a simpler song or modeling a melody more slowly, but by asking me to respond with more awareness of my own sensations. For instance, we once spent a full two hours synchronizing pick strokes and breath. Every up-stroke was accompanied by an inhalation, every downstroke by an exhalation. I felt rushed and anxious, for some unrelated reason. Anxiety prevented me from playing confidently. Mii decided that an exercise in synchronicity with myself would help. While I played, he insisted that the notes or melodies must not be proscribed, because a sound "suited to myself" would emerge once I brought my playing in line with my breath and eventually with my heartbeat. He called this an exercise in playing more naturally, and to extend the effect he had me switch from an electric to an acoustic *phin*, which he assured me was more "comfortable" and "natural." *Phin* and *khɛɛn* performance are often staged (for music videos and album cover art, e.g.) with acoustic instruments, or electric instruments unplugged, next to pristine bodies of water. This representation of nature is grounded in a purified conception of Isan as unpolluted. By playing in a way that activates this conception, the musician is supposed to be free to play precisely as they feel compelled to play, without conscious regard for technique. At Mii's suggestion, we listened together to the filthy water flowing through the canal, to the chickens and the traffic (perhaps this sound would train us?), and to our heartbeats. We tried to let our playing emerge freely from the climate. In fact, in all of our time studying together

Mii never once told me I played a wrong note. When something seemed off, and I asked Mii to point out the mistake, he invariably answered that whatever sounded right to my ears was correct. At times this was a disappointing response, especially when I heard my playing as clearly less "correct" than his. Nevertheless, the aim was to achieve a state that Mii understood to be one of freedom. Mii projected an independence, a freedom, that appealed to his listeners, and to Red Shirt protesters especially. Playing among the protest crowd, on the ground, Mii did not choose which melodies he would weave together in advance. He gauged the mood of the crowd, and responded through his improvisatory performance decisions. There was an appealing freedom in this. When Mii sensed the need to amp things up, he executed tricky maneuvers, like playing the strings of the *phin* with his teeth or holding the instrument behind his head, in the ostentatious style of rock guitarists, without seeming to break a sweat. For the crowd, in turn, Mii produced a purified sonority with overtones of rural subjectivity. He seemed unburdened.

I took a break to walk around Democracy Monument, then returned to hear Mii again. It was 3:45 p.m. The band had picked up steam, and Mii was now showboating, holding the *phin* over and behind his head without slowing the pace of the *lam phloen* riff on which he was jamming. Mii is, in a sense, as much a student of Carlos Santana as he is of *ajarn* Tongsai. His jam sessions could last ten minutes, with dramatic peaks such as the moment in *bo rák šiidam* when the percussion and *phin* rhythmically align for several measures. He seemed free, unconstrained. A quick, hard rain fell a few minutes before, during which Mii unplugged his effects pedals. Now the tone coming from his little amp and the gray speaker next to it sounded dry and clean. Mii grabbed a hula hoop and began swinging it around his torso, without pausing the music. He soloed faster and faster. The drummer pounded the bass drum that hung from his lower torso. The crowd clapped and danced, with elbows slightly bent, arms overhead, and fingers splayed and curved backwards. Mii wove fragments together in turbulent, emergent patterns, like the threads on his pants, freely. I knew how to play several of these melodies in isolation, although Mii's execution and skill at conjoining them was far faster and more elaborate. A Red Shirt on a motorcycle revved his engine behind the gyrating crowd, flag whipping in the wind. A second drummer, shirt soaked from the rain, kept pace. He had no kick drum, but used a cowbell to play fills. His cymbals were fully open and they hung ringing in the air. The masked young police officer played a single marching tom.

The crowd had grown to at least one hundred people, many of whom danced right in front of the band. One man, dressed as a Buddhist demon, hula-hooped. Another wearing a heavy motorcycle helmet snapped pictures with a small point-and-shoot camera. Mii, now picking up and down with blazing speed, sat on the curb while he played, as if to show off that he was relaxing despite the frenzy of his playing. Mii switched from one melodic fragment to the next at breakneck speed. The crowd's enthusiasm kept increasing. Mii's bamboo basket overflowed with bills large and small. The money flowed. He finished to rousing applause. I met him on the curb. He sat back and I asked, "was that fun?" He shook the sweat from his head, as if to distance himself from the question. Out of breath, he said in the space of a single exhalation: "Very tiring."

This chapter has outlined how *ajarn* Mii was drawn to the Red Shirt protests by the desire to meet moral and ethical imperatives—to serve listeners as an artist, to maintain the lineage of a rural Thai genre, to serve an abstract notion of standards, and to feel freedom, among others. Money was inseparable from this logic and its individual imperatives, since it afforded their fulfillment, and since it was part of rituals (such as donating to a performer) that accompanied performance. The glut of donations that Mii received for playing at protests reflected the audience's morality at least as much as Mii's entrepreneurial instincts. Mii's choice to pursue those donations contributed to the further fulfillment of the imperatives that structure his world. Money served morality, as morality at times served money. Mii was, in this regard, authentically motivated, although judging sincerity (as so many political observers did, so often) is in the end beside the point. Money and morality functioned in tandem as constraints that limited where and when Mii played, how his sonic niche was shaped, and how it circulated. Crucially, the logic of his protest performance was not necessarily shared by his listeners, nor by other protesters. The words, sounds, genres, and symbols that seem to bind and unify protesters into a movement might drift apart upon analysis. The Red Shirts, as with all protest movements, were *coordinated* more than unified. Mii's motivation for joining the movement seemed clear as a bell, superficially, but in fact it resulted from a fleeting quasi-coincidence of signifiers—fixed like a pure note imagined in the heterogeneous overtones of a clang—around morality and ethnoregional identity.

CHAPTER 14
Surveillance

To the left, a phalanx of police officers stood in line, frowning. Next to them, a radio station truck played music, and a crowd formed to dance.[1] One man, wearing a loudly inconspicuous floral-print shirt, gestured furtively with three fingers to an officer in the phalanx, who gave him a quick, quiet nod in response. The protests were surveilled at all times. (see Figure 14.1, at the end of this chapter)

~

The Thai army's psychological operations unit, called *pàtibàt kaanjìtwítyaa* or *por jor wor* (hereafter, PJW) was active during the protests. PJW, part of the second regiment of the Thai army's special warfare division based in the Central Thai province of Lopburi, deployed approximately thirty soldiers to broadcast music and sound throughout the March–May 2010 protests as a form of non-violent crowd control. These soldiers were like DJs in fatigues, performing in public places at moments of imminent conflict or panic. Although the unit has existed since 1963, and has years of experience in the provinces, Bangkok had never before been a major site for its musical operations. PJW soldiers emceed for approximately eight of the protest's ten weeks, working daily and often as a first line of defense against agitated Red Shirt protest crowds. The musical activities of PJW provide a unique vantage from which to eavesdrop on the relationship between the state and its discontents—to tune in to the trauma of political change so closely linked to the increased speakability of the politics of regional identity.

PJW's broadcasts at times created grim incongruities between musical sentiment and action. On April 10, for example, among the bloodiest days of the conflict, soldiers fired at protesters while "H.M. Blues," a gentle jazz piano tune written

---

1. This chapter is a partial excerpt from "A Division of Listening: Insurgent Sympathy and the Sonic Broadcasts of the Thai Military," originally published in *positions* Vol. 24:2, 403–33. Copyright 2016, Duke University Press. All rights reserved. Republished by permission of the copyright holder, Duke University Press. www.dukeupress.edu.

by King Bhumibol Adulyadej in the 1940s, drifted from a nearby army sound truck parked on a bridge. Its melody swung with cool indifference to the sharp popping of bullets in the darkness.[2] In addition to its role in conflict situations, PJW served as a preemptive peacekeeping force, using DJs and comedians to re-assure shoppers, tourists, and office workers in business districts where protesters had not yet gathered, but which they were rumored to want to occupy. Despite the dark irony of these performances, the unit was frequently successful, even as it performed on the thin line between control and chaos. For every performance, PJW gave painstaking attention to the demographics of its audience, directing sonic symbols toward ears tuned to specific frequencies of region, taste, experience, and humor. Such demographic attention might be described as a kind of "narrowcasting," or the tailoring of a broadcast to a highly specific listenership. PJW knew how to flatter its listeners by adjusting accent, song selection, and stage performance to suit a given crowd.

The Red Shirts held one of their first major demonstrations of the March-May 2010 protests just beyond the central gates of a military installation called RAB 11 on March 15, drawing several thousand energized demonstrators. The crowd trickled in throughout the late morning, as Red Shirt leader Veera Musikapong spoke laconically on a makeshift stage. Meanwhile, PJW dug in with truck-mounted speakers just inside the gates of the compound. They began with a mix of *phleeng rák châat*, compositions in various genres with lyrics that express unabashed love for Thailand and a desire for its unity. The performance was like a Thai cabaret show, as the unit set a mood by appealing to nationalism and "Thainess." The canon of *phleeng rák châat* includes a number of European-style anthems written in the 1930s, when Thailand adopted its first constitution. The architects of the country's political system, strongly influenced by fascist aesthetics, waged an intensive campaign to introduce the concept of national pride through music and drama.[3] The soldiers' gambit in beginning with these songs was to remind protesters that dissent was constrained by the need for national unity, and thus to make it difficult for them to act. The implicit message was to not create division by protesting in a manner that disrupted a clear, shared sense of national identity. Unity, as the PJW's own former theme song makes explicit in its lyrics, must be placed "above human life."

Speaking back to the Red Shirts, the military audio system boomed. Though it was impossible to see over the walls of the military base from the ground, aerial photographs showed that PJW had at least one large truck with speaker cabinets pointing forward from the top of the cab, some fifteen feet above the ground. The cabinets held four loudspeakers, each around three feet in diameter. Several soldiers

2. "Thai Army Clash with Red Protesters at Democracy Monument Pt 1" [*Video*], www.you-tube.com/watch?v=ztF6hUryt88&has_verified=1, accessed January 10, 2012.
3. Barmé, *Luang Wichit Wathakan and the Creation of a Thai Identity*.

sat among the equipment, while a line of three uniformed male soldiers and two fe-male soldiers in white blouses and black pencil skirts standing atop the truck took turns at the microphone. The company also included members whose job was to check the newswire and communicate with the other soldiers to update them on the unfolding protests.

Apparently anticipating less volume than PJW produced, the Red Shirts brought an audio setup that could not match that of the army. At the earliest protests, the Red Shirts relied on the ordinary speaker systems of taxis, which were only audible within a few meters of the vehicle.[4] But in combination, the two broadcast systems vying with each other led to cacophony. The protests in those tense early moments were anything but coherent. Sounds emerged from every-where, each threatening something emergent, if not dangerous—a stab of guitar seeming to tear open a song; hollers, firecrackers, engines roaring, the distant crackling thunder of an amplified orator. This continued until it all became rou-tine. The protest environment was one of urgent, delirious outbursts, even when nothing eventful was happening. It is no surprise that many protesters described being confused by the noise, rather than soothed by the *phleeng rák châat* that played amidst it.

"I could not hear clearly. . . . It was very noisy on this side," said one middle-aged motorcycle taxi driver who worked at a *win* (taxi stand) across the main road from RAB 11, and who joined the crowd outside the gates on March 15.[5] We spoke just a few weeks after the May crackdown, at a time when fear still palpably lingered. Motorcycle taxi drivers were a frequent presence at Red Shirt protest events, and many were nervous about being targeted by the authorities for their participation, whether or not they had broken any laws. In the after-math of what felt to many like a failure, the tone of these conversations was often anxious or resigned. "They [the army] had bigger equipment," explained the driver.

The first sign of success for PJW, by its own account, came not when the crowd was soothed but when Veera Musikapong, onstage, became uncharacteristically ag-itated when he realized that the military was drowning him out. He raised the tone of his remarks in response. Disrupting the Red Shirts' internal communications, es-pecially between leaders and demonstrators, was a victory of sorts, although many protesters I interviewed were quite angry about the tactic. The military, however, claimed victory for subduing crowds, not only for fracturing their communicative channels. The army's post hoc media campaign on radio and television reported that what eventually drew the protesters' attention in a more sustained fashion,

---

4. Journalist Nick Nostitz mentioned, in private conversation on October 19, 2010, that the Red Shirts' inferior sound system had been a source of great disappointment in March 2010.

5. Motorcycle taxi driver at *win* opposite RAB 11 gate, interview with the author, August 5, 2010. Name withheld at interviewee request. Translated from the original Thai.

transforming them from antagonists into audiences, was the entertainment value offered by the emcees of PJW. Live musical performance in Thailand, especially in the northeast, typically alternates between song and comedy, and PJW had spent days writing and rehearsing gags. Their material ranged from clean, "family-style" jokes to bawdy or misogynistic bits, which it interspersed between *luk thung* and *mor lam* songs selected by the unit's DJ. One gag delivered by Sergeant Major Surachaa Praponsri began: "Last night my wife told me to look after you, because my salary comes from your taxes." And, after a pause, "If I don't look after you, she won't sleep with me."[6]

Such banter not only emulated the kind heard at northeastern concerts, but came from the mouth of a speaker fluent in Isan dialect. This dialect is related to the Laotian language, and is symbolically and historically associated with rice farming and village life in the northeast. Middle-class Bangkokians interpret the Isan voice as coarse, while migrants from the region recognize their lives and trials in its grain. The elided R's and unique ending particles are common in street-corner conversation, in distinction to the long, trilled R's of classroom language instruction and government meetings. The meanings embedded in Thai dialects are an important dimension of the acid politics of class and regional difference. Sergeant Major Surachaa's joke, delivered with an Isan accent, struck a note of kinship between speaker and listener, while demonstrating a strategy of regional narrowcasting. The relationship of regionalism to class and political access marked so powerfully by accent could not be ignored as PJW deployed its carefully crafted messaging. Even when the unit succeeded in calming crowds, it exposed the true bases of unity, the true sources of listener attention, which scarcely included loyalty to the Thai state. Other members of the unit used similar tactics:

> Soontariya Gasa is the singer of the first Company of PJW's *luk thung* band. She selected some familiar songs such as Takkaten Chonlada's "I'm Not Your Girlfriend, I Can't Be Your Substitute" to sing for her Red brothers and sisters, and continued with "Siam is the Land of Smiles" by Pumpuang Duangjan. And in order to lower the degree of anger a step, Soontariya, who goes by the nickname "Green" (to emphasize that she's neither politically Yellow nor Red), speaks Isan, and chats with the protesters, who by and large come from Isan themselves. This wins them over in a big way.[7]

6. Panchai Pinchinda and Thipphimon Kiantiwathiratna, "PJW: The Thai Military's Calmmanding Force," Bangkok Biz News, March 17, 2010, www.bangkokbiznews.com//home/detail/life-style/lifestyle/20100317/105547/นักรบ-ปจว.--ม ˝อปลอบแห่งกองทัพไทย.html. Translated from the original Thai.

7. Ibid.

PJW recruits a diverse panel of soldiers precisely so that it can speak to audiences around the country in legible local accents. According to Major Gawseen Gampongyoot, "Using Central Thai, we don't reach the country folk. We have to use the local language because this is the only unit of the military whose mission is to create understanding within the population about these affairs."[8] The unit is fluent in demographic analysis, which it mobilizes as a modular voice of the state. Audiences, no matter how strongly they may wish to protest a set of policies, appreciate hearing their own intonation echoed back at them. The military gags, indeed, were met with laughter at RAB 11. Some Red Shirts were willing to assume the role of concertgoers, even though PJW's emcees worked openly on behalf of the military and government, and even as their sound masked the voices of the Red Shirts' own leaders.

Some Red Shirt protesters even gave credit to PJW for defusing a volatile situation by playing peaceful songs to calm the mood late in the rally, as tensions flared. According to the motorcycle taxi driver quoted above, when it became clear that the military would make no concessions to the Red Shirts, the protest leaders began threatening to break through the gates of RAB 11. At that moment, PJW improvised a program of calming speech and soothing music, telling the protesters at the front that they could come in and rest if they were hot and tired. As the driver recalled, "I was frightened then, frightened by the threats of the leaders, when they said that they would break in after two to three minutes. I was frightened, fearing what would happen there. But it was fortunate that the PJW arrived and made the situation calm down, with each side then returning to their own way." The March 15 rally ended without incident around 4:00 p.m., and the PJW were widely hailed as heroes. Several of the unit's members appeared in uniform on pro-government television in subsequent days to describe their own heroics. The daily Thai-language newspapers, also friendly to the government, published a spate of articles extolling PJW's psychological warfare broadcasts to a readership that, by and large, had no idea the group existed, especially not in its capacity as emcees. Appreciation for PJW, while not universal, most certainly crossed ideological lines.

Nevertheless, PJW's appearance did not necessarily bode well for the state. Interviewed afterward, protesters spoke dismissively about the broadcasting of *phleeng rák châat*, calling it a cheap and severe tactic used to silence them, not an irresistible gesture of brotherhood. It was not the nationalistic songs, but rather *luk thung* music that carried the day. Only when soldiers were seen as brothers and sisters of shared experience were they recognized as sympathetic figures. While the protesters listened to military broadcasts of *luk thung*, the same receptivity was not

---

8. Ibid.

extended to songs that appealed to their love for the nation, which in fact they heard as a disturbance.

The soldiers of PJW not only came to protests during tense moments, but also appeared in neighborhoods like Silom, an area secured early by the military, where protesters had been effectively kept out. Silom is a business district, and there PJW addressed nervous shoppers instead of political discontents. In Silom, the state committed armed defense resources to buoy consumer confidence. Their strategy was a direct and logical counter to the Red Shirts' own ploy of moving their rallies from conventional sites of political power such as the government house to areas of economic importance frequented by shoppers and businesspeople. The army thus transformed Silom preemptively into a razor-wire fortress, and deployed PJW as broadcasters who could put people at ease.

Retail spaces in Bangkok are sonically marked by incessant amplified chatter announcing sales, credit card offers, and late-model electronics. Typically, these announcements are made by mixed-gender groups of young people in formal attire stationed in front of a table with product literature. Having live hosts on the microphone lends the sound of retail space a warmth suggestive of human presence. The delivery is ambient, which is to say omnidirectional rather than focused. The shopper is not to be singled out by address; rather, she senses that today the market is *alive* with exchange. The level of politeness in shopping announcements varies significantly depending on how upscale the setting is. In cheaper malls, the ambient address may be more aggressive, while in fancier shopping centers it is likely to be softer and less direct.

On April 20, the soldiers of PJW structured their program with a careful ear toward the tenets of sales announcements. Gone were the Isan accents, the misogynist jokes, and the concert-like warm-ups. In their place was a dull, unobtrusive tag-team of male and female voices welcoming passersby, and offering deep apologies for the vicious-looking razor wire strung along the railing beneath the Skytrain. It was well after lunchtime, with long shadows on the pavement and the end of the workday on the horizon. The air was peaceful, with little sense of the conflict raging a mile away. In the shadow of office towers and next to Subway and KFC restaurants strolled Thais who identified as modern consumers, and who are accustomed to being addressed as such. PJW's psychological mission in this context was to maintain the flow of commerce by convincing people that the space they inhabited was safe from risk. Here, in the words of Major Gawseen, they "sold security like a product." The following conversation between two PJW announcers occurred on April 20:

MALE PJW: As far as convenience and safety, at this time I have to ask for your forgiveness.
FEMALE PJW: We ask for your forgiveness because, for those that walk past, while walking through you should watch out for the barbed wire barriers that are blocking the footpath. Be mindful of this wire because it's extra sharp. Be extra

careful as you walk. Leave at least. . . how many meters should they leave? Don't touch it at all because it's very sharp. It's quite dangerous.

MALE PJW: Brothers and sisters, please watch where you stand along the stairs to the BTS [Skytrain] going up and down. There are objects in the path, including barbed wire. And it's called barbed wire for a reason. This stuff is the barrier we put down. We ask for your forgiveness, brothers and sisters, with regard to the inconvenience in this area.

FEMALE PJW: That's right, please do avoid it.

MALE PJW: Because it is well-known that the situation up until now. . . you should know that when you come here we're taking care of you and keeping the peace.

FEMALE PJW: We're here to take care of you and keep the peace. To manage peace and order for our brothers and sisters, here in the Silom area. All the Thais and foreigners who came here today, I feel like I should ask for your apology. If you have problems or doubts, you can talk to the leader here.

MALE PJW: Today the street sellers are starting to come out, starting to sell things. Because this is a place of business. And especially a place of tourism. . . . Notice that the street stalls are full. This is a place of business. A place where tourists walk around. And for my Thai brothers and sisters, you can feel comfortable because of the studious efforts of the leader you see standing here. Our leader in uniform, with the baton and shield.

FEMALE PJW: No problem. You can chat with him. You don't have to be afraid, because we're concerned about the people. We want you to smile and feel comfortable. There's nothing to be afraid of.[9]

As the soldiers switched on a song, I chatted with a young marketer who worked at an office in the neighborhood. He had been watching the unit for several days, out of curiosity. He suggested to me that "this unit is more like a customer relationship program. . . . Their work is intended to make relationships with civilians, you know, in whatever way. . . . In marketing they call it an icebreaker, make everyone feel comfortable. I think they've been operating for a long time already, but we know about them in this moment because they've played an important role in the last couple of weeks."[10] The marketer had read about PJW in the newspaper, and was impressed with the unit's flexibility—they had also performed for Malay secessionists in southern Thailand, he pointed out—and furthermore with the difficult victory they had achieved in defusing the conflict on March 15. PJW staged a spectacle of peace and order. But in its actions, the fraying bonds of national unity also became clearly audible.

---

9. Translated from the original Thai.

10. Bystander who watched PJW on April 21, 2010, interviewed with the author on May 2, 2010. The bystander had read about PJW in the daily Thai-language newspaper *Thai Rath*. Name withheld at interviewee request. This conversation was in English.

Figure 14.1 A police officer observes a Red Shirt rally from an elevated platform. Photograph by the author.

CHAPTER 15
Outer Space

D oes distance afford panoramic listening, or wash away grain? The rallies rose
and receded massively, moving wavelike and then passing on. Congregations
of sound passed across roads and over trees, waves many kilometers long, landing
like dust beneath the feet of those who waited far off. Here heard the weary, undercover, tentative ones. Not all were involved, or always involved. Sometimes they
came closer. Finer detail might reveal something, but also might obscure something
else. Outer space was thick with the temptation of grain. The grain said come hear
(see Figure 15.1).

Figure 15.1 A sound recorder at the edge of a Red Shirt protest rally. Photograph by the author.

CHAPTER 16

The Vanishing Point of Audition

"The system, in a way, the logic is mundane, but. . . ."
"The system is eating itself up."
"Is there gonna be a shift, really?"

"When the Emergency Decree was still valid, they were not allowed to use a loudspeaker system, only the horns, but now they are allowed to use loudspeaker systems. So you had last on the 9th, they had a mobile stage, but they built speaker systems, so I expect to see speaker systems in Democracy Monument as well."

"The UDD is building the stage?"

"I don't know if they'll have a stage, but most likely a loudspeaker system. Before the Emergency Decree was over, they were not allowed. So you had all these speaker systems in the rally where the Emergency Decree was already lifted, but rallies inside the Emergency Decree had horns, not speaker systems."

"I had one tuned-up motorcycle about ten years ago, it was massive. Now with that one I couldn't get away in Thailand anymore. It didn't even slightly resemble the original. It was a bright lemon yellow color, I had different exhaust, different here, different there, it was massive. It's a huge business with the cars."

"They rent this speaker equipment. Somebody had to rent some big speaker system from the village level. All stages are always rented."

"They put them up so fast too!"

"Yeah. Because it's businesses that rent out stages. They're used for weddings, for village festivals, for concerts, for everything."

"And you see it all the time. Stages get put up everywhere for concerts, for advertising."

"Yeah. And they will rent from businesses which are close to them."

"Like personally close, like family?"

"Well, within the network, all the businesses are pro-Red and stuff like that."

"I have to get on my motorcycle. They're going to Democracy Monument."

"OK. I'll see you up there."

"It's all kind of like a secret code because there's so much that can't be said out loud that people kind of funnel it into these songs and these activities. The interesting thing about the way these protests work is that they're usually not vitriolic. I've seen people doing calisthenics, riding bikes they're doing today, going to the *wát* and praying. They do this just to kind of be together as kind of a social movement. But like they'll completely void it of any kind of political content because they're not allowed to talk about that stuff out loud, so they just get together and assume that people will know what they're there for without actually saying it."

Conclusion

On Constraints and Mediated Space

One evening in December 2010, I encountered Facebook founder Mark Zuckerberg on an unlit backstreet in Bangkok. It was as strange and sudden as that. He was surrounded by his entourage, walking to a private party. My wife and I were on our way to dinner at a restaurant a few minutes from home. Nearing it, we found the usually-quiet spot ringed with guards and surrounded by a press coterie. There was a buzz in the air. I asked one photographer, a young, smartly dressed Thai man, about the commotion. Was someone important coming? The man, after a moment of glancing around and seeming to consider whether he should say anything at all, whispered in my ear warily—not the guest's name, but that of his company: "Facebook. . ."

Zuckerberg, then a 26-year-old multibillionaire, was visiting Bangkok for a friend's wedding, and had rented the building. Serena and I could see through the slatted gates that an entire party was staged silently on the dark patio, still and ready. Moments later, Zuckerberg and his posse walked past us in the middle of the narrow road. I said his first name and he briefly turned toward me, before someone in his entourage shushed me harshly (the next twenty-four hours were filled with pangs of *l'esprit de l'escalier*). As the famous guest—in a sense the only guest—stepped onto the patio, the party-in-waiting sprang to life. The people who were posed silently inside let out a bright, loud cheer. Several grills shot up yellow flames, and the house lights flashed on festively. After witnessing this encounter from outside—alas, we were not invited to the party—we left for a different, familiar restaurant nearby. Excited about the unlikely encounter, we told our story to the waitress at the second restaurant. We expected her to be amazed or at least interested, but she gave us only a blank look. She did not know what Facebook was, let alone Zuckerberg. The distance between her and the young media tycoon's party was far greater than the five-minute walk from one restaurant to the other.

Her response should not have been surprising. In over a year of fieldwork, I witnessed how protesters had vastly different levels of access to media technologies. Even those platforms that the companies of Silicon Valley tend to market as universally accessible, as the tools of an integrated global village, do not in fact penetrate everywhere in the world. And even where they do penetrate, varying Internet connection speeds, economic inequality, different copyright laws, censorship, local communicative habits, and many other factors ensure that they will not do so evenly.[1] It is a basic premise of this book, reinforced by its chapter structure, that the mediated sonic niches of protest are heterogeneous and constrained, including by other niches. This condition extended to mediated communication throughout Thailand, far beyond the spaces of protest. Whatever this waitress's habits of media consumption and participation might have been, she was (at least in 2010) not part of Facebook's ambitious claim to be a "global community." The "mediated sonic spaces" and "uneven geography" described in the introduction to this book were constitutive of protest because they were constitutive of social life otherwise.

However, the politics and the publics of Thailand have transformed in tandem with its media environment in the years since my fieldwork. What have been the consequences of these transformations, and how might we understand them? On a trip to Bangkok in late 2016, I interviewed several activists, journalists, and academics about dissent in the aftermath of the 2014 military coup.[2] The junta that ousted prime minister Yingluck Shinawatra has since that time consolidated power, promising but failing to deliver national elections while writing a new, regime-friendly constitution.[3] Tacit (and arbitrarily executed) prohibitions against activism and anti-government speech have been made legally explicit, and are now enforced broadly and at times quite viciously.[4] Hopes for republicanism that began to shine through in 2011 have been quashed by the coup, and by the military-dominated regime that has installed itself since that time. One result is that public speech has become substantially more constrained even than it was in 2010 and 2011. The Red Shirt movement is now latent, at best. There are no more gatherings, no more showing of opinion, no radio stations, no gestures, no assemblies, not even at the furthest extremes of symbolic circuity, without risk of being hauled away

1. Paolo Gerbaudo, *Tweets and the Streets: Social Media and Contemporary Activism* (London: Pluto Press, 2012); Evgeny Morozov, *The Net Delusion: The Dark Side of Internet Freedom* (New York: PublicAffairs, 2011).

2. I have anonymized the subjects of these interviews, given the enormous sensitivity of the current political environment.

3. Richard C. Paddock, "Thailand Junta Seeks to Extend Its Power with Constitutional Referendum," *New York Times*, August 4, 2016.

4. Yukti Mukdawijitra, "A Professor Detained for His Thoughts," *Prachatai*, http://prachatai.org/english/node/7174?utm_source=dlvr.it&utm_medium=twitter, May 30, 2017. The article is about a professor who was arrested for posting illegal critical comments on Facebook. By anonymizing the name of the professor, whom the author visits in detainment, the piece also tacitly remarks upon a pervasive environment of fear and self-censorship under the junta.

for days-long questioning by the junta. Or worse.[5] Many intellectual and political radicals have left the country for Laos, Cambodia, France, Japan, or the United States. Others have stayed in the country and been brought in for "attitude adjustment" programs by the military, some repeatedly. A few of the holdouts have sent their families away, or had their bank accounts frozen. In order to remain free, most have been forced to sign contracts promising to quit their activism. Some, of course, are in prison. Thailand's politics and publics now face powerful new constraints.

The texture of everyday life in Bangkok has changed, too. A certain blankness falls on the places where dissent has thrived in the past. Ratchaprasong hums once more with commerce, but no longer with protest. This intersection, once alive with political aspiration, was the site of a major terrorist bombing in 2015, which killed 20 and injured 125. That attack, though not linked to the Red Shirts, was offered in an impoverished grammar of dissent—terrorism—that can flourish under authoritarianism. In the absence of a dialogic public sphere, dissent may logically take the form of horrific and spectacular violence. Meanwhile, conversations that ought to be full of optimism or at least political strategizing have been displaced by discussions about how to merely remain alive or avoid arrest. I asked one journalist, a veteran of the junta's attitude adjustment sessions who is still living in Bangkok, what he planned to do if the military ever sought his arrest or froze his assets, as it has done to so many others. Without speaking, he removed several heavy rings from his fingers, and pieces of gold bullion from his pocket, and dropped them on the table between us. A few ounces of precious metal were his emergency bank account, his ticket on a bus to Cambodia and then a new life, should it come to that. There is precious little space in contemporary Thailand for the development of anything like a political movement today.

Where does one go from here? Social media has become a risky, imperfect platform for open critical discussion. Although the junta has rigorously censored various websites and apps, expanded the Computer Crimes Act, and pressured Facebook and Google (among others) to aid them in restricting content, the prevalence of Internet access and use has nevertheless risen quickly. According to one report, the percentage of Thai households with at least one Internet-enabled device grew from 18.4 percent in 2012 to 59.8 percent in 2016.[6] It is possible, even likely, that the waitress who did not know who Mark Zuckerberg was in 2010 knows of him now, or at least that she uses Facebook. Activists, too, have become more dependent on social media. There is no other public forum readily available to them. Despite the junta's censorship, there are still opportunities for anonymity online,

5. "Thai junta allows a 'culture of torture,' says Amnesty," *Al Jazeera*, http://www.aljazeera.com/news/2016/09/thai-junta-culture-torture-amnesty-160928054932041.html, September 28, 2016.
6. "The State of Internet Censorship In Thailand: A research study by the Open Observatory of Network Interference (OONI), Sinar Project, and the Thai Netizen Network," March 20, 2017, https://ooni.torproject.org/post/thailand-internet-censorship/#key-findings.

and even for occasional flashes of critical expression, given enough caution. Some, who I spoke to in 2016, including erstwhile Red Shirts, were even optimistic about digital activism, seeing it as a frontier rather than a refuge. There was a general sense that the new stars of political dissent were those who had a charismatic—and often humorous—online presence. But most were less sanguine, describing digital activism as something of a rigged game. One journalist told me that:

> A big chunk of [activism] has migrated into . . . cyberspace. Facebook in particular is very active. Most interestingly, those guys in exile, notably Somsak [Jeamteerasakul], who is in Paris. Check his followers, it's huge, like four hundred thousand now. This guy is an academic superstar. Somsak along with Pavin [Chachavalpongpun]. We don't have a government-in-exile. What we have now is a virtual resistance from people in Europe, in the United States. . . . So we could say that despite the banned political gathering of more than four people, that conversation is still being conducted. But when you ask why I'm not optimistic, I don't see how anyone could possibly oust the military regime. . . . I think the victory for the junta-sponsored constitution camp and then the death of the king, which means people are in a very prolonged mourning period. I think that has dealt a death blow to any hope that the military regime will be ousted. . . . I just went to the [office of the BBC in Thailand, which had been closed the previous day by the junta for airing a banned documentary about the new king]. I can show you the picture. The place is shut. The sign has been removed so you can't even tell. . . . Basic liberties, civil rights cannot be taken for granted. At the same time people manage to engage in not just conversations but networking. Which is really strange and there's a big caveat. The junta-appointed, rubber-stamped parliament will have a new cyber bill and let's see what effect there will be. They will have more power to more decisively block websites, for example. We can expect further attempts to curb the public sphere in cyberspace. . . . It is heavily surveilled. If you look back, this didn't exist even in 2006. We didn't see any sort of burgeoning public sphere, to use Habermas's terminology. But it exists today and the conversation is ongoing. As of yesterday, the military regime decided to block the [BBC] biography of the new king, but of course people know that they can still access it if they know how, or if they have saved it. And that's the strength of social media. But on the other hand it's also a weakness. Because people feel as if they are already resisting, but in fact the physical reality looks very orderly, and quiet. . . .[7]

This journalist identifies an emergent public sphere in which the rhetorical distinction between "real" and "virtual" life (so easy to problematize) is effectively reified by the law. Fleshy bodies can no longer gather in groups larger than four people. But there is no limit to online gathering, precisely because the architecture of social media affords connection but not communication, in Morris's terms.[8] And

7. Anonymous, interview with the author, December 7, 2016.
8. Morris, "Theses on the New Öffentlichkeit."

architecturally, for the junta, digital media have thus far proved quite manageable. If the military government perceives that a line has been crossed in a Facebook post, for example, it has the technical means to block the offending content, as well as the legal tools to arrest the offender. The journalist suggests, in this way, that the digital realm (architecturally and legally developed as a space of mere *connection*) can be made to appear open, while the "physical reality" (more robustly understood as spaces of potential *communication*) can be closed off. Digital connection is subject to intensive surveillance. Today there is no lawlessness spreading through the air like a mist. In the spaces managed by the junta, dissidents *suffer* visibility, because they are immediately and archivally visible to (as well as identifiable by) the state. Among Somsak's four hundred thousand followers, surely, there are many men wearing floral-print shirts and gesturing furtively, their hiddenness accomplished by the technology itself.

The journalist continued:

> After the ouster of the Yingluck administration in 2014, the Red Shirts [became] a more monolithic group. So there's that sort of less visibility of the shades [between different Red Shirts]. Whereas back in 2011, it wasn't just on Facebook. People occupied real space at different areas. Of course they had their own niches. It's harder to differentiate now that they're all hiding or continuing to exist or fleeing into cyberspace. With the physical reality during the protests you could see, say, what sort of background these people were from, middle-class or rural poor, which provinces. On Facebook it's not really visible because a number of them do not use their real name or divulge much information.

The weakness of political dissent in post-coup Thailand, even in a moment of sharply increased digital connectivity, raises a vital question: what is the value of networked protest? Moreover, what kind of locally specific analyses must we conduct to understand how the digital realm is constituted in a given place? Recent literature on political movements and social media has tended to describe it as inherently subversive or at least connective. Tufekci, despite claiming to seek a middle ground between technological optimism and pessimism, assigns new media some essentially positive attributes: ". . .in the context of rebellion and protest, digital technologies play a fundamentally communitarian role. Digital media also allow individual expressiveness. Through this expressiveness and community building, digital affordances and core goals of most protesters are interlaced."[9] Elsewhere, she adds that "technology is helping create new ways of organizing and communicating."[10] In fact, such affordances are far from universal. Different political contexts absorb and utilize digital technology in different ways. Close

---

9. Tufekci, *Twitter and Tear Gas*, 111.
10. Ibid., 116.

anthropological analysis of vernacular expressions of dissent is therefore vital. In Thailand, as this book has described, heterogeneous forms of media were instrumental in the development of the Red Shirt movement. But under the junta, none of the attributes of new media described by Tufekci are present. Instead, the military government has successfully isolated key dissidents and fractured their alliances, faring far better in its repression of protest during a time of greater digital connection than the previous regime had. "States are catching up on social media," note Youmans and York, "using them to gather intelligence and spread proregime propaganda."[11] The Thai junta has applied draconian laws unevenly, so that no one ever quite knows where they stand, or when it is safe to speak. Digital technology has worsened this condition in Thailand, and no subversive network has yet emerged to challenge it. Youmans and York detail how media companies, being profit-driven, develop the architecture of their products to make money, not to facilitate activism.[12] Thus social media platforms are typically only friendly to activism by accident, if at all, and future changes to their architecture (such as a crackdown on pseudonymous accounts) may have incidentally disastrous consequences for political movements. Moreover, the Thai government has facilitated the spread of certain technologies that are more readily controllable, while restricting others. In this way, platform architecture is not only unpredictable for activists who might wish to use it, but actively influenced by the state. In Thailand, there is precious little room for the kind of practical maneuvering that, for example, Brunton and Nissenbaum schematize in their *Obfuscation: A User's Guide to Privacy and Protest.*[13]

Under the junta, there is little grain to hear; heterogeneous niches are thwarted. Sound and protest are severely and, for now, quite effectively constrained. It may be worth asking whether it is no coincidence that the coup took place just as digital media was expanding in Thailand. The emerging public that the journalist above describes—one marked by increased visibility—is precisely the kind of public in which the current junta can better assert its control. Social media, through a sample of three years, has provided sweeping tools for an undemocratic Thai government to manage and mitigate dissent. Thus far, the junta's opposition can claim no analogous victories.

Many people, in many geopolitical contexts, have suggested that platforms like Line, Facebook, and WhatsApp do not necessarily privilege progressive dissent. Morozov compares the effects of online surveillance to a panopticon.[14] This is no longer a new or surprising observation. But what if these platforms are not just aids to authoritarianism but catalysts of its rise? It is not clear that the Thai junta

11. William Lafi Youmans and Jillian C. York, "Social Media and the Activist Toolkit: User Agreements, Corporate Interests, and the Information Infrastructure of Modern Social Movements," *Journal of Communication* 62 (2012): 315–29.
12. Ibid.
13. Finn Brunton and Helen Nissenbaum, *Obfuscation: A User's Guide to Privacy and Protest* (Cambridge, MA: MIT Press, 2015).
14. Morozov, *The Net Delusion*, 145.

could operate as it now does without the affordances of social media. In particular, the Computer Crimes Act and the Cyber Scout program, which enlists teenaged volunteers to monitor the online activity of fellow citizens, have been powerful weapons of control and prosecution.[15] The tools for the Cyber Scout program became available around 2010, not only to the government but to a growing number of Thai people; the junta merely exploited these tools better than anyone else. We may ask what kinds of governing regimes tend to assume power when the public sphere is mediated and in part constituted by technologies that afford an enhanced visibility of dissident actors?

Perhaps this difficult question provides a figure for comparison. The United States presidential election of 2016 was won by the campaign that most cannily navigated the abiding media environment, as US elections are typically won, ethics and legality be damned. But the same campaign also anticipated how a public sphere full of connection (but bereft of communication) could be dominated by the bare act of winning. Winning became not a precursor to governing but a *substitute* for governing. The only governmental responsibility became the monitoring and management of a sphere of connections to ensure a self-interested self-perpetuation. As in Thailand, this condition preceded the rise of the administration that seemed to epitomize it. Political participation in the United States has long since been explained as a kin of modern sports fandom, supported by an endless stream of quantitative analysis that is less predictive of outcomes than productive of its own epistemological supremacy. Whatever might happen between my writing these words and your reading them, the mediated public sphere remains in thrall to this condition, and vulnerable to the modes of power it abets. The Thai junta diverges in many ways from the Trump administration. And yet both owe an enormous debt to the contemporary condition of social media, both for their initial ascendance and their perpetuation thereafter.

Given this, how might sound, protest, and constraint still be thought optimistically, or at least strategically? On January 21, 2017, at the Women's March in Washington, D.C., marchers teemed past Trump International Hotel, clogging the street and sidewalk in front of it. The collective chant of "asshole" created a low, steady rumble in the canyon of buildings. Inside the hotel, from a suite high up, a few children appeared in one window, peering down at the crowd, probably not hearing. The chant was nevertheless remarkable in its massiveness. It was a statement of resistance and of intimidation, and an act of substantial political force. But it was not yet dialogic. It did not manage to escape the channels that constrained it. The people in the hotel were not hailed by its address. And the Women's March as a whole was meanwhile criticized for making implicit claims to its own proportional representation without acknowledging, for example, how it enjoyed leeway that

15. Saksith Saiyasombut, "Become A Cyber-Scout, Clean Up Thailand's Internet!," December 18, 2010. https://saiyasombut.wordpress.com/2010/12/18/become-a-cyber-scout-clean-up-thailands-internet/

protests led by or identified with people of color had been denied.[16] The distinct factions that make up a coalitional left were not made any less heterogeneous by a voicing of the fact that Donald Trump is an asshole. The sound of the chant therefore did not unsettle the constraints that enabled its circulation. The asshole chant left room for future strategic adjustments that might take more careful stock of who can speak in which idioms, and of who gives audience. In both Thailand and the United States, on the left, there is work to do: personal reflection, media analysis, listening. The different contexts can be compared, and further triangulated with other places and movements. A radical politics today, in any sonic expanse or niche of dissent, still must begin like Sombat sitting thoughtfully on the red couch in his office, listening, with the birds singing softly outside. We must know the parameters of the political game more intimately than those who lay them out. We must recognize when our shouts have been given license, and what we win and lose by having that license. Awake to our visibility, we must strive to be mutually audible.

We must study quiet in order to know when it might become noise. But we must also intuit, like Mae, that our voices are not ours, that we may speak fearlessly but never under circumstances of our own choosing. Constraints are the condition of possibility for sound to be mobile, and for movements to move, just as the mobility promised by sound and dissent is precisely what makes them each vulnerable to constraint. The sound of our voice is contingent and radically limited. Someday we may come to sing perfectly, only to return to the fields as fading stars. We must learn to dwell in this uncertainty, and to sing on.

16. Lavanya, Ramanathan, "Was the Women's March Just Another Display of White Privilege? Some Think So," *Washington Post*, https://www.washingtonpost.com/lifestyle/style/was-the-womens-march-just-another-display-of-white-privilege-some-think-so/2017/01/24/00bbdcca-e1a0-11e6-a547-5fb9411d332c_story.html?utm_term=.fca823d67a9c

BIBLIOGRAPHY

I. ENGLISH-LANGUAGE BOOKS AND JOURNAL ARTICLES

Ahmed, Sara. *Living a Feminist Life*. Durham, NC: Duke University Press, 2017.

Althusser, Louis. "Ideology and Ideological State Apparatuses." In *Lenin and Philosophy and Other Essays*. New York: Monthly Review Press, 2001: 85–126.

Amporn Jirattikorn. "Lukthung: Authenticity and Modernity in Thai Country Music." *Asian Music: Journal of the Society for Asian Music* 37(1) (2006): 24–50.

Anderson, Benedict. *Imagined Communities: Reflections on the Origin and Spread of Nationalism*. London: Verso, 2006.

Anderson, Benedict. "Withdrawal Symptoms: Social and Cultural Aspects of the October 6 Coup." *Bulletin of Concerned Asian Scholars* 3 (1977): 13–30.

Asian National Media Barometer. "Asian Media Barometer: A Locally Based Analysis of the Media Landscape in Asia—Thailand 2010."

Augoyard, Jean-François, and Henry Torgue. *Sonic Experience: A Guide to Everyday Sounds*. Kingston, ON: McGill-Queen's University Press, 2005.

Auslander, Philip. *Liveness: Performance in a Mediatized Culture*. London: Routledge, 1999.

Baker, Chris, and Pasuk Pongpaichat. *A History of Thailand*. New York: Cambridge University Press, 2009.

Barmé, Scot. *Luang Wichit Wathakan and the Creation of a Thai Identity*. Singapore: Social Issues in Southeast Asia–Institute of Southeast Asian Studies, 1993.

Barz, Gregory. "Meaning in Benga Music of Western Kenya." *British Journal of Ethnomusicology* 10 (2001): 109–17.

Bijsterveld, Karin. "Acoustic Cocooning: How the Car Became a Place to Unwind." *The Senses & Society* 5(2) (2011): 189–211.

Bijsterveld, Karin. *Mechanical Sound: Technology, Culture, and Public Problems of Noise in the Twentieth Century*. Cambridge, MA: MIT Press, 2008.

Blacking, John. *How Musical Is Man?* Seattle: University of Washington Press, 1973.

Bodden, Michael. "Rap in Indonesian Youth Music of the 1990s: 'Globalization,' 'Outlaw Genres,' and Social Protest." *Asian Music* 36(2) (Summer/Fall 2005): 1–26.

Bowie, Katherine. *Rituals of National Loyalty*. New York: Columbia University Press, 1997.

Brinkema, Eugenie, and Evan Johnson. "Critique of Silence." *differences* 22(2–3) (2011): 211–34.

Brown, Courtney. *Politics in Music: Political Transformation from Beethoven to Hip-Hop*. Atlanta, GA: Farsight Press, 2007.

Brown, Wendy. "Neo-liberalism and the End of Liberal Democracy." *Theory and Event* 7(1) (2003): 1–29.

Brunton, Finn, and Helen Nissenbaum. *Obfuscation: A User's Guide to Privacy and Protest*. Cambridge, MA: MIT Press, 2015.

Butler, Judith. "Bodies in Alliance and the Politics of the Street." *European Institute for Progressive Cultural Policies*, September, 2011.

Butler, Judith. *Notes Toward a Performative Theory of Assembly*. Cambridge, MA: Harvard University Press, 2015.

Castells, Manuel. *Networks of Outrage and Hope: Social Movements in the Internet Age*. Cambridge, MA: Polity Press, 2012.

Chambers, Paul Wesley. "Thailand in Crisis: Resurgent Military, Diminished Democracy, Civil War?" Briefing prepared for the United States National Intelligence Council and US Department of State, Washington DC, April 19–20, 2010.

Chion, Michel, Claudio Gorbman, and Walter Murch. *Audio Vision: Sound on Screen*. New York: Columbia University Press, 1994.

Clewley, John. "The Many Sounds of Siam: Thai music ranges from Classical to Bikers' Rock." In *The Rough Guide to World Music: Europe, Asia and Pacific*, edited by Simon Broughton, Mark Ellingham, and Jon Lusk. London: Rough Guides, 2009: 440–48.

Connor, Steven. "The Helping of Your Good Hands: Reports on Clapping." In *The Auditory Culture Reader*, edited by Les Back and Michael Bull. New York: Berg, 2004., 67–76.

Connors, Michael Kelly. *Democracy and National Identity in Thailand*. London: RoutledgeCurzon, 2003.

Cusick, Suzanne. "An Acoustemology of Detention in the 'Global War on Terror.'" In *Music, Sound, and Space: Transformations of Public and Private Space*, edited by Georgina Born. Cambridge: Cambridge University Press, 2013.

Daughtry, Martin. *Listening to War: Sound, Music, Trauma, and Survival in Wartime Iraq*. New York: Oxford University Press, 2015.

de Certeau, Michel. *The Practice of Everyday Life*. Berkeley: University of California Press, 1984.

Dolar, Mladen. *A Voice and Nothing More*. Cambridge, MA: The MIT Press, 2006.

Drott, Eric. *Music and the Elusive Revolution: Cultural Politics and Political Culture in France, 1968–1981*. Berkeley: University of California Press, 2011.

Dyson, Frances. *Sounding New Media: Immersion and Embodiment in the Arts and Culture*. Berkeley: University of California Press, 2009.

Elinoff, Eli, and Claudio Sopranzetti, "Provincializing Bangkok: Isan from 'Not Yet' to 'Now.'" *South East Asia Research* 20(3): 299–303.

Evers, Hans-Dieter, and Rüdiger Korff. *Southeast Asian Urbanism: The Meaning and Power of Social Space*. Hampshire, UK: Palgrave Macmillan, 2001.

Eyerman, Ron, and Andrew Jamison. *Music and Social Movements: Mobilizing Traditions in the Twentieth Century*. New York: Cambridge University Press, 1998.

Garofalo, Reebee, ed. *Rockin' the Boat: Mass Music and Mass Movements*. Cambridge, MA: South End Press, 1992.

Geertz, Clifford. *The Interpretation of Cultures: Selected Essays*. New York: Basic Books, 1973.

Gerbaudo, Paolo. *Tweets and the Streets: Social Media and Contemporary Activism*. London: Pluto Press, 2012.

Gershon, Ilana. "Neoliberal Agency." *Current Anthropology* 52(4) (August 2011): 537–55.

Giles Ji Ungpakorn. *A Coup for the Rich: Thailand's Political Crisis*. Bangkok: Workers Democracy Publishing, 2007.

Giles Ji Ungpakorn. *Thailand: Class Struggle in an Era of Economic Crisis*. Hong Kong: Asia Monitor Resource Center, 1999.

Gitelman, Lisa. *Always Already New: Media, History, and the Data of Culture*. Cambridge, MA: MIT Press, 2006.

Goffman, Erving. *Frame Analysis: An Essay on the Organization of Experience*. Boston, MA: Northeastern University Press, 1986.

Goodman, Steve. *Sonic Warfare: Sound, Affect, and the Ecology of Fear.* Cambridge, MA: The MIT Press. 2009.

Greenhouse, Carol, ed. *Ethnographies of Neoliberalism.* Philadelphia: University of Pennsylvania Press, 2009.

Guilbault, Jocelyne. *Governing Sound: The Cultural Politics of Trinidad's Carnival Musics.* Chicago: University of Chicago Press, 2007.

Haberkorn, Tyrell. "Engendering Sedition: Ethel Rosenberg, Daranee Charnchoengsilpakul, and the Courage of Refusal." *positions: east asia cultures critique* 24(3) (August 2016): 621–51.

Haberkorn, Tyrell. "Hannah Arendt, Nidhi Eoseewong, and the Spectre of Totalitarianism in Thailand." *The Asia-Pacific Journal: Japan Focus* 12(14) (No. 4, 2014): 1–6.

Haberkorn, Tyrell. *Revolution Interrupted: Farmers, Students, Law, and Violence in Northern Thailand.* Madison: University of Wisconsin Press, 2011.

Habermas, Jürgen. *The Structural Transformation of the Public Sphere An Inquiry into a Category of Bourgeois Society.* Cambridge, MA: MIT Press, 1991.

Haraway, Donna. *The Haraway Reader.* New York: Routledge, 2004.

Harvey, David. *A Brief History of Neoliberalism.* Oxford: Oxford University Press, 2005: 19.

Harvey, David. *Spaces of Global Capitalism: Towards a Theory of Uneven Geographical Development.* London: Verso, 2006.

Havel, Václav. *The Power of the Powerless: Citizens Against the State in Central-Eastern Europe.* Armonk, NY: M.E. Sharpe, 1985.

Hayashi, Sharon, and Anne McKnight. "Good-bye Kitty, Hello War: The Tactics of Spectacle and New Youth Movements in Urban Japan." *positions: east asia cultures critique* 13(1) (Spring 2005): 87–113.

Hecker, Hellmuth. *Angulimala: A Murderer's Road to Sainthood.* Kandy, Sri Lanka: Buddhist Publication Society, 1984.

Heller, Michael C. "Between Silence and Pain: Loudness and the Affective Encounter." *Sound Studies* 1(1) (2015): 40–58.

Heilbronner, Oded. "Resistance Through Rituals—Urban Subcultures of Israeli Youth from the Late 1950s to the 1980s." *Israel Studies* 16(3) (Fall 2011): 28–50.

Heinrich Böll Stiftung Southeast Asia Foundation. "New Media and Political Mobilization." 2012.

Helmreich, Stefan. "An Anthropologist Underwater: Immersive Soundscapes, Submarine Cyborgs, and Transductive Ethnography." *American Ethnologist* 34(4) (November 2007): 621–41.

Helmreich, Stefan. "Gravity's Reverb: Listening to Space-Time, or Articulating the Sounds of Gravitational-Wave Detection." *Cultural Anthropology* 31(4) (2016): 464–92.

Helmreich, Stefan. *Sounding the Limits of Life: Essays in the Anthropology of Life and Beyond.* Princeton, NJ: Princeton University Press, 2016.

Hemmasi, Farzaneh. "Intimating Dissent: Popular Song, Poetry, and Politics in Pre-Revolutionary Iran." *Ethnomusicology* 57(1) (Winter 2013): 57–87.

Herzfeld, Michael. *Siege of the Spirits: Community and Polity in Bangkok.* Chicago: University of Chicago Press, 2016.

Hirschkind, Charles. *The Ethical Soundscape: Cassette Sermons and Islamic Counterpublics.* New York: Columbia University Press, 2006.

Horning, Susan Schmidt. "Engineering the Performance: Recording Engineers, Tacit Knowledge and the Art of Controlling Sound." *Social Studies of Science* 34 (2004): 711.

Human Rights Watch. "Descent into Chaos: Thailand's 2010 Red Shirt Protests and the Government Crackdown." May 2011.

Jaiser, Gerhard. *Thai Popular Music.* Bangkok: White Lotus, 2012.

Jasper, James. *The Art of Moral Protest: Culture, Biography, and Creativity in Social Movements*. Chicago: University of Chicago Press, 1999.

Kane, Brian. *Sound Unseen: Acousmatic Sound in Theory and Practice*. New York: Oxford University Press, 2014

Kasian Tejapira. "Toppling Thaksin." *New Left Review*. May 22, 2006.

Keyes, Charles. *Finding Their Voice: Northeastern Villagers and the Thai State*. Seattle: University of Washington Press, 2014.

Klima, Alan. *The Funeral Casino: Meditation, Massacre, and Exchange with the Dead in Thailand*. Princeton, NJ: Princeton University Press, 2002.

Koerth-Baker, Maggie. "The Loudest Sound in the World Would Kill You on the Spot." *Five Thirty Eight*, July 7, 2016.

LaBelle, Brandon. *Acoustic Territories: Sound Culture and Everyday Life*. New York: Continuum, 2010.

Laclau, Ernesto. *On Populist Reason*. London: Verso, 2002.

Laclau, Ernesto, and Chantal Mouffe. *Hegemony and Socialist Strategy*. London: Verso, 1985.

Larkin, Brian. "Techniques of Inattention: The Mediality of Loudspeakers in Nigeria." *Anthropological Quarterly* 87(4) (Fall 2014): 989–1015.

Latour, Bruno. *Science in Action: How to Follow Scientists and Engineers Through Society*. Milton Keynes, UK: Open University Press, 1987.

Laurence, Felicity, and Oliver Urbain, eds. *Music and Solidarity: Questions of Universality, Consciousness, and Connection*. New Brunswick, NJ: Transaction Publishers, 2011.

Lefebvre, Henri. *The Production of Space*. Hoboken, NJ: Wiley-Blackwell, 1992.

Lefebvre, Henri. *Rhythmanalysis: Space, Time, and Everyday Life*. London: Bloomsbury Academic, 2004.

Lévi-Strauss, Claude. *Tristes Tropiques*. New York: Pocket Books, 1977.

Leichtman, Ellen C. "The Different Sounds of American Protest: From Freedom Songs to Punk Rock." In *Popular Culture, Crime and Social Control*, edited by Mathieu Deflem. Bingley, U K: Emerald Group Publishing Limited, 2010: 173–91.

MacLachlan, Heather. *Burma's Pop Music Industry: Creators, Distributors, Censors*. Rochester, NY: University of Rochester, 2011.

Manabe, Noriko. "The No Nukes 2012 Concert and the Role of Musicians in the Anti-Nuclear Movement." *The Asia-Pacific Journal: Japan Focus*. Accessed January 9, 2013.

Manabe, Noriko. *The Revolution Will Not Be Televised: Protest Music After Fukushima*. New York: Oxford University Press, 2015.

Manuel, Peter. "World Music and Activism Since the End of History." *Music & Politics* XI(1) (2017).

Martin, Bradford D. *The Theater Is in The Street: Politics and Public Performance in Sixties America*. Amherst and Boston: University of Massachusetts Press, 2004.

Mazzarella, William. "Totalitarian Tears: Does the Crowd Really Mean It?" *Cultural Anthropology* 30(1) (February 2015): 91–112.

McAlevey, Jane F. *No Shortcuts: Organizing for Power in the New Gilded Age*. New York: Oxford University Press, 2016.

McCargo, Duncan, and Krisadawan Hangladarom. "Contesting Isan-ness: Discourses of Politics and Identity in Northeast Thailand." *Asian Ethnicity* 5(2) (2004): 219–34.

McLuhan, Marshall. "The Medium Is the Message." In *Understanding Media: The Extensions of Man*. New York: Signet, 1964: 23–35, 63–67.

Meintjes, Louise. "Paul Simon's Graceland, South Africa, and the Mediation of Musical Meaning." *Ethnomusicology* 34(1) (Winter 1990): 37–73.

Miller, Terry. "From Country Hick to Rural Hip: A New Identity Through Music for Northeast Thailand." *Asian Music* 36(2) (Summer–Autumn 2005): 96–106.

Miller, Terry E. *Traditional Music of the Lao: Kaen Playing and Mawlum Singing in Northeast Thailand.* Westport, CT: Praeger, 1985.

Miller, Terry, and Sean Williams. *The Garland Encyclopedia of World Music IV: Southeast Asia.* New York: Garland, 1998.

Mitchell, James. "Isaan Lives: Hongthong Dao Udon: From singing star to political prisoner." *Isaan Record,* http://isaanrecord.com/2016/09/12/isaan-lives-hongthong-dao-udon-from-singing-star-to-political-prisoner/.

Mitchell, James. "Kon Baan Diaokan or 'We're from the Same Village'—Star/Fan Interaction in Thai Lukthung." *Perfect Beat* 12(1) (2011): 69–89.

Mitchell, James. *Luk Thung: The Culture and Politics of Thailand's Most Popular Music.* Seattle: University of Washington Press, 2016.

Mitchell, James. "Red and Yellow Songs: A Historical Analysis of the Use of Music by the United Front for Democracy against Dictatorship (UDD) and the People's Alliance for Democracy (PAD) in Thailand." *South East Asia Research* 19(3) (2011): 457–94.

Moro, Pamela. "'Songs for Life': Leftist Thai Popular Music in the 1970s." *Journal of Popular Culture* 20(3) (1986): 93–113.

Morozov, Evgeny. *The Net Delusion: The Dark Side of Internet Freedom.* New York: PublicAffairs, 2011.

Morris, Rosalind. "Giving Up Ghosts: Notes on Trauma and the Possibility of the Political from Southeast Asia." *positions: asia critique* 16(1) (Spring 2008): 229–58.

Morris, Rosalind. *In the Place of Origins: Modernity and Its Mediums in Northern Thailand.* Durham, NC: Duke University Press, 2000.

Morris, Rosalind. "Theses on the New Öffentlichkeit." *Grey Room* 51 (Spring 2013): 94–111.

Morton, David. *The Traditional Music of Thailand.* Berkeley, CA: University of California Press, 1976.

Muehlebach, Andrea. *The Moral Neoliberal: Welfare and Citizenship in Italy.* Chicago: University of Chicago Press, 2012.

Naruemon Thabchumpon, and Duncan McCargo. "Urbanized Villagers in the 2010 Thai Redshirt Protests: Not Just Poor Farmers?" *Asian Survey* 51(6) (2011): 993–1018.

Novak, David. *Japanoise: Music at the Edge of Circulation.* Durham, NC: Duke University Press, 2013.

Ochoa Gautier, Ana María. "Acoustic Multinaturalism, the Value of Nature, and the Nature of Music in Ecomusicology." *boundary* 2 43(1) (2016):107–41.

Ochoa Gautier, Ana María. *Aurality.* Durham, NC: Duke University Press, 2015.

Ochoa Gautier, Ana María. "Sonic Transculturation, Epistemologies of Purification and the Aural Public Sphere in Latin America," *Social Identities: Journal for the Study of Race, Nation and Culture,* 12(6) (2006): 803–25.

Ortiz, Horacio. "Financial Value: Economic, Moral, Political, Global." *Hau: Journal of Ethnographic Theory* 3(1) (2013): 64–79.

Pasuk Pongpaichat. "Confronting Thailand's Inequality Through Fiscal Reform." *East Asia Forum.* January 14, 2012.

Pasuk Pongpaichat, and Chris Baker. *Thaksin: Second Edition.* Seattle: University of Washington Press, 2010.

Pattana Kitiarsa. "Modernity, Agency, and Lam Sing: Interpreting 'Music-Culture' in Northeastern Thailand." *Crossroads: An Interdisciplinary Journal of Southeast Asian Studies* 17(2) (2006): 34–65.

Pavin Chachavalpongpun. *Good Coup Gone Bad: Thailand's Political Development Since Thaksin's Downfall.* Singapore: Institute of Southeast Asian Studies, 2014.

Pavin Chachavalpongpun. "Royal Motherhood Statement," August 4, 2011, http://asiapacific.anu.edu.au/newmandala/2011/08/04/royal-motherhood-statement/.

Pavin Chachavalpongpun. "'Unity' as a Discourse in Thailand's Polarized Politics." *Southeast Asian Affairs* 10 (2010): 332–42.

Peddie, Ian, ed. *The Resisting Muse: Popular Music And Social Protest.* Burlington, VT: Ashgate, 2006.

Persons, Larry Scott. "The Anatomy of Thai Face." *MANUSYA: Journal of Humanities* 11(1) (2008): 53–75.

Plate, Tom. *Conversations with Thaksin.* Tarrytown, NY: Marshall Cavendish Corp., 2011.

Pornprapit Phoasavadi. "From Prachan to Prakuad: The Process of Officializing Traditional Music Competition in Contemporary Bangkok." PhD dissertation, University of Washington, 2005.

Pruett, David. "When the Tribe Goes Triple Platinum: A Case Study Toward an Ethnomusicology of Mainstream Popular Music in the U.S." *Ethnomusicology* 55(1) (February 2011): 1–30.

Ranciere, Jacques. *Dissensus: On Politics and Aesthetics.* New York: Bloomsbury, 2010.

Reynolds, Craig J. "The Social Bases of Autocratic Rule in Thailand." In *Bangkok May 2010: Perspectives on a Divided Thailand*, edited by Michael John Montesano, Pavin Chachavalpongpun, and Aekapol Chongvilaivan. Singapore: Institute of Southeast Asian Studies, 2012: 271.

Rodgers, Tara. "Toward a Feminist Epistemology of Sound: Refiguring Waves in Audio-Technical Discourse." In *Engaging the World: Thinking After Irigaray*, edited by Mary Rawlinson. Albany: State University of New York Press, 2016: 195–214.

Sakakeeny, Matt. *Roll With It: Brass Bands in the Streets of New Orleans.* Durham, NC: Duke University Press, 2013.

Salazar, Noel. "Towards an Anthropology of Cultural Mobilities." *Crossings: Journal of Migration and Culture* 53(1) (2010): 53–68.

Salazar, Phillipe-Joseph. "Figuration—A Common Ground of Rhetoric and Anthropology." In *Culture+Rhetoric*, edited by Ivo Strecker and Stephen Tyler. Oxford, New York: Berghahn Books, 2009: 150–165.

Savitri Gadavanij. "Discursive Strategies for Political Survival: A Critical Discourse Analysis of Thai No Confidence Debates." PhD dissertation, University of Leeds, 2002.

Schafer, R. Murray. *The New Soundscape: A Handbook for the Modern Music Teacher.* Toronto: Berandol Music Limited, 1969.

Schafer, R. Murray. *The Soundscape: Our Sonic Environment and the Tuning of the World.* Rochester, VT: Destiny Books, 1993.

Scott, James C. *The Moral Economy of the Peasant: Rebellion and subsistence in Southeast Asia.* Princeton: Princeton University Press, 1976.

Scott, James. *Weapons of the Weak: Everyday Forms of Peasant Resistance.* New Haven, CT: Yale University Press, 1985.

Sitrin, Marina. *Horizontalism: Voices of Popular Power in Argentina.* Oakland, CA: AK Press, 2006.

Smith, Bruce R. "Into the Wild Blue Yonder: The Challenges of Acoustic Ecology," In *Hearing Cultures: Essays on Sound, Listening, and Modernity*, edited by Veit Erlmann. London: Berg, 2004.

Smith, Neil. "Neo-Critical Geography, Or, The Flat Pluralist World of Business Class." *Antipode* 37(5) (2005): 887–99.

Smith, Neil. *Uneven Development: Nature, Capital, and the Production of Space.* London: Verso, 2010.

Sophorntavy Vorng. "Bangkok's Two Centers: Status, Space, and Consumption in a Millennial Southeast Asian City." *City & Society* 23(sup. 1) (2011): 66–85.

Sopranzetti, Claudio. "Motorcycle Taxi Drivers, Mobility and Politics in Bangkok." PhD dissertation, Harvard University, 2013.

Sopranzetti, Claudio. *Owners of the Map: Motorcycle Taxi Drivers, Mobility, and Politics in Bangkok*. Oakland: University of California Press, 2017.

Sopranzetti, Claudio. *Red Journeys: Inside the Thai Red-Shirt Movement*. Bangkok: Silkworm Books, 2012.

Sreberny-Mohammadi, Annabelle, and Ali Mohammadi. *Small Media, Big Revolution: Communication, Culture, and the Iranian Revolution*. Minneapolis: University of Minnesota Press, 1994.

Stanyek, Jason, and Sumanth Gopinath, eds. *The Oxford Handbook of Mobile Music Studies*. New York: Oxford University Press, 2014.

Stanyek, Jason, and Benjamin Piekut. "Deadness: Technologies of the Intermundane." *The Drama Review* 54(1) (Spring 2010): 14–38.

Steingo, Gavin. "Sound and Circulation: Immobility and Obduracy in South African Electronic Music." *Ethnomusicology Forum* 24(1) (2015): 102–23.

Sterne, Jonathan. *The Audible Past: Cultural Origins of Sound Reproduction*. Durham, NC: Duke University Press, 2003.

Sterne, Jonathan. "Quebec's #casseroles: On Participation, Percussion, and Protest." *Sounding Out!* June 4, 2012, http://soundstudiesblog.com/2012/06/04/casseroles.

Sterne, Jonathan. "Sounds Like the Mall of America: Programmed Music and the Architectonics of Public Space." *Ethnomusicology* 41(1) (Winter 1997): 22–50.

Sterne, Jonathan, ed. *The Sound Studies Reader*. New York: Routledge, 2012.

Sterne, Jonathan. "The Theology of Sound: A Critique of Orality." *Canadian Journal of Communication*, 36 (2) (2011): 207–225.

Sulak Sivaraska. "Crisis of Thai Identity." In *National Identity and Its Defenders: Thailand, 1939–1989*, edited by Craig J. Reynolds. Bangkok: Silkworm Press, 1991: 41–58.

Sutharin Koonphol. "Concept and Practice of 'Public Space' in the City of Bangkok, Thailand: a Case Study based on Sanam Luang." PhD dissertation, University of London, 2001.

Taffet, Jeffrey E. "My Guitar is Not for the Rich: The New Chilean Song Movement and the Politics of Culture." *Journal of American Culture* 20 (1997): 91–103.

Tausig, Benjamin. "A Division of Listening: Insurgent Sympathy and the Sonic Broadcasts of the Thai Military." *positions: asia critique* 24(2) (2016): 403–33.

Tausig, Benjamin. "Sound and Movement: Vernaculars of Sonic Dissent." *Social Text* 36(3) (2018).

Taylor, Diana. *The Archive and the Repertoire: Performing Cultural Memory in the Americas*. Durham, NC: Duke University Press, 2003.

Thak Chaloemtiarana, Charnwit Kasetsiri, and Thinaphan Nakata. *Thai Politics: Extracts and Documents, 1932–1957*. Bangkok: Social Sciences Association of Thailand, 1978.

Thompson, Emily. *The Soundscape of Modernity: Architectural Acoustics and the Culture of Listening in America, 1900–1933*. Cambridge, MA: The MIT Press, 2004.

Thongchai Winichakul. *Siam Mapped: A History of the Geo-Body of a Nation*. Honolulu: University of Hawaii Press, 1997.

Toop, David. *Sinister Resonance: The Mediumship of the Listener*. New York: Continuum, 2011.

Tse-Hsiung Lin. "Mountain Songs, Hakka Songs, Protest Songs: A Case Study of Two Hakka Singers from Taiwan." *Asian Music* 42(1) (Winter/Spring 2011): 85–122.

Tufekci, Zeynep. *Twitter and Tear Gas: The Power and Fragility of Networked Protest*. New Haven: Yale University Press, 2017.

Turino, Thomas. *Music as Social Life*. Chicago: University of Chicago Press, 2008.

Ubonrat Siriyuvasak. "Commercialising the Sound of the People: Pleng Luktoong and the Thai Pop Music Industry." *Popular Music* 9(1) (1990): 61–77.

Warner, Michael. *Publics and Counterpublics*. New York: Zone Books, 2005.

Wong, Deborah. *Sounding the Center: History and Aesthetics in Thai Buddhist Performance*. Chicago: University of Chicago Press, 2001.

Wong, Deborah. "Thai Cassettes and their Covers: Two Case Histories." *Asian Music* 21 (1) (Autumn 1998): 78–104.

Youmans, William Lafi, and Jillian C. York. "Social Media and the Activist Toolkit: User Agreements, Corporate Interests, and the Information Infrastructure of Modern Social Movements." *Journal of Communication* 62 (2012): 315–329.

Yuangrat Wedel. *Modern Thai Radical Thought: The Siamization of Marxism and Its Theoretical Problems*. Bangkok: Thai Khadi Research Institute, Thammasat University, 1982.

II. THAI-LANGUAGE BOOKS, JOURNAL ARTICLES, AND GOVERNMENT PUBLICATIONS

"Act to 'Manage Gatherings in Public Places'" ("ร่างพระราชบัญญัติจัดระเบียบการชุมนุมในที่สาธารณะ พ.ศ. . . . ."), http://www.parliament.go.th/ewtadmin/ewt/parliament_parcy/ewt_news.php?nid=3175&filename=index08, accessed March 4, 2013.

Annusorn Unno. "We Come in Peace: The Peaceful Methods of the Red Shirts." In *Truth For Justice: The Situation and Consequences of the Protest Dispersal, March-May 2010*. Bangkok: People's Information Center, 2012. (อนุสรณ์ อุณโณ. "We Come in Peace: สันติวิธีฉบับคนเสื้อแดง." ใน *ความจริงเพื่อความยุติธรรม: เหตุการณ์และผลกระทบจากการสลายการชุมนุม เมษา - พฤษภา 53*.)

Chayanit Poonyarat. "'Thirteen Secrets' and Peaceful Methods in Thai Society." Warasan Sathaban Phrapokkhlao 8(1) (2010). (อาจารยช·ญานิษฐ·พูลยรัตน์·. "'13 ความลับ' และสันติวิธีในสังคมไทย." สถาบันพระปกเกล้า 8(1) (2010).)

Charoen Phengmun. "Community Radio and the Development of Local Politics." *COLA Local Administration Journal* 8(2) (2015). (เจริญ เพ็งมูล, วิทยุชุมชนกับการพัฒนาทางการเมืองท้องถิ่น.)

"The Development of 'Songs for Life.'" ("พัฒนาการเพลงเพื่อชีวิต"), http://www.9dern.com/rsa/view.php?id=90, accessed January 30, 2013.

"February 25 Retracing the Opening of the First Radio Station in Thailand." http://www.vcharkarn.com/vblog/109877. (25 กุมภาพันธ์ ย้อนอดีต เปิดสถานีวิทยุฯ ครั้งแรกในไทย.)

"Horizontal Line: The Flat Strategies of Horizontalided." ("แกนนอน: วิถีระนาบ Horizontalidad"), http://www.tonkla.org/tag/แกนนอน/, accessed February 21, 2012.

Institute for the Heroes of Democracy. *Heroes of April 10: The Dead Have Faces; The Murdered Have Lives*. Bangkok, 2010. (ทีมข่าวไทยอีนิวส์. วีรชน *10* เมษา: คนที่ตายมีใบหน้า คนที่ถูกฆ่ามีชีวิต. กรุงเทพ, 2010.)

Manot Joramat. "Laws About the Peace and Order of the People." *The Scales of Justice*. Book 5, Year 12 (May 1965). (มาโนช จรมาศ "ข้อกฎหมายเกียวกับความสงบเรียบร้อยของประชาชน." ดุลพาห เล่ม 5 ปี 12 พ.ค. 2508.)

Nidhi Eosriwong. "The Red Shirt Movement and Thai Politics and Society." *Matichon*. May 19, 2011. (นิธิ เอียวศรีวงศ์ "ขบวนการคนเสื้อแดงกับสังคม-การเมืองไทย." มติชน. 26 กันยายน พ.ศ. 2554.)

Office of Academic Technology and Society. *Mawlum Cing Isan—Bodies and Voices in a Modernized Performing Art from Northeast Thailand*. University of Technology, Suranari, Nakhon Ratchasima 2001. (สำนักวิชาเทคโนโลยีสังคม. คนซึ่งอีสาน ร่างกาย กามารณ์ อัตลักษณ์ และเสียงสะท้อนของคนทุกข์ในหมอลำซึ่งอีสาน. มหาวิทยาลัยเทคโนโลยีสุรนารี, นครราชสีมา 2544.)

Pattana Kitiarsa. "Popular Music, Emotional Labor, and Isan Diaspora." http://chornorpor.
blogspot.com/2012/03/popular-music-emotional-labor-and-isan_13.html, 2011.
(พัฒนา กิติอาษา. "ดนตรีอีสาน แรงงานอารมณ์ และคนพลัดถิ่น.")

Pattarawut Bunpraseri. "Local Media in Mass Media: The Case of Mor Lam." Master's Thesis,
Institute for the Development of Mass Media in Thailand, 2008. (ภัทราวุธ บุญประเส
ริฐ. "การใช้สื่อพื้นบ้านในการสื่อสารทางการเมือง ศึกษากรณีหมอลำ.")

Sangsit Piriyarangsaan. *Police, People of Influence, and the Hidden Economy.* Bangkok: SUP
Books, 2005. (สังศิต พิริยะรังสรรค์. ตำรวจ ผู้มีอิทธิพล และ เศรษฐกิจมืด, ศึกษา ม
ะเร็งร้ายของสังคมด้วยแว่นขยายทางวิชาการ. ก.ท.ม.: หนังสือSUPอีน 2005.)

"Special Order of the Prime Minister, 1/2010, on the Establishment of a Center for the
Resolution of the Emergency Situation." ("คำสั่งนายกรัฐมนตรี ที่ พิเศษ ๑/๒๕๕๓ เรื่
องการจัดตั้งศูนย์อำนวยการแก้ไขสถานการณ์ฉุกเฉิน"), http://www.ratchakitcha.
soc.go.th/DATA/PDF/2553/E/045/3.PDF, accessed January 4, 2013.

Si Klayonsut. "The Peace and Order of the People." *The Scales of Justice,* Book 1, Year 3, January,
1956. (สีห์ คลายนสูตร. "ความสงบเรียบร้อยของประชาชน." ดุลพาห เล่ม 1 ปี _
ม.ค. 2499.)

Somsak Jeamteerasakul. "'We Fight': Political Royal Songs and the Politics of 1975–1976."
somsakwork.blogspot.com (blog), November 16, 2007. (สมศักดิ์ เจียมธีรสกุล.
"เราสู้: เพลงพระราชนิพนธ์การเมืองกับการเมืองปี 2518–2519.")

"Tongsai Taptanon" ("ทองใส ทับถนน"), http://www.tlg.rmutt.ac.th/wp-content/uploads/
2011/06/67—ครูทองใส-ทับถนน.pdf, accessed January 28, 2013.

Uchent Chiangsen, ed. *19–19: Pictures, Lives, and Battles of the Red Shirts From October 19, 2006
to May 19, 2010.* Bangkok: Fa Diaw Kan, 2011. (อุเชนทร์ เชียงเสน:บรรณาธิการ. 19–
19: ภาพ ชีวิต และการต่อสู้ของคนเสื้อแดง จาก 19 กันยา 49 ถึง 19 ะพฤษภา 53.
กรุงเทพ: ฟ้าเดียวกัน, 2011.)

Wad Rawi, ed. *Crisis Nineteen.* Bangkok: Sribanya Publishing 2011. (วาด รวี วิกฤต 19.
กรุงเทพ: ศรีปัญญา, 2011.)

Wanich Charungkichanan. "The Royal City." In *Wanich 60.5: Watching the Passing of a Life
at 60.5 Years.* Bangkok: Open Books, 2010. (วานิช จรุงกิจอนันต์. "เมืองหลวง." ใน
Wanich 60.5: มองผ่านชีวิตหกสิบปีครึ่ง. กรุงเทพ: Bangkok: Open Books, 2011).

Wichai Noparasmi. *Jit Pumisak: People Need To Keep Standing by Fighting.* Bangkok: Fa Diaw
Kan, 2008. (วิชัย นภารัศมี: บรรณาธิการ. จิตร ภูมิศักดิ์ คนยังคงยืนเด่นโดยท้าทาย.
กรุงเทพ: ฟ้าเดียวกัน, 2008.)

III. BILINGUAL PUBLICATIONS
Constitution of Thailand.
Radio and Television Broadcasting Services Act, B.E. 2551 (2008).
Thai Public Broadcasting Service Act.

IV. ENGLISH-LANGUAGE PERIODICALS, NEWS CHANNELS, AND WEBSITES
Asian Correspondent
Bangkok Post
BBC
Channel Four (UK)
CNN
Comic Vine
Facebook
Five Thirty Eight
The Guardian (UK)

Isaan Record
Monrakplengthai.com
The Nation
New Mandala
New York Times
Prachatai English
Voice of America

V. THAI-LANGUAGE PERIODICALS, NEWS CHANNELS, AND WEBSITES
ASTV Manager
Bangkok Biz News
Channel News Asia
Fa Diaw Kan
Facebook
Khao Sot
Mahachon
Muslimthaipost.com
Matichon
Nopeter.org
Norporchoreu.com
Prachatai
Sansiri.com
Siam Rath
Straits Times
Surin108.com
Topicthailand.com

LIST OF INTERVIEWS
Ae Porntip and Nattawut Skidjai, May 23, 2010.
Anonymous (Motorcycle taxi driver at *win* opposite RAB 11 gate, no nickname given), August 5, 2010.
Anonymous (Vendor, no nickname given), May 20, 2011.
"Art," (bystander who watched PJW on April 21, 2010), May 2, 2010.
"Daeng" (car audio installer), March 30, 2011.
"Dear," (Red Sunday composer) December 17, 2010.
"Doctor," January 23, 2011.
Garrity, Peter, January 5, 2011.
Jenphop Jopgrabuanwan, December 5, 2010.
Jin Gammachon, December 19, 2010.
Kittisak Janpeng ("Diew"), March 23, 2012.
Kong Rithdee, July 28, 2010.
Nostitz, Nick, October 19, 2010.
Om Khaphatsadi, June, 2011.
Orn, August 15, 2010.
Orn, August 22, 2010.
Pae Bangsanan, August 2012.
"Pat," January 10, 2011.
"Pat," January 16, 2011.
"Pat," February 11, 2011.

"Pat," February 17, 2012.
"Pat," April 25, 2011.
Pom Krongthong, December, 2011.
Pravit Rojanaphruk (journalist, *The Nation*), August 17, 2010.
Sombat Boonngamanon, September 1, 2010.
"Tata," October 2010.
Vermeij, Eef (archivist), June 17, 2011.

INDEX

CPSIA information can be obtained
at www.ICGtesting.com
Printed in the USA
BVHW012249220919
559036BV00002B/3/P